THE PROFESSIONAL PRACTICE SERIES

The Professional Practice Series is sponsored by the Society for Industrial and Organizational Psychology (SIOP). The series was launched in 1988 to provide industrial/organizational psychologists, organizational scientists and practitioners, human resource professionals, managers, executives, and those interested in organizational behavior and performance with volumes that are insightful, current, informative, and relevant to organizational practice. The volumes in the Professional Practice Series are guided by five tenets designed to enhance future organizational practice:

1. Focus on practice, but grounded in science
2. Translate organizational science into practice by generating guidelines, principles, and lessons learned that can shape and guide practice
3. Showcase the application of industrial/organizational psychology to solve problems
4. Document and demonstrate best industrial and organizational-based practices
5. Stimulate research needed to guide future organizational practice

The volumes seek to inform those interested in practice with guidance, insights, and advice on how to apply the concepts, findings, methods, and tools derived from industrial/organizational psychology to solve human-related organizational problems.

Previous Professional Practice Series volumes include:

Published by Jossey-Bass

Organization Development
Janine Waclawski, Allan H. Church, Editors

*Creating, Implementing, and Managing
Effective Training and Development*
Kurt Kraiger, Editor

The 21st Century Executive
Rob Silzer, Editor

Managing Selection in Changing Organizations
Jerard F. Kehoe, Editor

Evolving Practices in Human Resource Management
Allen I. Kraut, Abraham K. Korman, Editors

Individual Psychological Assessment
Richard Jeanneret, Rob Silzer, Editors

Performance Appraisal
James W. Smither, Editor

Organizational Surveys
Allen I. Kraut, Editor

Employees, Careers, and Job Creation
Manuel London, Editor

Published by Guilford Press

Diagnosis for Organizational Change
Ann Howard and Associates

Human Dilemmas in Work Organizations
Abraham K. Korman and Associates

Diversity in the Workplace
Susan E. Jackson and Associates

Working with Organizations and Their People
Douglas W. Bray and Associates

Implementing Organizational Interventions

Implementing Organizational Interventions

Steps, Processes, and Best Practices

Jerry W. Hedge

Elaine D. Pulakos

Editors

Foreword by Eduardo Salas

JOSSEY-BASS
A Wiley Company
www.josseybass.com

Published by

JOSSEY-BASS
A Wiley Company
989 Market Street
San Francisco, CA 94103-1741

www.josseybass.com

Copyright © 2002 by John Wiley & Sons, Inc.

Jossey-Bass is a registered trademark of John Wiley & Sons, Inc.

Jossey-Bass books and products are available through most bookstores. To contact Jossey-Bass directly, call (888) 378-2537, fax to (800) 605-2665, or visit our website at www.josseybass.com.

Substantial discounts on bulk quantities of Jossey-Bass books are available to corporations, professional associations, and other organizations. For details and discount information, contact the special sales department at Jossey-Bass.

We at Jossey-Bass strive to use the most environmentally sensitive paper stocks available to us. Our publications are printed on acid-free recycled stock whenever possible, and our paper always meets or exceeds minimum GPO and EPA requirements.

Library of Congress Cataloging-in-Publication Data

Implementing organizational interventions : steps, processes, and best practices / Jerry W. Hedge and Elaine D. Pulakos, editors; foreword by Eduardo Salas.
    p. cm.—(The professional series) (The Jossey-Bass business & management series)
    Includes bibliographical references and index.
    ISBN 0-7879-5722-4 (alk. paper)
    1. Organizational change. 2. Corporate reorganizations.
I. Hedge, Jerry W. II. Pulakos, Elaine Diane. III. Series.
IV. Series: The Jossey-Bass business & management series.
HD58.8 .I47 2002
658.4'063—dc21

2001008202

FIRST EDITION
HB Printing 10 9 8 7 6 5 4 3 2 1

The Jossey-Bass
Business & Management Series

The Professional Practice Series

SERIES EDITOR

Eduardo Salas
University of Central Florida

EDITORIAL BOARD

Timothy T. Baldwin
Indiana University, Bloomington

Wayne F. Cascio
University of Colorado

Kenneth P. De Meuse
University of Wisconsin, Eau Claire

Jerry W. Hedge
Personnel Decisions Research Institute, Inc.

A. Catherine Higgs
Allstate Insurance Company

Kenneth Pearlman
Lucent Technologies

James W. Smither
LaSalle University

Scott I. Tannenbaum
The Group for Organizational Effectiveness
State University of New York, Albany

Contents

Foreword

Implementing any kind of organizational intervention is easier said than done. Interventions are hard and labor-intensive, and they take time, resources, and commitment. Yet they are essential for long-term organizational effectiveness and survival, and they are critical for moving organizations forward and solving many of their key problems. As I/O psychologists, we regularly recommend a variety of interventions—from mergers and acquisitions to training programs, staffing and employee development, compensation systems, strategic planning processes, and others. Whatever the intervention we recommend, its effectiveness depends on a number of individual, group, organizational, legal, and environmental variables. The key challenge in implementing interventions is managing these complex human, political, and cultural factors in a manner that facilitates success. Of course, most implementations never go as planned. Some fail miserably, others simply fade away. Why? Can this situation be avoided? What have we learned about how to succeed from the industrial/organizational psychology literature and the experience of I/O psychologists who have spent their careers implementing interventions? This book addresses these questions.

Jerry Hedge and Elaine Pulakos have assembled a collection of readable, insightful, and useful chapters on implementing organizational interventions. This is no small accomplishment, given the complexity of the topic. The chapter authors highlight what needs to be done or what one needs to be aware of when implementing diverse interventions. They provide implementation examples, tips, guidelines, and practical advice—all in the spirit of giving practitioners the tools they need to succeed. The volume will help HR practitioners, managers, and executives implement organizational interventions successfully.

On behalf of the editorial board of the Professional Practice Series, I hope this new volume adds value to the practitioner's tool kit. We continue to seek topics and publish volumes that address the needs of those in practice. This volume is an exemplary model of what we are after. Jerry and Elaine, well done. And to the authors, thank you for your insights.

February 2002   EDUARDO SALAS
                                                   University of Central Florida
                                                   Series Editor

Preface

Successful implementation of organizational interventions requires careful planning and coordination during all stages of design, development, implementation, and institutionalization. Finding the best way to ensure successful implementation and achieve the intended results is not a particularly straightforward process because numerous individual, organizational, and environmental variables are likely to have an effect. At the same time, the literature on implementation tends to offer only general guidance—"You have to obtain management buy-in," "You have to communicate about the new systems and processes," and so forth. Although it is certainly true, such general guidance does not provide specific steps and strategies that will help practitioners to ensure the success of their interventions. There is a need for more specific implementation models and strategies. Furthermore, different types of organizational interventions present unique problems and issues.

Overview

The present volume, *Implementing Organizational Interventions: Steps, Processes, and Best Practices,* seeks to address the void in the implementation literature and to provide concrete models, strategies, and guidance for effective implementation of organizational interventions. The core chapters of the volume are organized around specific content areas. Each one focuses on the primary steps involved, issues that must be considered, and decisions that must be made for successful implementation of one type of organizational intervention. In addition, the authors highlight implementation issues and lessons learned by giving examples of situations they have encountered in the course of implementing their own interventions.

In the introductory chapter, Jerry Hedge and Elaine Pulakos briefly review current thinking and research on implementing organizational interventions gathered from the organizational change, organizational innovation, and marketing literatures. The aim is to provide some background and context for thinking about implementation issues. Then, because all the interventions discussed in this volume do represent a form of organizational change, this introductory chapter is followed by a chapter on implementing organizational change in the broader sense. The principles discussed in Chapter Two, by Carolyn Gallagher, Lennox Joseph, and Maria Park, have implications for all organizational interventions and therefore may provide readers with some initial insights and a useful frame of reference for the eight more focused chapters that follow.

In Chapter Three, Mitch Marks discusses the merger and acquisition integration process, noting that most mergers and acquisitions fail to achieve their desired outcomes. He then presents some of the key implementation issues and describes the opportunities available for I/O psychologists to intervene to help make mergers and acquisitions meet their financial and strategic objectives.

In Chapter Four, Ben Dowell describes succession planning as one of the most challenging strategic actions to be taken in today's rapidly changing business environment. He explores the decisions that one should make to design and implement a succession planning system that will enhance the probability of success of an organization's future leaders.

In Chapter Five, Dave Dorsey reviews the current organizational IT landscape and some of the critical factors related to IT project success and failure. This chapter underscores the notions that implementing IT cuts across technological, human, and organizational subsystems and that customer-focused, human-centered approaches are critical.

In Chapter Six, Paul Mulvey and Gerry Ledford suggest that if successful design and implementation practices are used, reward systems become powerful management tools that will significantly influence employee decisions and work behavior. The chapter highlights the key challenges that reward system designers and implementers face, and the many decisions associated with each type of compensation system.

In Chapter Seven, Nancy Rotchford discusses the development and implementation of practical, usable performance management systems that fit the culture and business needs of the organization. She highlights the necessity of making trade-offs between psychometric requirements and the cultural and business constraints within which the system must work in order to maintain and strengthen performance and increase productivity.

In Chapter Eight, Mark Teachout and Craig Hall describe practical issues that are important to the successful implementation of training programs, using the ADDIE (assess, design, develop, implement, evaluate) model as a guide to discuss each instructional phase.

In Chapter Nine, Nancy Tippins reviews the steps involved in the successful implementation of a large-scale selection program and alerts the reader to issues that should be considered before moving a selection procedure into operational use. She suggests that success depends as much on the project management and interpersonal skills of the I/O psychologist as the technical I/O skills.

In Chapter Ten, Scott Eggebeen discusses the added challenges associated with global implementation. He looks at general human resource practices across borders and provides more detail on the cross-cultural implications of specific interventions.

In Chapter Eleven, the concluding chapter, Elaine Pulakos and Jerry Hedge briefly summarize the salient issues raised in the book. They then focus on the need to understand an organization's culture clearly if one wishes to implement an organizational intervention successfully.

Intended Audience

It is our hope that a volume in the SIOP Professional Practice Series on implementation will appeal to a wide audience. Professionals in an organization will learn about useful guidelines for embedding new systems and other interventions into the organizational culture, no matter whether they support a particular function (for example, hiring, training, and so on) or several functions. External consultants will get a better idea about what others have done to implement organizational interventions, what the literature suggests, and the critical issues. Researchers will learn about a number of practical issues and unanswered questions that need to be explored in a variety of content areas.

Acknowledgments

We were fortunate in our choice of chapter authors. The authors of the nine core chapters were knowledgeable and articulate, and in those rare instances when the editors were presumptuous enough to suggest minor adjustments, were gracious in their receptivity to feedback. These authors made our jobs both easy and enjoyable. We thank them for their contributions to the science and practice of I/O psychology. We would also like to thank the series editor, Ed Salas, and the acquisitions editor, Julianna Gustafson, for their guidance, counsel, and insight.

February 2002   JERRY W. HEDGE
                                                                    Minneapolis, Minnesota

                                                                    ELAINE D. PULAKOS
                                                                    Arlington, Virginia

The Authors

JERRY W. HEDGE is president and chief operating officer of Personnel Decisions Research Institutes. He has worked in both the public and private sectors, planning, implementing, and evaluating research in the areas of job analysis, performance measurement, personnel selection and validation, training evaluation, and attitude assessment. He is a fellow of the Society for Industrial and Organizational Psychology and the American Psychological Association, and currently serves on the editorial board of SIOP's Professional Practice Series. He received his Ph.D. in industrial/organizational psychology (1982) from Old Dominion University, and his B.A. degree in psychology (1976) from Texas Lutheran College. He has published numerous journal articles and book chapters during the course of his career.

ELAINE D. PULAKOS is vice president and director of the Washington, D.C., office of Personnel Decisions Research Institutes. She received her B.A. degree (1980) from the Pennsylvania State University and her M.A. (1983) and Ph.D. (1984) degrees from Michigan State University. She is a fellow of the American Psychological Association and Society for Industrial and Organizational Psychology and has served as president, member-at-large, secretary, and program chair of the latter. Her interests focus on the areas of staffing, performance management, and employee development. She has published extensively in these areas, including a recent book with Daniel Ilgen titled *The Changing Nature of Performance: Implications for Staffing, Motivation, and Development*. Pulakos has consulted with numerous public and private-sector organizations, crafting solutions and designing and implementing operational human resource systems to meet their specific needs.

DAVID W. DORSEY is currently a research scientist at the Washington, D.C., office of Personnel Decisions Research Institutes. He received his Ph.D. (1997) in industrial and organizational psychology with a graduate minor in computer science from the University of South Florida. His research and consulting interests cover a range of topics from information technology and computational modeling to performance measurement and job analysis. He has been an invited speaker on issues such as advanced information technologies, and his work has been highlighted in professional journals such as the *Journal of Applied Psychology* and *Personnel Psychology*.

BEN E. DOWELL is vice president, Center for Leadership Development, for the Bristol-Myers Squibb Company, where he leads a group that provides consulting support to management on the development, renewal, and continuity of leadership and operating culture in the company. Before joining Bristol-Myers Squibb, Dowell held a number of management development and human resource generalist positions at Pepsico in the Frito-Lay, Pepsico Foods International, and Pizza Hut divisions. Earlier, he was assistant professor of administrative sciences at Kent State University's Graduate School of Business and managing partner of The Kent Group, a consulting firm he cofounded. He received his Ph.D. in industrial/organizational psychology from the University of Minnesota.

SCOTT L. EGGEBEEN is senior director, Global Core Human Resources, at Booz Allen & Hamilton, a leading global management and technology consulting firm. He is also an adjunct professor at New York University. Previously he worked for Merrill Lynch, NYNEX, and AT&T. He has extensive experience implementing succession planning, executive assessment and development, selection testing, employee opinion surveys, performance appraisal, compensation, benefits, recruiting, and employee relations. He is a member of the American Psychological Association and the Metropolitan New York Association for Applied Psychology. He received his Ph.D. in psychology from Columbia University, where he has also appeared as guest lecturer. With coauthor Joel Moses, Eggebeen contributed a chapter on executive assessment and succession planning to *Evolving Practices in Human Resource Management,* an earlier volume in this series.

CAROLYN A. GALLAGHER is an independent management consultant specializing in change management. She has over twenty years of management and consulting experience and is an experienced management coach. Gallagher holds an M.B.A. in management from St. Thomas University, where she is presently a member of the faculty. Her clients have included a number of Fortune 500 companies. Most recently she has been consulting on change management with the World Bank in its Africa, Asia, and Middle East regions.

CRAIG R. HALL is a performance adviser for Performance Consulting and Learning Technology at USAA, where he is involved in all aspects of performance systems and instructional design, including development and evaluation of technology-based training. Earlier he was a research scientist at the USAF Research Lab, where he developed and evaluated simulation-based (virtual reality) instruction for intelligence agents. Hall also spent ten years at HongkongBank as a computer analyst and auditor, participating in the development of banking applications and auditing computer operations and installations in the United States, Southeast Asia, Canada, and Australia. He earned his Ph.D. in instructional systems at Florida State University.

LENNOX E. JOSEPH is senior change consultant at the World Bank Group and an organization development consultant and trainer in private practice in Washington, D.C. Previously, he was president and CEO of NTL Institute for Applied Behavioral Science and president and senior consultant of the Inguz Group of Ohio. An expert in organizational development and change—specializing in organizational transformation and renewal, creation of learning systems, strategic repositioning, and in integrating diversity values into strategic plans—he has done extensive work internationally. He is an adjunct professor at American University, Washington, D.C., a board member of the REAP Gallery for Creating and Managing Change (Seattle), Path Setters (Santa Cruz, California), Turtle Studios (Alexandria, Virginia), and on the editorial board of Diversity Factor (Philadelphia). He earned his Ph.D. at Case Western Reserve University.

GERALD E. LEDFORD JR. is practice leader, Employee Performance and Rewards, at Nextera's Sibson Consulting Group. He is a nationally recognized authority on approaches to improving organizational effectiveness and employee well-being, including compensation. Before joining Sibson in 1998, he was a key contributor at the Center for Effective Organizations, the University of Southern California. Ledford received his Ph.D. in psychology from the University of Michigan. He has published over seventy articles and chapters and eight books and monographs, most recently *The Rewards of Work: What Employees Value,* which was cosponsored and published by WorldatWork. A frequent speaker at professional and business forums, including WorldatWork events, his research and opinions are often cited in newspapers, magazines, radio, and television news.

MITCHELL LEE MARKS, who received his Ph.D. in organizational psychology from the University of Michigan, is a San Francisco–based consultant who has been at the center of some of the most prominent mergers and acquisitions in the United States and abroad. He also advises organizations on large-scale change, corporate culture, and team building. His clients span all industry sectors and range from small start-ups to large multinational firms. He has authored four books, including *Joining Forces: Making One Plus One Equal Three in Mergers, Acquisitions, and Alliances* with Philip H. Mirvis, and several articles. He is a frequent speaker to professional groups and has lectured at the Harvard Business School.

PAUL W. MULVEY is associate professor in the College of Management at North Carolina State University. His research and consulting focuses on reward systems and team performance issues. He has presented numerous papers at national and international conferences and published articles in journals including *Academy of Management Journal, Academy of Management Executive, Compensation and Benefits Review, Journal of Social Psychology, Organizational Behavior and Human Decision Processes, Small Group Research,* and *WorldatWork Journal.* Mulvey recently coauthored *The Rewards of Work: What Employees Value,* which was cosponsored and published by WorldatWork. He is currently a Park Faculty Scholar at North Carolina State University.

MARIA VERONICA PARK is senior management consultant with the World Bank, working in the areas of strategic organizational diagnosis and change, work-life policies and programs, and internal and external client satisfaction. She is responsible for the World Bank's institutional staff survey program. She has led the design, development, and execution of numerous survey evaluation efforts. She is also responsible for the evaluation and monitoring of the work-life policies and programs. She received her Ph.D. in industrial and organization psychology from the University of Illinois, Champaign-Urbana.

NANCY L. ROTCHFORD obtained her Ph.D. in psychology from the University of Illinois. Since beginning her career in 1982, she has been employed by Bank of America, Boeing, and Microsoft. She has been responsible for developing and implementing performance management systems, employee selection systems development, validation and implementation, quality of service assessment, and employee survey and 360-degree feedback development and execution. She has had numerous affiliations in her nineteen-year career, including board of directors and chairperson of The Mayflower Group and board of directors of the Northern California Human Resources Council, Personnel Testing Council of Northern California, Society for Industrial and Organizational Psychology, and the American Psychological Association.

MARK S. TEACHOUT is assistant vice president of Performance Consulting and Learning Technology at USAA, where he provides leadership and direction for all performance consulting, learning technology, curriculum, and staff development. Earlier, he was a senior scientist at the USAF Research Lab. He led research and development projects in training, program evaluation, test development and validation, and performance measurement and improvement, for which he received the Scientific Achievement Award for outstanding research. He has published numerous articles and reports and is a frequent speaker at conferences on improving training and performance in the workplace. He received a Ph.D. in industrial/organizational psychology from Old Dominion University. Among his many affiliations, he is on the editorial board for the Solutions Series of SIOP. He is adjunct professor at St. Mary's University, San Antonio.

NANCY T. TIPPINS is president of the Selection Practice Group of Personnel Research Associates (PRA), where she is responsible for the development and execution of firm strategies related to employee selection and assessment. Earlier, she worked at GTE, Bell Atlantic, and Exxon Company and managed numerous large-scale selection projects. Tippins is active in professional affairs, including the Society for Industrial and Organizational Psychology (SIOP), the American Psychological Association (APA), and various private industry groups. She is a fellow of SIOP and APA and received her Ph.D. in industrial and organizational psychology from the Georgia Institute of Technology.

Implementing Organizational Interventions

Implementing
Organizational
Intervention

CHAPTER 1

Grappling with Implementation
Some Preliminary Thoughts and Relevant Research

Jerry W. Hedge
Elaine D. Pulakos

It is an organizational reality that the adoption and implementation of almost any system, process, or tool is likely to clash with certain organizational interests and internal alliances. Various groups in organizations may resist change because it upsets the status quo they are comfortable with, or because it interferes with the pursuit of their personal agendas. Although such resistance is unrelated to the technical merits of an intervention, it nevertheless undermines successful implementation. Thus, marketing efforts that spotlight an intervention's technical superiority may not only fail to convince people of its merits but also fail to motivate them to adopt it.

Obviously, the people, the environmental context, and the technical merits of an intervention all contribute to its successful development and implementation. This may be why the techniques advocated by industrial/organizational psychologists are used less often than might be expected, given their scientific foundation. Johns (1993) suggested that the technical merits of an intervention have little relationship to the likelihood of its actual adoption and long-term success, and argued that it is not the complexity of the science that is at the heart of many implementation failures but the lack of understanding by psychologists of how organizations identify and select business solutions.

Although considerable attention and numerous volumes have been devoted to the development of technically sound interventions, comparatively little attention has been paid to figuring out how to make them work in organizations. This is, perhaps, because developing interventions is relatively easy compared with implementing them. Consider, just as one small example, the relative ease with which a set of performance appraisal rating scales can be developed compared with the much more onerous task of getting supervisors in organizations to rate employees in a manner that truly discriminates effective from ineffective performers.

But if the organizational interventions we develop are ever to have the full impact they could, then the complexities associated with their implementation must be dealt with head-on. Specific models and guiding principles like those already in the development literature must be devised for implementation. Although there is a significant literature on change management, innovation adoption, and other related topics, this book is the first to translate broad implementation principles that have been offered into practical and concrete steps for specific organizational interventions.

In the following section we offer a brief overview of some of the main principles culled from the different literatures to guide implementation success.

Insights from the Organizational Change Literature

Organizational change and development is more complex than merely choosing a new approach for modifying an organization's structure, people, or technology. Forces operating at the individual, group, and organizational levels influence management's selection of a particular approach. Often, managers are attracted to the latest workplace fad or fashion, without examining its proven effectiveness or how well it fits the situation. Beer and Eisenstat (1996) suggested that too often companies adopt in a top-down manner programs such as total quality, employee involvement, incentive compensation, and reengineering, and then find that they fail to yield benefits commensurate with the time and money invested in them.

Kiechel (1979) surveyed management consultants and concluded that over 90 percent of American companies were unsuccessful in carrying out changes in corporate strategies. Lawler and Mohrman (1987) noted similar findings with quality circles in the United States; they described a process that began with enthusiasm, was followed by implementation failure, and was then abandoned before any payoff could be realized. Beer and Eisenstat (1996) cited more recent studies reporting that more than 70 percent of all corporations adopting total quality management or reengineering programs said these programs did not live up to expectations.

Certainly, initial enthusiasm and acceptance are insufficient to manage change through all the stages required for successful implementation. Even carefully adopted changes are sometimes abandoned. This may be due in part to the fact that when popular programs are introduced, many of the implementation steps that must be advocated by management and embraced by the members of the organization are overlooked. For example, O'Neill, Pouder, and Buchholtz (1998) noted that managers often express surprise about unexpected developments that arise after implementing strategies touted as successful elsewhere. This should not be so surprising, however, because the administrative details that form the fabric necessary for embedding the system into an organization will almost always be less visible than the strategies themselves. Thus, preliminary acceptance and even enthusiastic embrace of an intervention at introduction fail to ensure real organizational change.

Obviously, most changes produce resistance in the individuals or groups affected by them. The organizational change literature (see, for example, King, 1990; Hultman, 1998) suggests possible reasons for resistance to change, including the vested interests of organizational members, fear of uncertainty, misunderstandings, social disruption, inconvenience, organizational incompatibility, lack of top-level support and commitment, and rejection of outsiders. Exhibit 1.1 describes these variables in greater detail.

A number of years ago, Margulies and Colflesh (1982), writing about planning and implementing a new technology, offered some

Exhibit 1.1. Reasons for Resistance to Organizational Change.

- **Vested interests of organizational members:** Change affects the status quo and employees worry that positions may be eliminated or they may be terminated or reassigned. Not surprisingly, then, change is likely to meet with resistance.

- **Fear of uncertainty:** Employees in most jobs establish a routine; they become familiar with the expectations and responsibilities of the job. Simply put, the known is more comfortable than the unknown.

- **Misunderstandings:** Whenever situations change, misunderstandings may arise—often because of lack of clarity. Misunderstandings are especially likely between higher management and those on whom change is imposed.

- **Social disruption:** Comfortable patterns of communication and information flow are established after working with other employees over time. Changes tend to disrupt such established patterns of interaction.

- **Inconvenience:** The normal routine of performing a job is affected when new processes or procedures are introduced. If the change is merely perceived as an inconvenience that may be enough to elicit resistance.

- **Organizational incompatibility:** Poor fit (or poor perceived fit) between the current organizational structure and the new strategy and its desired outcome may create strong resistance among organization members.

- **Lack of top-level support and commitment:** If employees perceive a lack of enthusiasm, support, or commitment from management (especially top management) they may be less likely to embrace the change themselves.

- **Rejection of outsiders:** When change is introduced by an external change agent, there may be resistance merely because the individual is considered an outsider who cannot possibly know what is best for the organization.

recommendations based on their own successful experiences, including the following:

- Successful change programs depend on informed and motivated persons in the organization.
- Key management should initiate and support the change process.
- Cooperation must come from all levels in the organization.
- Management should be routinely engaged in monitoring the new system to ensure its continued alignment with the organization's goals and objectives.
- People likely to be affected by the change should be involved early in the process.
- Honest and open sharing of plans is crucial to minimize the feelings of threat that come up in the face of technological change.

More recently, Beer and Eisenstat (1996) offered similar advice, outlining three basic principles derived from the organizational behavior and development literature that they believe should characterize successfully implemented change processes:

- The change process should be systemic (that is, the broader perspective of issues related to organizational alignment or fit should be taken into account).
- The change process should invite open discussion of barriers to effective implementation (that is, any successful implementation plan must anticipate potential impediments).
- The change process should develop a partnership among relevant stakeholders (that is, change requires people at all levels of the organization to adapt).

The authors concluded, however, that these basic principles appear to be rarely followed in actual intervention practice.

As Porras and Robertson (1992) noted, any change program must pay attention to both individual and organizational needs. The personal benefits to be gained, and the likely problems to be confronted, should be communicated early in the process to establish an atmosphere of trust. In addition, employees and work groups may wish to participate in planning, analyzing, and coordinating the change effort. This participation, in turn, may offer employees some insight into the need for change and help minimize resistance.

Insights from the Organizational Innovation Literature

Beyer and Trice noted in 1978 that up to that time any real focus on implementation had been directed at understanding and overcoming initial resistance to change by organizational members. They suggested that more attention had been given to how changes are initiated than to the processes and mechanisms involved in actually putting them in place. These authors pointed to the innovation literature as providing a particularly relevant body of research helpful in understanding the implementation process. In this body of literature, *innovation* is defined as a technology, product, or service that is used for the first time by members of an organization, whether or not other organizations have used it previously.

Numerous models have characterized the organizational innovation process. For example, Hage and Aiken (1970) identified a four-stage model (evaluation, initiation, implementation, routinization); Zaltman, Duncan, and Holbek (1973) proposed a two-stage model of design and implementation; and Nord and Tucker (1987) adopted a four-stage model (diagnosis, design, implementation, stabilization). Regardless of the model used, the conclusion is the same: most of the research has focused on the design component and relatively little research has been done on implementation.

Nord and Tucker (1987) suggested that this was unfortunate because implementation activities have much more to do with an innovation's success than design activities. They concluded that implementation is the "payoff" stage of the innovating process. Once the innovation is made, the process of embedding it into organizational life becomes the central activity. Therefore, the authors examined the available research and suggested a number of characteristics that might be critical to successful implementation. They categorized these overall as characteristics of the innovation, characteristics of the organization, and characteristics of relevant interpersonal processes. Exhibit 1.2 lists and describes in brief some of the variables in each of these categories.

Exhibit 1.2. Variables That May Affect Innovation Implementation Success.

Characteristics of the Innovation

- **Routine or radical:** Routine innovation is something new yet similar to what the organization has done before. Radical innovation is new and different from what has been done previously; it may require changes in employee behavior and organization structure.

- **Technical or administrative:** Technical innovations originate in the organization's technical core and include ideas for a new product, process, or service; they tend to succeed with low formalization, distribution of power, and decentralization. Administrative innovations originate in the organization's administrative core and pertain to recruitment policies, resource allocation, and structuring of tasks, authority, and rewards; these are best carried out with high formalization, centralization, and tight structures.

- **Central or peripheral:** Central innovations involve major day-to-day work of the organization and affect activities of almost everyone. Peripheral innovations are associated with specific or limited projects in groups or units; they do not have a central impact on the whole organization or a critical impact on work units.

Characteristics of the Organization

- **Structure:** Organic structures are usually characterized by participative processes and free-flowing communication; mechanistic structures are governed by rules and procedures that reduce ambiguity and potential conflict, and provide clear guidance.

- **History:** To some degree, all organizations are unique and many elements of an organization's history influence its current behavior.

- **Strategy:** The strategy is the organization's main objectives, purposes, goals, and policies.

- **Size:** Smaller organizations may be more facile in their ability to design and implement innovations, but large organizations may have more available tools with which to facilitate implementation.

- **Culture:** Shared key values and beliefs may help or hinder innovation adoption.

- **Organizational learning:** Employees' shared new understandings about the relationship between actions and their outcomes.

Exhibit 1.2. Variables That May Affect Innovation Implementation Success, Cont'd.

Characteristics of Interpersonal Processes

- **Employee involvement:** Employee participation in the change event may facilitate implementation success, or even reshape the innovation.

- **Politics and influence:** Individual pursuit of self-interest, whether or not that self-interest conflicts with larger organizational interests.

- **Communication:** Frequency, methods, and direction of information flow may affect employee commitment to successful innovation implementation.

- **Leadership styles:** The underlying need structure of the individual leader, which motivates various behaviors in leadership situations, can affect perceptions of the leader's commitment to the innovation and the subsequent support among organizational members.

Klein and Sorra (1996) argued that an organization's inability to benefit from adopting an innovation more likely reflects a failure of implementation than a failure of the innovation itself. The authors believe that implementation effectiveness is influenced by both an organization's climate and the perceived fit of that innovation to users' values.

They described an organization's climate for the implementation of a given innovation as employees' shared perceptions of the degree to which their use of the innovation was expected, supported, and rewarded by the organization. The fit between the users' values and the intended innovation was defined in terms of the degree to which users believe the innovation would foster (or inhibit) the fulfillment of their values. Klein and Sorra encouraged organizations to foster a fit between climate, innovation, and values by providing participation opportunities for employees at all levels and educating them about the organizational need for the innovation.

Taking a Marketing Perspective

Leonard-Barton and Kraus (1985) stated that individuals responsible for guiding a technical innovation's transition into operational use are often more adept at overseeing its development than its implementation. Certainly, competencies required for development and adoption of an innovation are different from those necessary for ensuring its acceptance. Consequently, they recommended that the organization adopt a marketing perspective as perhaps the best framework through which to accomplish implementation.

In clarifying their recommendations, they also differentiated the notion of a marketing perspective from a selling perspective. Whereas selling starts with a finished product, marketing begins with gathering information on user needs and preferences. They concluded that a marketing approach was the proper framework to adopt when it comes to change initiatives because it looks at how to position a product in relation to all other products vying for attention. A marketing perspective also emphasizes the importance of understanding available or required distribution channels and the infrastructure needed to support product use. Further, Leonard-Barton and Kraus (1985) noted that a marketing perspective encourages implementation managers to involve users in the early identification and strengthening of fit between a product and their own needs, prepares users to operationalize the innovation, and shifts "ownership" of the innovation to users.

The authors suggested that many implementation efforts have failed because the importance of preparation for implementation is underestimated. As we noted earlier, an innovation's technical superiority and even its strategic importance do not guarantee its acceptance or continued use. Yet it is this misperception that leads individuals and organizations to "overcommit" to the purchase or development of a technology but "undercommit" to its implementation. Just as marketing managers carefully plan the details for gathering critical product information, so implementation managers must develop a framework to guide decisions about when and how to collect needed information from relevant users.

Leonard-Barton and Kraus (1985) emphasized the importance of identifying the individuals or groups whose acceptance is essential for the success of the intervention. Thus, it must be decided who to approach, when, and with which arguments. Certainly, both top management and end users must buy into the innovation to make it succeed, but marketing an idea to these two groups requires very different approaches. Top management, with an eye on the bottom line, tends to focus on return on investment and payback. Involving end users in the decision-making process whenever possible instills a sense of ownership of the intervention. Leonard-Barton and Kraus's simple message is that it is overly optimistic to believe that an innovation will sell itself, and it is equally dangerous to oversell the potential impact of a new system.

Conclusion

Beer and Eisenstat (1996) noted that the constantly changing work environment—with global competition and rapidly changing technology—is forcing corporations to rethink their strategies and realign their organizations to implement these strategies. They stated that corporate leaders may have to learn to reformulate strategy and realign their organizations routinely if they are to thrive, or even survive, in such a turbulent environment. Because of this rapidity of change, individuals and organizations also must become more proficient at successful implementation of programs, techniques, and procedures required to help organizations stay viable. When implementation is viewed as the transition process from the decision to acquire a new technology, process, or tool to its incorporation in day-to-day work, the cyclical, never-ending nature of the process becomes more apparent.

Consequently, it will become more and more crucial to understand the factors that affect implementation success in today's world of work. The importance of the implementation component of any program, practice, or technique seems indisputable. But extensive coverage of the topic has yet to emerge in the research or practice literature. The remaining chapters in this volume describe different types of organizational interventions, the implementation activities involved, lessons learned, and specific, practical guidance for the reader that should facilitate implementation success and enhance our understanding of implementation processes.

References

Beer, M., & Eisenstat, R. A. (1996). Developing an organization capable of implementing strategy and learning. *Human Relations, 49,* 597–619.

Beyer, J. M., & Trice, H. M. (1978). *Implementing change: Alcoholism policies in work organizations.* New York: Free Press.

Hage, J., & Aiken, M. (1970). *Social change in complex organizations.* New York: Random House.

Hultman, K. (1998). *Making change irresistible: Overcoming resistance to change in your organization.* Palo Alto, CA: Consulting Psychologists Press.

Johns, G. (1993). Constraints on the adoption of psychology-based personnel practices: Lessons from organizational innovation. *Personnel Psychology, 46,* 569–592.

Kiechel, W. (1979). Playing the rules of the corporate strategy game. *Fortune, 24,* 110–115.

King, N. (1990). Innovation at work: The research literature (pp. 15–59). In M. A. West & J. L. Farr (Eds.), *Innovation and creativity at work: Psychological and organizational strategies.* New York: Wiley.

Klein, K. J., & Sorra, J. S. (1996). The challenge of innovation implementation. *Academy of Management Review, 21,* 1055–1080.

Lawler, E. E., & Mohrman, S. A. (1987). Quality circles: After the honeymoon. *Organizational Dynamics, 15,* 42–54.

Leonard-Barton, D., & Kraus, W. A. (1985). Implementing new technology. *Harvard Business Review, 63,* 102–110.

Margulies, N., & Colflesh, L. (1982). A socio-technical approach to planning and implementing new technology. *Training and Development Journal, 36,* 16–29.

Nord, W. R., & Tucker, S. (1987). *Implementing routine and radical innovations.* San Francisco: New Lexington Press.

O'Neill, H. M., Pouder, R. W., & Buchholtz, A. K. (1998). Patterns in the diffusion of strategies across organizations: Insights from the innovation diffusion literature. *Academy of Management Review, 23,* 98–114.

Porras, J. I., & Robertson, P. J. (1992). Organizational development: Theory, practice, and research (pp. 719–822). In M. D. Dunnette & L. M. Hough (Eds.), *Handbook of industrial and organizational psychology* (2nd ed.). Palo Alto, CA: Consulting Psychologists Press.

Zaltman, G., Duncan, R., & Holbek, J. (1973). *Innovations and organizations.* New York: Wiley.

CHAPTER 2

Implementing Organizational Change

Carolyn A. Gallagher
Lennox E. Joseph
Maria Veronica Park

An organization's change process is often very rewarding and satisfying. Sometimes, however, it seems as if the process is under siege, facing complex challenges and doomed to have little impact. The reason is simple: organizational change runs contrary to the human need for consistency and stability. Hence, the change agent must understand the delicate balance between consistency and change, both individually and organizationally. This chapter focuses on how to implement change intervention processes in organizations in the face of this need to maintain balance.

The chapter offers practitioners the knowledge, tools, and techniques needed to succeed in implementing change in organizations. It is organized into five sections:

- "Putting Organizational Change in Context" briefly looks at the beginnings of organizational change, defines terms, and identifies the key values relevant to change.
- "The Change Process" presents a model of a change implementation process.
- "Key Principles in Implementing Change" provides some organizational do's and don'ts on change.

- "Methodologies for Change" highlights useful change methods.
- "Measuring Change Implementation" discusses ideas on measuring change implementation in organizations.

Putting Organizational Change in Context

This section provides a brief overview of some of the main trends in organizational change and discusses the different dimensions of change implementation in organizations. It is in how we view and define organizational change that we lay the foundation for powerful change processes and their ultimate impact on an organization.

The idea of social planning and hiring experts to solve problems goes back a couple of centuries. But the notion that social scientists can plan, participate in, and actively change an organization only took root in the middle of the twentieth century. It was then that executives and social practitioners saw the possibility of merging and reconciling the field of social practice with the science of human and organizational behavior. It was a slow realization that employees could intentionally determine the form and shape of their collective future, and that it was in the organization's interest for them to do so. Also during this period there was a shift from the concept of nonintervening social scientists to social scientists having a valued, even critical, role to play in the guidance and management of organizations. This drew attention to the technical questions of how to plan and create change in organizations. By the early 1960s the discussion shifted from who should be involved in processes of change planning and its overarching values and purposes to how to plan particular changes in particular settings and situations.

The late 1960s and 1970s saw a wave of liberal movements that brought to the fore the language and rhetoric of power, and questioned the realities of existing relationships in society and in organizations. These realizations led to a focus on self-expression and transparency in organizations, tightening the gap between espoused values and actual values. By the 1980s organizational change efforts centered on humanizing the workplace.

Now in the first years of the third millennium, the emphasis is on treating planned change in organizations not as a value in itself but as an artifact of management. We find a greater emphasis on the technical application of change practices than on change itself and an institutionalization of change in culturally diverse organizations. Hence, today one can look to the following values in implementing change in organizations:

- *Ownership:* Change and change implementation processes need to be "owned" or "desired" by organizational members rather than by a few senior-level executives alone.
- *Hard data:* Data need to be collected to support change implementation initiatives. The data must come from different informants and be validated as some of the dominant ways that the organization thinks about itself and its work.
- *Integrity:* Certain core organizational values must be held as nonnegotiable in the change process.
- *Diversity:* Heterogeneity in organizations, and the need to respond to it for employee and business reasons, must be assumed.
- *Empowerment:* Individual needs (identity recognition, personal-professional development, and self-autonomy and self-expression) must be balanced with organizational demands in order to facilitate and regulate the collective whole.
- *Learning:* It must be understood that all true change involves learning and that as individuals and organizations learn about themselves and how they do their work they improve their performance.

Change is a journey that involves moving from a present state through a transition process to a future or desired state. Organizational change is a business process in an organization where there is a clearly articulated plan to achieve the desired end. The desired state is often referred to as the *vision*. When the journey is a simple one—for instance, involving improvements in present policies or increased efficiencies through new procedures—it is considered first-order or incremental change. In this type of change, the underlying foundations of work (that is, the purpose of the work, its ranking in the value chain, beliefs about how the work should be done) remain unchanged. The goal of the change effort is to help the organization do differently what it has always done.

There is also second-order change. Here the change is not incremental but discontinuous and revolutionary, radically affecting how people think about their work and their role in relation to it. This type of change process redefines the psychological and sociocultural context of the work, and when successfully carried out changes the business processes surrounding the organization's deliverables. This is transformative or radical change, because the assumptions themselves that govern work change along with the organization's culture.

Both of these types of change can occur through a voluntarily planned approach or as a result of external forces that cause an organization to rethink its work processes. The latter is considered *reactive change,* because the organization is responding to stimuli outside its control. Determining whether a change process is incremental or transformative, reactive or proactive has an impact on the design and implementation of the change process. In all scenarios certain elements and developmental phases remain the same, although how they get implemented may vary considerably. These elements and developmental phases constitute a change implementation process.

The Change Process

We have created a simple change model as a framework for considering the typical processes and pitfalls that occur in creating change in organizations. In our model, four sets of people must work closely together: client, change consultant, champion, and staff and managers.

The client (for example, the president of the company, senior vice president, or manager) is the individual who expresses a need for a new or renewed organization and contracts for help in creating it. The change consultant (external or internal) is the architect of the change process. He or she works closely with the client to determine what initial plan will best meet the client's requirements. A consultant cannot create the change without the collaboration of champions and of staff and managers. Even though these roles are presented individually here, in reality it is the ability of these people to work as a team that creates successful change.

Exhibit 2.1 shows these roles in a change implementation process and the phases of a change process. A discussion of these roles and phases follows.

Exhibit 2.1. Change Roles and Phases of Change.

People	Roles	Phase
Client	• Expresses dissatisfaction with status quo • Imagines the possibility of something different • Champions project from beginning to end • Lets go of organizational control that stifles change • Aligns, blends emerging structure with process, systems, cultural, political, technical landscape	Initiate
Change Consultant	• Translates clients wants, needs into preliminary change plan (the what) • Provides technical expertise in design and implementation of change • Determines organizational readiness for changes and intervenes to increase readiness when needed • Coaches leaders, champions, and change team in change leadership, change management, and dealing with resistance • Spearheads change communication and influences processes to engage the system in ongoing change	Plan
Champions	• Focus on specific tasks in change implementation • Act as feedback loop for change process; initiate midcourse corrections • Validate the change process • Determine how work will be done • Assume responsibility of change management in their own venues • Engage wider circle of staff in accomplising change • Respond to resistance with information, assurance, support and incorporate it into change plans • Celebrate successes	Implement
Staff and Managers	• Provide information about what needs to be changed and how • Work in areas of their expertise to institutionalize change • Operate as reality check on change processes • Celebrate successes	Institutionalize

Client

Ideally, the client plays two primary roles. His or her initial responsibility is to express why there is discontent with the status quo. There may be a need for a change in attitudes or behaviors, a feeling that the present structure does not meet organizational needs, or a realization that needs have changed over time, rendering the present structure, systems, processes, and behaviors irrelevant. The client works with the change consultant to determine the roots of the dissatisfaction and is committed to discovering the real issues, and not just the symptoms, to be addressed. Second, the client expresses some idea of the desired goals or end state. The more details a client can provide on the desired future—or vision—the greater the likelihood that it will be achieved. The consultant often has to coach and counsel the client into clearly articulating this initial vision.

The client also offers a primary check on the organizational realities that need attention in creating the change. It is this awareness—sometimes learned, often intuitive—that is a key signpost for the change consultant. The client remains a sounding board throughout the change process and is usually the overall champion for the project.

Change Consultant

With technical knowledge in change design and planning, the change consultant translates the client's needs and desires into initial plans that respond to the organization's financial, political, technical, sociocultural, structural, and even spiritual realities. The change consultant also calculates the cost of the change against these realities and gauges the organization's readiness for change, thus helping the organization to address issues such as these: What time commitment will be needed? What level of disruption do the change plans create in the environment? Is this disruption valid, or is it too much or not enough? Is the vision for the future sufficiently articulated and will it be compelling and motivating for staff? Are communication plans in place to allow staff ownership of the process? What strategy is needed to influence key decision makers and resisters in the organization?

Despite the natural inclination to resist change, many people actually have an inherent psychological "space" for change. This space is directly proportional to the level of dissatisfaction they are experiencing. If the change process seems valid but the psychological space is insufficient for change, the consultant may need to create more of it. This can be done by raising the client's awareness of the deliverables or feelings that are not being addressed or highlighting the possibilities that remain unfilled. One effective way to do this is by benchmarking the organization against best practices and opening the client's eyes to what is truly possible. Readers interested in more information on benchmarking are directed to *Benchmarking for Best Practices* (Bogon & English, 1994).

During initial phases of the change process, the consultant is a primary interface with the client, providing status reports through regular change design team meetings attended by individuals with leadership functions in the change process. As the process continues, the flow of communication normally becomes more relaxed and everybody communicates with the client as needed.

Consultants do not disappear once change plans are produced but rather remain very much connected to the project through the implementation, completion, and acknowledgment phases. They oversee from the conceptual perspective whether things are going according to plan. Often the consultant must alter the plans as new information emerges during the change process. This is important, because change implementation must itself model the ability to change as the environment dictates what it is willing to accept.

Champions

Champions are key advocates designated to work on specific tasks in change implementation. They are selected because they have a reputation for successfully delivering projects and are respected in the organization. They have an active role in transforming the change plans into structures, systems, policies, and procedures. They are the implementers of the change process and builders of change in the organization. Their work varies from laying the foundation and groundwork for change to constructing the pillars—behavioral, technological, political, financial, spiritual, and emotional—to support the changing organization. Together with the change consultant they sequence the change, continually negotiating conflicting priorities between the change implementation process and daily operations of the business.

The task at hand during this phase of the change process is to translate plans into reality, as detailed in Figure 2.1. All plans should be validated with the individuals and groups they affect. This means assembling work groups, introducing them to the change process, selling the change idea, engaging them in deciding on a path forward, and identifying the key blocks to the plans. In this phase, implementation of the intervention is key and maintaining a specific work plan with a time frame becomes increasingly important.

Figure 2.1. Stepping-Stones in Change Implementation.

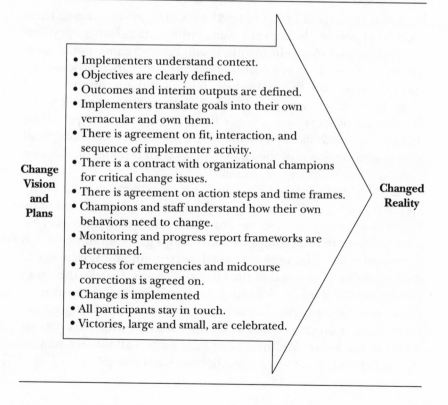

Change Vision and Plans

- Implementers understand context.
- Objectives are clearly defined.
- Outcomes and interim outputs are defined.
- Implementers translate goals into their own vernacular and own them.
- There is agreement on fit, interaction, and sequence of implementer activity.
- There is a contract with organizational champions for critical change issues.
- There is agreement on action steps and time frames.
- Champions and staff understand how their own behaviors need to change.
- Monitoring and progress report frameworks are determined.
- Process for emergencies and midcourse corrections is agreed on.
- Change is implemented
- All participants stay in touch.
- Victories, large and small, are celebrated.

Changed Reality

As new procedures are recommended, structures are created, and technology is introduced, the champions work with the consultant to develop the strategy to influence key organizational stakeholders. Having champions also increases the number of individuals getting involved, and ideally, creates an infectious spirit of change in the organization.

We cannot overemphasize the importance of communicating during the change implementation process. The organization must remain aware of what is occurring. A communications plan helps disseminate information on the change process and is the critical tool to managing increasing resistance in the organization. Champions must be skilled in identifying key resisters, listening to their opinions, and using their ideas in strengthening the change process for greater sustainability in the future.

Staff and Managers

Staff and managers help create the change by working in their areas of expertise (human relations, information technology, survey analysis, and so on) in the newly emerging organizational infrastructure. They serve as a reality check on the change process, but also help make sure that individual changes and improvements and ongoing organizational processes fit together. They institutionalize the change process by dealing with all the operational problems that interfere with its implementation. Their operational comments are important aspects of the change process and should not be seen as complaints simply to be dismissed.

It is during this stage of a change process that the change team members (client, change consultant, champions, staff and managers) begin an overall assessment of the change initiative and express pride in their accomplishments and regrets about plans that remain unfilled. The period of final assessment and review marks the beginning of the end of the change process. Usually the client determines that it is best to turn the organization's attention to more pressing concerns. The actual transition from the change implementation process occurs when the client claims, "This is it, for better or for worse. We might not have gotten all that we wanted but we certainly have more now than we had before."

Assumptions of Change Implementation

Five main assumptions contribute to effective implementation of change:

- *Intentionality:* At the very moment one starts thinking about a change, one begins to manifest the desired change. Therefore, it is important from the initial stages in thinking about change to be intentional about what is being created, how it is being created, and the purposes it will serve.

- *Teamwork:* No one individual creates a successful and noteworthy change process. Change occurs when a group draws together its collective resources to create and achieve a possibility that previously it was unable to imagine.

- *Creation of new identities:* A critical part of every successful change process we have observed is that a new identity is created for the organization, task group, or individual. Simultaneously there is the discarding of an old identity that is seen as no longer beneficial. Letting go of old identities and creating new ones is an important part of organizational change.

- *Importance of change leaders:* The personality and character of those who hold change management leadership roles are as important as the change methodologies in contributing to successful change. Behavior role modeling by senior management is important for organizational change to occur.

- *Survival:* Whatever exists in an organization exists for a specific reason and was created to deal with a specific challenge (real or imagined) that the organization once faced. Hence, it is important to remember the original purposes of the structure (or system, process, procedures, behaviors, or attitudes) that exist today. Asking such questions allows us to appreciate the past and see the new organization emerging based on the strengths of the old. Two good resources on these change issues are *Organizational Culture and Leadership* (Schein, 1997) and *Appreciative Inquiry: Change at the Speed of Imagination* (Watkins & Mohr, 2001).

Key Principles in Implementing Change

Two sets of key principles are important regardless of the content or magnitude of the change undertaken. One set relates to understanding the context of change, the second to the management and motivation of the human resources needed to mobilize and implement the change effort. In this section, we discuss these two principles along with some related implementation advice.

Context of Change

To understand the context of change it is first necessary to be clear about what is driving change. Is the change *vision-driven* or *gap-driven,* and what is the impact of these on the implementation and design of the change process? Second, because change happens in a work system, how does the nature of the system affect the way we design and carry out the implementation process? And third, what and where is the resistance and how can it best be used to facilitate the desired end-state?

Vision-Driven or Gap-Driven Change

Vision-driven change is based on a vision—a shared and detailed picture of the desired reality for the organization that is unfettered by the dilemmas of the present. It is not designed just to solve today's problems but to inspire a completely new approach to the organization's future. When an organizational change is vision-driven or when an organization elects to change with a vision in mind, it is deciding to *design* rather than *problem-solve* its way into the future. The organization realizes that it cannot "fix" itself to achieve the future it desires but rather requires something more radical. The book *Visionary Leadership: Creating a Compelling Sense of Direction for Your Organization* (Nanus & Bennis, 1995) provides more detail about the characteristics of this type of change.

Gap-driven change is also based on a vision, but rather than focusing on the vision to pull an organization forward there is an extra step in the process. There is the desired state, the status quo, and a discrepancy between the two—a gap between what is and what is desired. The vision is still there but the primary focus of the change effort is on closing the gap. This means problem solving, something most organizations are quite good at and enjoy doing.

Gap-driven change is positive in that it calls on the organization to do something it already knows well, without the sense of inadequacy and ambiguity that venturing into the unknown can bring. The downside is that implementation of a gap-closing strategy can degenerate into a series of problems to be solved, and the vision is lost. Closing the gap encourages incremental strategies and may miss the breakthrough thinking that a vision inspires. *Terms of Engagement: Changing the Way We Change Organizations* (Axelrod, 2000) offers more information on gap-driven change.

Both vision-driven and gap-driven change are effective strategies. The choice is made based on the magnitude of the change needed, the experience of the system with change efforts, and the energy and determination of the leadership.

> Remember to match the approach to the readiness of the organization. If problem solving is a strong competence and a vision is too much of a stretch, then an organization might choose a gap strategy and work with leadership to stay open to possibilities.

Maintaining a Systems Perspective

It is important to maintain a systems perspective while creating change in an organization. A system is an arrangement of interconnected and interdependent elements whose purpose in an organizational setting is to create outputs. The elements work together, and when one element is changed all others are affected and so is the overall ability of the system to produce. The awareness that everything is interconnected means that change planners must think through the system's existing interrelationships and anticipate the dynamics and conflicts that will arise.

Some systems are more complex than others, with multiple feedback loops that provide information on performance and intricate interdependencies that are not easily detectable. In these kinds of systems, the effects of change are hard to predict and even keen observers will not be able to explain some outcomes fully. For instance, in a large cultural survey project in a multinational corporation, monthly support group meetings were held with high-level representatives of each vice presidency in order to deal with the systemic issues that existed throughout the institution but were experienced differently in each vice presidency. This was one way to coordinate the change efforts throughout the organization and it also provided important feedback to the change design team on how the implementation of the change was occurring and what adjustments were needed in the future.

Multiple feedback loops are a key element in bringing about change in complex organizations; they provide critical ongoing progress data that reinforce the changes. An example of a simple feedback loop would be to maintain conversation space on a Web site for comments on the change implementation process. A more complex feedback loop would be to organize a forum with panelists from different divisions to brief staff on the changes occurring and to inform the designers about where necessary connections are not being made.

Generally, the organization's complexity and interrelatedness are underestimated. Change efforts aim for specific outcomes in a specific time frame and produce those along with unintended outcomes. It is important to remember that the process of adaptation and change is really never finished. As much as the organization needs stability and wants the turmoil of change to be over with in order to return to "situation normal," life is always evolving. The change effort needs to hold the organization's longing for stability and the reality of continual change in balance to help the organization cope.

One example of this paradox is the shift from design to implementation. The perception is that design is finished before implementation begins. But in reality, design is never finished and the implementation phase makes this point clearly. Unforeseen problems, unintended outcomes, and the passage of time all ensure that the organization will continually outgrow its planned design. The more complex the organization, the more likely it is that design will continue throughout the implementation phase.

> Keep implementers connected with each other so they can
> exchange stories and commiserate. And keep the energy
> flowing. Large initiatives should be broken down into
> elements; each element is an opportunity for success and an
> energy infusion. Quick wins help keep the energy level high
> and the organization motivated.

Valuing Resistance to Change

Healthy systems have a built-in bias for the status quo. After all, the purpose of a system is to produce a deliverable, and any challenge to production or how production is accomplished is a threat. The response to threat is resistance; it is the system's way of saying no.

Resistance is a biological programming that exists at both the organizational and individual levels and may take many forms. A group facing a significant change may resist by denying that change is necessary or by asking for unreasonable amounts of data to "prove" that the status quo is unsatisfactory. Staff might be physically or mentally absent. They may organize to fight the change, activate their personal networks against the change, or attempt to ignore the whole thing. They may attack the credibility of the leader, turn on each other, or be passive-aggressive in the implementation of the change commitments.

To some degree, many forms of resistance can be anticipated and appropriate responses can be programmed into a change design and implementation. For instance, it is helpful to have a comprehensive strategic change communication plan (SCCP) that provides as much hard data as possible. This plan maps the content and tone of the communications media with the different behavioral and psychological responses at every stage of the change process. The plan should be designed so that its strategic thrust is to confront the dissatisfaction of the organization; elicit, receive, and acknowledge responses from employees; stimulate and challenge staff to be involved; and focus and inspire individuals to action.

It is impossible to anticipate all the resistance to be encountered, and so it is useless to try to manage it all. But like other elements in a system, resistance can be handled by attentive listening, vigilance, observation, and midcourse correction. *Coaching Change: Breaking Down Resistance and Building Up Hope* (Bandy, 2000) and *Making Change Irresistible: Overcoming Resistance to Change in Your Organization* (Hultman, 1998) offer specific strategies in handling resistance.

Participation is one design choice that is particularly helpful in dealing with resistance. Change "done" to an individual or an organization heightens resistance; opportunities for meaningful choices and input in design and implementation lessens resistance.

Consider resistance as a force protecting something of value in the organization. Engage the resistance and assess whether the specific component that is being valued is an element that needs to be incorporated into the change implementation plans.

Management and Motivation of the Human Resource

The most elegantly designed plan is completely dependent on people for its implementation. We identify four principles in this regard. The first has to do with the critical role of the leader; in the best change implementation processes, the change leaders not only advocate the change but also become symbolic of it. The second principle examines the role of the individual in change and the personal adaptation that is necessary to embody change in one's own work experiences. Third is the element of participation or providing opportunities for those who will have to live with the changed reality to help in its creation. The fourth principle is to plan for the critical transition period between letting go of today and moving forward with tomorrow.

Change Leadership

It is important to have solid credible change leadership. In times of change trust is fragile. The staff seeks reassurance from a source they feel they can rely on, someone they feel is truthful, who will tell them the real story including the risky parts. They want to be treated as adults. In addition, each person has his or her own reservations and questions about the change and looks to the leader's words and behavior for answers and reassurance. When the leader fulfills this role, he or she becomes a symbol of the change effort and the vision.

The successful leader is optimistic, not defensive, and genuine, able to share his or her hopes and concerns with integrity, and sufficiently self-confident to reassure staff that everyone is in it together. Congruence in leadership is critical; words and behavior must match—"the talk must be walked." The leader interacts with all organizational members, telling them what they need to know, weaving together a picture that includes everyone and what they are expected to do. This is a tall order for most managers, and many are not equal to the challenge. For those whose expertise is in planning, monitoring, and controlling, the uncertainty that change brings can ignite a firestorm of behaviors and fears that send exactly the wrong messages to staff. Managing through change is the best these leaders can do.

Individuals with organizational stature, especially in senior management positions, must be given the mantle of change leadership. If there is a natural leader at the forefront of a change effort, his or her skills should be put to use. Otherwise, it is important to recognize the strengths in the present leadership and make the best use of those strengths in planning the change effort. Once individuals understand their role as change leaders, and the criticality of this role to successful implementation, most are willing to try approaches different from their daily management style. A coach usually gives great support. Coaches can help change leaders anticipate trouble spots, work through their own feelings about change, and respond to staff's anxieties. With experienced, thoughtful support, many managers can succeed in leading change.

With or without support, change leaders have the greatest impact on creating change when they are willing to change themselves and to grow during the change process. The organization sees this, respects it, and criticizes it, but it always takes notice that change is indeed happening. Conversations with the leader about personal change must explicitly address what that person wants and can expect in the change process and his or her personal comfort level with the support arrangements that have been made. If this kind of frankness is not possible with the leader, the change impact will be compromised. The organization needs clear vision, flexibility, and a steady hand on the rudder to ensure the success of any change effort. If conversations about these issues are problematic among the change leaders, consultants, and champions it is unlikely that they will occur with staff and in organizational units. *Beyond Change Leadership: Advanced Strategies for Today's Transformational Leaders* (Anderson & Anderson, 2001) and *Trust and Betrayal in the Workplace* (Reina & Reina, 1999) provide additional insights into helping managers become change leaders.

Organizational change sparks personal change, and when the leader of a change implementation process is a strong model of personal change the door is open for other participants to change as well. The leader whose behavior is congruent with the changes under way sends a powerful message. He or she models the post-change expectations for managers and sets the tone for the future.

Choose and groom strong individuals to lead a change process. They should be given personal and organizational support. They should be encouraged to focus on their own personal learning and change in addition to tasks and specific responsibilities associated with their role as a change leader. They should learn to inventory the learning (both positive and negative) and express it as they implement the change initiative. The leadership should also be spread around, expanding the base as implementation develops, because building a critical mass of leaders is important.

Personal Adaptation to Change

Adapting to change is a personal growth process that has professional and career ramifications. Support to help people adapt to change needs to be built into the change implementation process from the very beginning. Team building methods help newly created teams, and many group techniques are available to raise and address problems. For example, rather than expecting staff merely to read about a new work flow, it is helpful to organize role-play sessions. Team members can play out the new process with one of them acting the part of the product and the rest acting out the steps in the process. As the "product" moans and groans or celebrates its treatment at each step, the players experience the new flow and see possibilities to improve the process even further. This "becoming the process" enables staff to imagine life after change and adjust to how they will personally fit into the new environment.

When management pays attention to what is happening with staff at a personal and emotional level, it lessens anxiety, stretches their imagination, lets them know that management is concerned with their well-being, and increases ownership of the change process. If there is no encouragement or care for the personal adjustment process, implementation will be slow and staff may remain paralyzed by their own resistance.

In every change process, a small percentage of people simply do not fit into the new environment. To keep that number to the absolute minimum, the personal change process must be intentional and supported by the organization.

Invest heavily in attending to individual needs during change. It is important to be gentle with employees and appreciate their struggles in the change process. Support structures should be provided to help them work through their feelings about the change.

Participation

When staff participate in the process, they gain the time to adjust emotionally to change and are directly involved in decision making. If participation options are not offered early, disagreement and silent minorities will surface later. If input opportunities are offered only at the time of implementation, it will be too late for meaningful input.

Some believe that participation can slow down change processes with lengthy discussion and searches for consensus. Sometimes this is true, but it does not have to be. There are many ways to achieve agreement quickly, as shown in Figure 2.2. Participation builds understanding, creates teachers and communicators to spread the word, and anticipates questions and problems. It is an investment that pays off in broader acceptance and understanding—saving time during implementation.

Participation does not eliminate or even decrease the need for strong leadership. The more participation there is in an effort, the more important it is that the leader be clear on the vision, the reason for change, and what comes next, and remain in touch with progress or problems.

Transition Planning

Transition planning recognizes that the organization is moving away from a current state and embracing a new vision. When man-

Figure 2.2. Tools for Agreement in a Hurry.

	Ownership	
	Higher	**Lower**
Quality: Higher	• *Force field analysis*—Identify drivers and constraints for key alternatives. • *Multiple test*—Eliminate alternatives based on how they satisfy tests (low cost, short time, low political impact). • *Dot prioritizing*—Polling process with adhesive dots based on specific criteria. Save the high scores. • Groupware.	• *Third-party validation*—The expert decides among alternatives.
Quality: Lower	• *Toss out*—Indicate three least-favorite options; throw out the aggregate least favorites.	• *Straw poll*—There is a show of hands or secret ballot to eliminate alternatives. • *Straight voting*—Majority wins.

Build ownership and enhance the impact of the change by involving staff early and often in its design, planning, and implementation. To the degree possible, work groups should be allowed to plan their own "how" and implement it with a minimum of fuss.

agement focuses on a vision it is easy to overlook the needs of staff for an orderly parting with the past. But new ways cannot be established until the staff let go of the old. Transition planning helps the organization let go of past ways of working.

To move forward staff must leave behind procedures they created, roles they developed, skills they mastered, meaningful relationships, and the fit they have developed with a work group or supervisor. These are significant losses, difficult to balance against a future that may be enticing but unknown. Until the passing of the old (structures, systems, procedures, policies, roles, relationships) is acknowledged and even grieved, the organization will not be ready to go on to something new. Attempting to short-circuit the transition process or overselling the future desired state (while the organization tenaciously clings to the old ways of doing things) does not help staff adapt to their losses.

The transition plan must answer key questions of staff who are letting go of their past. These are often very personal questions. Who am I now that I have a different role? Do I still have a contribution to make? Am I still important? How do I fit into the new environment? Who will I work with? Who will the boss be, and will she appreciate me? The plan should include such things as training for new skills, developing processes for creating new work teams, choosing leaders, defining new roles, and ensuring that staffs are ready and prepared to succeed. Also useful in transition planning is to plan methods of rewarding success using a process that matches the desired organization rather than the organization that is being left behind. Some of these are described in Exhibit 2.2.

The transition plan, nested in the implementation schedule, must continually reinforce the organization in moving toward its vision.

Exhibit 2.2. Rewarding Behavior in a Change Process.

Category	Example Behaviors	Rewards
Vision	• Behavior that exemplifies key tenets of the vision • Contribution that extends the vision down in the organization	• Public institutional acknowlegment • The "Prince" award • Work posted on change Web site
Managing Resistance	• An observable personal change • Leadership—patient and consistent explanation of change benefits—addressing the hard questions • Turnaround results in productivity	• Story featured in house organ or change newspaper • Special membership in elite organization—the "Not the French Resistance" • Awarding of "survivor" benefits spot award or nonmonetary • Story, legendary turnarounds in a special change "chronicle" after the change is completed
Transition	• Assisting others in adjustment to change • Early achievement of change productivity goals	• Competition and awards for goal achievement: 75 percent there; 90 percent there; on target • Best practice awards—inclusion in best practice database • Team awards: dinners, boat trip, activities • A day off
Stabilizing	• Longer-term perseverance and delivery on goals	• The long-distance runner award: victory tape, bonus • Promotion • Spot ansd performance awards • Team awards—financial and activities

Develop a comprehensive communications and education plan for leaders, participants, and all staff members. Progress should be reported on often through success stories and stories of best practice. Achievers should be rewarded and successes celebrated as widely as possible, because it is never just one person or one group that creates success. Success depends on foundational and interrelated efforts.

Finally, we offer this short list of perspectives to avoid, or as we term them, "implementation don'ts":

- *Do not dawdle; implement as quickly as possible.* The organization is likely to be fatigued and anxious about changes to come. Everyone wants to get back to work—facilitate that as much as possible.
- *Do not lock in a design.* Any design element is open to refinement during implementation. Within the general structure, organizational members should be encouraged to personalize and shape the home they will eventually inhabit.
- *Do not blame.* It is a rare change effort that goes according to plan and there are many reasons for outcomes to change during implementation. Sometimes the reasons are progress or a better way and sometimes the reasons are troublesome, including sabotage. All are learnings to be understood and incorporated into change implementation. Blaming and judging preempts learning and has no place in implementation.
- *Do not change key leadership if it can possibly be helped.* Leaders are the touchstone for the vision and make the "big picture" case for change. They manage boundary relationships and often hold the institutional memory of what was intended.
- *Do not forget to capture knowledge as change is implemented.* It is important to retain "one of everything," including both the formal and informal. Whatever the results, it will be important to remember what was done and how the organization went about it. What does not work today could well be appropriate tomorrow.
- *Do not let implementation just fade away.* Completion of the effort should be celebrated. The ending should be as clear as the beginning was.

Methodologies for Change

Modern management's bias is to use tools and technologies to create change in organizations. However, tools and technologies succeed by increasing efficiency in already existing systems rather than altering the complex social relations and the important workplace issues that must be addressed in any change process. Still, some methodologies can enhance the impact of change interventions in organizations. But it is important to be clear about the criteria for choosing methodologies and the guidelines for their use.

Criteria for Choosing Change Implementation Methodologies

There is no one best methodology for the design and implementation of change that is applicable to all situations. Which methodology to choose for a change process depends on several variables, some of which have already been addressed: type of change envisioned (vision-driven or gap-driven change), level of the system being targeted (unit, department, or whole organization), type of resistance expressed (both at the individual and group level), time frame (or rather, time pressure), and technological capabilities of the organization.

The methodology chosen must allow all parties to have input into the change process. Representatives from each stakeholder group should meet and even engage in some preparatory work building common ground or using Future Search techniques. For specific techniques and practices in Future Search see *Discovering Common Ground* (Weisbord & Janoff, 1993) or *The Search Conference* (Emery & Purser, 1996).

Given the time pressure and the technology capacity of the organization, it might be useful to do some of the interventions online, but these must be combined with face-to-face interaction. With vision-driven change, the methodologies must be more facilitative, allowing staff the time to buy into the change process.

General Guidelines in Using Methodologies

Several guidelines should be followed no matter the methodology used. As a rule of thumb, the first step, even before choosing a methodology, is to determine the key goals and expectations of the change process. A clear goal statement informs the staff about what to expect from the change and minimizes their anxiety during interventions. This occurs best in dialogue with the recognized change leaders and with a commitment from the decision makers of the organization. A clear goal statement sends a message to staff that there is organizational support for change.

Suggested guidelines for the use of methodologies include these:

- *Congruency:* The implementation should be in the direction of the change and the methodology should therefore introduce some of the change goals in its actual use. For example, if the organization is working on a diversity goal, then culturally diverse teams and diverse technologies should be used in the implementation phase of the change process.
- *Involvement:* All players need to be in the room at the same time.
- *Data points:* Always generate your own data and always collect your data from all representative groups in the client organization.
- *Consensual validation:* Data generated with other groups in the organization should be validated through data feedback meetings or in the communications plan. Response should be invited. This helps build ownership for the change implementation process.
- *Communication:* The reasons why certain methodologies were chosen and others were omitted should be explained. For instance, it helps staff to know that executives recognize that there is a problem among the management ranks and that the retreat they are attending is a team-building exercise.
- *Methodology versus change goal:* It is important for managers to be careful of fad methodologies, where the methodology becomes the end result rather than leading to the desired change.
- *Consciousness awareness:* Methodologies that respond to the unspoken needs of the organization should be used. The organization's social, emotional, and technological capital for the vision should be built. If safety is an issue in data gathering and analysis, then more anonymous groupware computer systems instead of hard copies may be used to collect and analyze data.

A Methodological Approach

In order to help readers better understand the use of methodologies in implementing change we describe here an approach that involves several methodologies. Two of these methodologies work well in the design stage and in the analysis stage: Large Group Participation and Appreciative Inquiry (AI). We will walk through one case study to illustrate how these two methodologies may be used in a change initiative.

Let us take the example of an organization that faced issues common to many present-day organizations: increasing work demands, diminishing quality and staff capacity for life-work balance, high stress, take-home laptops that extended the day, job security concerns, limited budgets, and lack of prioritization among managers who worked seventy- to ninety-hour weeks. Employees felt overwhelmed, with no control over their lives and little support or guidance from their managers to regain priorities and balance. Furthermore, there was a low level of confidence that colleagues and management would respect staff interests when making work decisions. Generally there was a sense of despair in the organization that this was the way things were and there was no real hope for change. What could one do to transform this work situation into one with a productive, committed, and supportive workforce?

Most organizations would first contract with a consultant to help address these issues. We have found that a team of internal and external change consultants working together brings a balanced perspective to the design, analysis, and implementation of change interventions. The internal consultants have the history of the organization and the political knowledge essential to get things done. They also provide the continuity from the feedback and follow-up sessions to the institutionalization of the change across the organization. External consultants bring fresh perspectives, including knowledge of what has worked in other organizations, the experience of different work cultures, and "out of the box" thinking. Most especially, they bring hope that things can change if people think about their work differently.

The consultant team lays out a work program for the change process and communication plan to be used throughout the process and tests this with a group of stakeholders. This is a crucial step and often neglected by change teams. A well-thought-out communication process puts order to the vast amount of information generated in implementation efforts and explicitly links outcomes to interventions. If the outcomes are not explicitly linked to the intervention through appropriate communication channels, staff will only remember that they invested time and energy that resulted in no obvious benefits.

The entire organization is actively involved in all phases of the process, and communication is key in establishing a spirit of openness and transparency. This was especially important here because lack of trust of senior management and of the organization's ability to change was rampant in this organization. As part of the communication plan, an organizational Web site may be established to keep interested parties informed of every step of the change. The site includes the change process status, current happenings, and provides a vehicle for those unable to participate to offer their comments and suggestions through an "interactive" comment box. Other methods of communication include oral presentations by champions, quarterly letters from the CEO, newsletters, and town hall meetings. Bit by bit, because of the constancy and consistency in the presentation of the change, employees begin to internalize that a change process is occurring and take notice with renewed hope for the future.

Before convening each meeting with staff, the consultant team creates the agenda to achieve the identified goals and expectations and determines if there are any other efforts across the institution addressing similar goals. It is common to find efforts across smaller work groups to address the same goals the organization is attempting to address. Sharing these best practices creates hope and encourages change in the larger work environment, giving staff a mental model of how things can be done.

With the groundwork laid (expectations clarified, goals identified, work program detailed, communication plan implemented, related practices introduced), the specific intervention begins. With this organization, we chose the Large Group Participation methodology because it helped with the fragmented nature of the organization and increased networking among the divisions, which raised optimism for the change. Large Group Participation gathers key stakeholders together in conference. It is particularly useful in understanding an organization as a whole system and ensuring broad ownership of end results. In this case, a consultant planned a large group diagnosis meeting early in the process to identify the critical collective issues that needed to be addressed throughout the institution. A diagonal "slice of staff" across the organization met and provided a comprehensive assessment as a microcosm of the organization. This group of people identified issues, detailed them, and determined priorities with agreement on how to proceed. When they are carefully designed and facilitated, such large conferences can address very complicated issues (for example, mapping a complex work process) in a short period of time. Accomplishing the same work in this organization with interviews, focus groups, and analysis would have taken weeks and may never have produced any agreement or shared understanding.

The large group method is ideal in environments with multiple stakeholders where there is a tight deadline and ownership of change is important. However, the method is not an ideal choice when time for ideas to mature or time to evoke new strains of thought needs to be built into an iterative process. *Whole-Scale Change: Unleashing the Magic in Organizations* (Dannemiller Tyson Associates & Wheatley, 2000) and *Large Group Interventions: Engaging the Whole System for Rapid Change* (Bunker & Alban, 1966) offer further discussion of large group pros and cons.

Appreciative Inquiry (AI) was also used in this organizational diagnosis. This methodology differs from the conventional problem-solving technique, which identifies the problem, analyzes issues, generates solutions, and designs action plans, always keeping the focus on the problem. In contrast, AI centers on what is valued and well perceived. Information is gathered through interviews and storytelling and is used to help the group collectively visualize what the future could be. AI is powerful and effective because it enables group members to design their future based on what contributed to their peak performance in the past. It raises commitment from all of the involved parties, and successful implementation becomes likely because changes are not mandated from above but result from collective agreement.

What were the steps in this approach? First, the individuals in the group were asked to identify the factors that made their environment desirable. These sessions were devoted to describing the factors that gave life and energy to the work environment. Through open dialogue, all members of the group defined their ideal environment and agreed on a shared vision of how they wanted their work environment to be. This meant they had to merge individual ideas. AI methodology makes a deliberate attempt to create an atmosphere supporting dialogue and acceptance of differing viewpoints. This, in turn, facilitated ownership of the change plans and increased the trust that was so lacking in this organization.

Methodologies such as Appreciative Inquiry allow organizations to accept and incorporate the change process into daily operations with much less trauma than when the change is seen as a top-down dictum designed to fix the organization. Watkins and Mohr (2001) in their work *Appreciative Inquiry: Change at the Speed of Imagination* provide a thoughtful discussion of how to create organizational change using this methodology.

Measuring Change Implementation

Measurement is often difficult in change situations because what needs to be measured is the *impact* of change, something that is invisible. For instance, how does one measure change in organizational culture? Nonetheless, it is important to assess the impact of the change not just to satisfy key decision makers but to demonstrate progress and allow executives to know when it is time to move on.

Measuring the change progress itself facilitates the change momentum. It should be an ongoing process providing feedback at different stages of the implementation. The success of the change initiative is facilitated by incoming information from the work environment that validates or invalidates the perceptions of the design team members and what they think is happening.

Typical methods to measure impact are carrying out interviews, surveys, and observations and collecting hard data. Whatever the methodology used, the data collected must be closely tied to the goals and expectations that were identified earlier by the key decision makers. Often in large organizations a regular staff survey (every eighteen to twenty-four months) is the vehicle used to get the organization's opinion on how a change plan has been progressing and its impact over time. During a complex change process, it is also useful to do a change assessment survey every six to eight months; staff are surveyed on their perceptions of progress on key success indicators.

It is important to plan regularly to collect data that track the change, what is going well or not well, and how staff feel as they experience the changes in their work environment. Such midcourse assessment allows for reflection, renewal, and reinforcement of accomplishments during the change process.

Measuring the impact of change need not be a complex process and should include the following steps:

- *Developing key success indicators early in a change process.* This helps ground the change process and in the turmoil of change keeps people focused on the prize.
- *Employing different forms of measurement.* Staff surveys, learning forums, joint problem solving, and debriefings should all be used in addition to social gatherings designed around having conversations on the impact of the change.
- *Collecting data at different levels of systems.* Instruments for data collection should address the different levels of systems. Essentially, how is the change being experienced at the individual level, the unit level, the divisional level, and by the entire organization?
- *Searching out and using organizational indicators already in place.* Data on sick leave, staff turnover in the organization as a whole and among different social groups (women, minorities, the physically challenged), disability ratios, use of vacation time, number of hours spent on the Internet—all contribute to a picture of whether the change is in the organization's best interest.
- *Receiving measurement as feedback to the change process rather than a good or bad judgment on how things are going.*

In measuring a change process one should be mindful that change is as much a political process as a social and technological one. When individuals' power bases are under threat, they are not inclined to look favorably on the very processes that they perceive will diminish their power. The measurement of a change process must truly measure the changes that are occurring in the system rather than critique the change process. One can always learn how to implement change processes better, but the true test of the change process is in the legacy it leaves to the organization.

Additional Resources

Ackoff, R. (1999). *Recreating the corporation: A design of organizations for the 21st century.* New York: Oxford University Press.

Argyris, C. (1993). *Knowledge for action: A guide for overcoming barriers to organizational change.* San Francisco: Jossey-Bass.

Block, P. (1999). *Flawless consulting: A guide to getting your expertise used* (2nd ed.). San Francisco: Jossey-Bass.

Block, P. (2000). *The flawless consulting fieldbook and companion: A guide to understanding your expertise.* San Francisco: Jossey-Bass.

Dannemiller Tyson Associates. (2000). *Whole-scale change toolkit.* San Francisco: Berrett-Koehler.

Hanson, P. G., & Lubin, B. (1995). *Answers to the questions most frequently asked about organization development.* Thousand Oaks, CA: Sage.

Janoff, S., & Weisbord, M. R. (1995). *Future search.* San Francisco: Berrett-Koehler.

Jaworski, J. (1998). *Synchronicity: The inner path of leadership.* San Francisco: Berrett-Koehler.

Markham, D. J. (1999). Spirit-linking leadership: Working through resistance to organizational change. Mahwah, NJ: Paulist Press.

Quinn, R. (1996). *Deep change: Discovering the leader within.* San Francisco: Jossey-Bass.

Schwartz, P. (1996). *The art of the long view: Planning for the future in an uncertain world.* New York: Doubleday.

References

Anderson, D., & Anderson, L. A. (2001). *Beyond change management: Advanced strategies for today's transformational leaders.* San Francisco: Jossey-Bass.

Axelrod, R. (2000). *Terms of engagement: Changing the way we change organizations.* San Francisco: Berrett-Koehler.

Bandy, T. (2000). *Coaching change: Breaking down resistance and building up hope.* Nashville, TN: Abingdon Press.

Bogon, C., & English, M. (1994). *Benchmarking for best practices.* New York: McGraw-Hill.

Bunker, B. B., & Alban, B. (1966). *Large group interventions: Engaging the whole system for rapid change.* San Francisco: Jossey-Bass.

Dannemiller Tyson Associates, & Wheatley, M. (2000). *Whole-scale change: Unleashing the magic in organizations.* San Francisco: Berrett-Koehler.

Emery, M., & Purser, R. E. (1996). *The search conference: A powerful method for planning organizational change and community action.* San Francisco: Jossey-Bass.

Hultman, K. (1998). *Making change irresistible: Overcoming resistance to change in your organization.* Palo Alto, CA: Consulting Psychologists Press.

Nanus, B., & Bennis, W. (1995). *Visionary leadership: Creating a compelling sense of direction for your organization.* San Francisco: Jossey-Bass.

Reina, D. S., & Reina, M. L. (1999). *Trust and betrayal in the workplace.* San Francisco: Berrett-Koehler.

Schein, E. H. (1997). *Organizational culture and leadership.* San Francisco: Jossey-Bass.

Senge, P. M. (1999). *The dance of change: Challenges of sustaining momentum in learning organizations.* New York: Doubleday.

Watkins, J. M., & Mohr, B. (2001). *Appreciative inquiry: Change at the speed of imagination.* New York: Wiley.

Weisbord, M. R., & Janoff, S. (1993). *Discovering common ground.* San Francisco: Berrett-Koehler.

CHAPTER 3

Mergers and Acquisitions

Mitchell Lee Marks

Seventy-five percent of mergers and acquisitions fail to achieve their financial or strategic objectives. Although there are many reasons for this dismal track record—including paying the wrong price and buying the wrong player—studies show that it is *the process through which organizations are integrated* that determines eventual success or failure (see, for example, Wright, Hoskisson, & Businetz, 2001; Elsass & Veiga, 1994; Hitt, Hoskisson, Ireland, & Harrison, 1991). Yet most executives tend to deny the psychological and cultural issues that arise when two previously independent organizations are combined into one. As a result, leaders underestimate and underfund the work of integration.

This chapter presents interventions to facilitate the merger and acquisition integration process. These interventions are not "rocket science"—that is, they are neither complicated nor esoteric. Rather, the interventions described here are basic staples of the modern managerial repertoire. Why then do mergers and acquisitions so frequently fail to achieve their financial and strategic objectives? The answer lies in their implementation. As we will see, the very nature of how mergers and acquisitions are conceived runs counter to effective intervention. Add to this the psychological dynamics of combining—including the tendency for buyers to dominate the action and for sellers to experience the loss of their job security or corporate identity in a manner likened by many to the Kubler-Ross model of death and dying—and the work of implementing straightforward interventions becomes very difficult.

Based on firsthand experience in over seventy-five organizational combinations—and on my review of others' work in this area—this chapter reports primary interventions that industrial/organizational (I/O) psychologists and other transition managers can make to minimize unintended consequences, such as employee distraction from performance and culture clash, and maximize the likelihood of the combined organization being more than the sum of its parts. To be sure, there is no one-size-fits-all prescription for successful integration of complex work organizations. And it would be imprudent to think that the work of joining organizations and their employees together could be described in a single chapter. However, these pages present some of the key implementation issues and opportunities for I/O psychologists to intervene to help make mergers and acquisitions meet their financial and strategic objectives.

Combination Phases

For the past twenty years my colleague Philip Mirvis and I have been involved in an action research program to investigate and address human, cultural, and organizational aspects of corporate combinations (Marks & Mirvis, 1998). Early in our investigations, we collaborated with the Management Analysis Center of Cambridge, Massachusetts, in a study of corporate combinations in banking and finance (1985). This research showed that significant differences could be found between "typical" and "successful" cases when the distinct phases gone through in the transition from independent to integrated entities were separated (see Exhibit 3.1).

In the *precombination phase* the deal is conceived and negotiated by executives and then legally approved by shareholders and regulators. In the *combination phase* integration planning ensues and

Exhibit 3.1. Combination Phases.

Phase	Typical Emphasis	Successful Emphasis
Precombination	Financial	Strategic
Combination	Political	Combination planning
Postcombination	Damage control	Flexibility

implementation decisions are made. In the *postcombination phase* the combined entity and its people regroup from initial implementation, and the new organization settles in.

Precombination Phase

Much of the emphasis in the typical merger or acquisition during the precombination phase is on the financial implications. Buyers concentrate on the "numbers": what the target is worth, what price premium if any they should pay, what the tax implications are, and how to structure the transaction. The decision to do a deal usually is thus framed in terms of the combined balance sheet of the companies, projected cash flows, and hoped-for return on investment.

Two interrelated human factors accentuate this financial bias. First, members of the buy team in most instances have financial positions or backgrounds. They bring a financial mind-set to their study of a partner, and their judgments of synergies are mostly informed by financial models and ratios. They often do not know very much about, say, engineering, manufacturing, or marketing, and do not bring an experienced eye to assessments of a partner's capabilities in these regards. Then there is the tendency for so-called hard criteria to drive out soft factors. If the numbers look good, any doubts about such things as organizational or cultural differences tend to be scoffed at and dismissed. This was clearly the case in the merger that brought German and American automobile manufacturers together in the Daimler-Chrysler combination.

In successful cases, by contrast, buyers bring a strategic mind-set to the deal. But there is more to it than an overarching aim and intent. Successful buyers also have a clear definition of specific synergies they seek in a combination and concentrate on testing them well before momentum builds and negotiations commence. Here too human factors play a part. For instance, members of the buy team in successful cases come from technical and operational as well as financial areas. And during the scouting phase, they dig deep into the operations and markets of a candidate in order to gauge its fit. Years ago, Citibank went on a buying spree of European financial institutions. Most of these deals led to financial success because Citibank identified and stuck to clear selection criteria (only going after "turnaround" situations) and broadened team membership beyond traditional financial roles.

Sensible buyers consider carefully the risks and problems that might turn a strategically sound deal sour. This does not mean that the financial analyses are neglected or that they are any less important to success. On the contrary, what puts mergers and acquisitions on the road toward success is both an in-depth financial understanding of a proposed combination and a serious examination of what it will take to produce desired financial results.

Combination Phase

After legal clearance is received and the deal becomes a reality, politics predominates in typical cases. Often this is pure power politics: the buyer decides how to put the two organizations together. USAir's purchase of Piedmont Airlines is a classic example. The buyer had a poor reservations system and woeful customer service, so much so that passengers called it "Useless Air." Piedmont had a better system and a cheerful staff. Nonetheless, USAir mandated the adoption of its system.

Political game playing runs rampant in many combinations as individuals jockey for power and positions and management teams fend off overtures for control from the other side by hiding information or playing dumb. Transition task forces have usually been convened to recommend integration options, but personal empire building and conflicting group dynamics block their efforts to seek and capture the true synergies. Meanwhile, cultures clash as people focus on differences between the partners and which side won which battles rather than join together to build a sense of one team going forward. In one health care merger, the two sides could not even agree on starting times for meetings— one organization's managers began 9:00 A.M. meetings promptly whereas the other's managers only left their offices at the top of the hour, collected their papers, chatted with their assistants, and grabbed a cup of coffee before arriving at the conference room around 9:15. In their premerger culture this was no problem, because everyone involved knew that 9:00 A.M. meetings actually began at 9:15. But it infuriated counterparts from the partner organization, who described the tardiness as "disrespectful" and "undisciplined." Of course, the latecomers regarded their new partners as "uptight" and having "misplaced priorities."

In successful combinations, an emphasis on planning prevails. There are always political gambits for self-preservation, but much of the energy that usually goes into gamesmanship gets directed more positively into combination planning. Leadership clarifies the critical success factors to guide decision making and oversees the planning process to ensure that sources of synergy are found. Managers and employees come together to discuss and debate combination options, and when the process is well managed, high-quality combination decisions result. In Pfizer's acquisition of Warner-Lambert, for example, sixteen functional integration teams were created in research and development alone. Before convening the teams, executives clarified strategic decision-making criteria to be used to avert politically charged recommendations, hand-picked team leaders who were more diplomatic than dominating, freed up resources so that each team could have a facilitator, and sponsored an off-site meeting to identify and address potential hindrances to an effective team process.

Postcombination Phase

Up to eighteen months after a combination, we hear executives moan that their best talent has jumped ship, productivity has plummeted, and culture clash remains thick. Often this is because executives grow impatient with planning and hurry implementation so much that the two companies fail to integrate, with resulting serious declines in everything from employee morale to customer satisfaction. There are options for damage control in this situation, but obviously the better course of action is to preclude the need for damage control by following a successful road map from the start. With a sound strategy guiding the precombination phase employees gain confidence in their leadership, knowing that organizational enhancements are likely to result from the combination. This strategy guides decision making during the combination phase and lessens the "It's us against them" battles and the political gambits. Then, in the postcombination phase, flexibility guides implementation. Midcourse corrections are common in successful combinations. Employees take these in stride when they understand the strategic thrust of a deal and perceive planning to occur through an aboveboard process.

A Diagnostic Approach to Facilitating Mergers and Acquisitions

The three phases of a combination do not have discrete boundaries. Planning activities traditionally conducted in the combination phase—once both government and shareholder approval has been received—increasingly are being started in the precombination phase. AOL and Time Warner began integration planning well before federal regulators blessed the deal. Integration teams were launched in the Pfizer–Warner-Lambert deal months before legal approval came through. In addition, implementation activities once relegated to the postcombination phase are being accelerated into the combination phase as executives rush to cut costs to meet Wall Street's expectations of postmerger financial performance. Reorganization and reductions in workforce greeted employees at subsidiary CNN only days after AOL's acquisition of Time Warner became legal. Certainly, as megamergers bring huge organizational entities together, implementation will occur at various speeds in specific functions, lines of business, and geographical units.

Despite the blurring of the phases of a combination, it is helpful to consider them individually when preparing an intervention. Knowing the challenges of each phase increases the likelihood that a firm will be able to marshal resources to identify and address actions required to combine complex organizations. Yet it is not enough to understand at a generic level the issues and opportunities of each phase. Every combination is different—with distinct purposes, partners, personalities, and parameters. As with any organizational intervention, a diagnosis is required to identify the specific dynamics of the deal and focus resources on the issues that matter most for eventual success.

The diagnostic methods available to I/O psychologists in a merger are similar to those they use in other contexts—individual and focus group interviews, questionnaires, observations, archival data, and so on. Unfortunately, however, most mergers and acquisitions are conceived in a manner that makes conducting a thorough diagnosis impractical. Mergers and acquisitions are very secretive events. To prevent insider trading or even a preemptive bid from a competitor, executives must keep the number of people in the know to a bare minimum. With rare exceptions, as the deal is being conceived and negotiated the buying CEO is surrounded only by strategic and financial advisers (who, incidentally, are rewarded for *doing the deal* and not necessarily for *making the deal work*); no I/O psychologists are in the room to bring up matters like retention of key talent or the inevitable culture clash.

Even after the deal is announced and approved, internal I/O psychologists and human resource professionals face an uphill battle in conducting a thorough and reliable diagnosis. Executives on the buying side lurch into crisis mode as they rush to integrate operations while trying to deal with day-to-day business matters. Driving in two lanes at once, they quickly become overwhelmed and make little time for the data collection needs of I/O psychologists. Meanwhile, executives and employees in the acquired organization are in a state of shock, reeling at the loss of their identity and independence. They may not trust or confide in internal I/O psychologists from the lead company even when diagnostic activities are well intentioned (see, for example, Marks & Mirvis, 2001). Then, as the dust begins to settle and implementation occurs in the postcombination phase, executives like to pretend that the whole thing is over and done with. They wishfully claim that employees have put the merger behind them and are ready to move forward when in most combinations employees actually are coping with the lingering effects of job insecurity, transition mismanagement, and culture clash. And the employees' path to moving forward is blocked by an unclear vision or the absence of a compelling strategic vision for the future. So although a diagnosis could identify some genuine inhibitors to the desired postcombination organization, some executives regard employee research as a nonessential distraction in an environment of limited resources.

A discussion of organizational diagnosis is beyond the scope of this chapter. However, in the cases presented here diagnoses were vital to the selection of interventions to minimize the unintended consequences of integrating organizations while maximizing the opportunity to use the combination to build a better organization.

Precombination Phase

The precombination phase encompasses strategy setting, scouting, partner evaluation and selection, and deal making. Obviously, the quality of work conducted in this phase has a substantial influence on the eventual results. The typical acquisition program has a few key weak points during the precombination phase (see Exhibit 3.2).

Issue: Poor Business Strategy or Weak Core Business

To begin with, some buyers are not sure what they want to do in the marketplace and tend to follow the industry fashion when it comes to mergers or acquisitions. This is particularly true in the case of industries where the market leaders make aggressive moves and the followers either have to catch up or leave the game. More frequent are cases where a buyer has access to a mountain of cash and no means of growing internally. Here the buyer rolls the dice in its choice of investment and selection of a partner. And although the game can be exciting, it seldom yields any sustained payoff.

Another problem is when buyers choose to acquire as a substitute for fixing current business problems. At a manufacturing firm, a dying business line received "life support" from an acquisition in the form of new sales staff with new customer contacts. As it turned out, however, the patient was terminally ill with worn-out technology. Neither aggressive staff nor new customers could keep the business alive. Better to have fixed or closed these failing businesses than try to revive them with an infusion.

At other times, the core assumptions behind the combination are flawed. Kodak's acquisition of Sterling Drug, for example, never produced the synergies that Kodak anticipated would propel it into the very profitable pharmaceutical segment producing

Exhibit 3.2. Issues and Interventions in the Precombination Phase.

Issue	Intervention
There is a poor business strategy or weak core business.	Look for a new employer or client.
Combination strategy or rationale is not widely understood or supported.	Build understanding of and support for combination strategy and rationale.
There is pressure to do a deal and hurry due diligence.	Add I/O perspective to partner selection process.

ethical drugs. After five years of poor earnings, Kodak acknowledged its mistake and divested Sterling.

Intervention: Abandon Ship

When an organization is following the wrong business strategy or is suffering from a critical weakness in its core business, then an acquisition will not remedy the situation. But many executives would rather take their cash, purchase a thriving competitor, and hope that the healthy patient cures the sick one. Of course, things turn out just the opposite of what had been hoped for—the improper strategy or the core business problem contaminates the previously healthy target. Acquisitions or mergers made in such situations are doomed to failure. There is little or nothing an I/O psychologist can do to shore up the ailing organization if senior leadership does not own up to the inherent business problems. The best advice to give here is to jump ship before the acquisition claims careers.

Issue: Combination Strategy or Rationale
Not Widely Understood or Supported

Equally debilitating is when the basic rationale underlying the decision to look for an acquisition or merger partner is not clear, or when the fundamental criteria for selecting a target are not broadly understood. In some instances, corporate planners do not fully think through why they are acquiring a particular company and how that company fits specifically with their strategy. Literally, they set out to find a target when they are not clear about why they want to join forces with it. In other cases, the small inner circle of senior executives and advisers clarifies a sound strategy for growth and a solid rationale for selecting a particular target, yet the secrecy enveloping the deal prevents other key managers from understanding and supporting the rationale for it.

Intervention: Develop a Shared Perspective of the
Combination's Rationale and Its Desired Results

A few years ago, I received a call from the CEO of a high-technology firm who had recently announced his company's first major acquisition. The company, a computer hardware maker, was strong in the middle and upper segments of its product market. Margins were high in these segments, yet most of the industrywide growth was occurring in the lower end. Working with external advisers, the CEO concluded that he had to acquire a firm with expertise at the lower end in order to achieve his company's expectations for revenue growth. There simply was not enough time in the Internet age to meet revenue expectations through internal growth.

After negotiating the deal amid great secrecy, the CEO announced the acquisition. On their own initiative, several senior executives from the acquiring company holed themselves away in a conference room where they hammered out what they called the "integration plan." When the CEO read the plan he found that, among other things, it called for the elimination of the to-be-acquired firm's R&D function. This would have defeated the very purpose for doing the deal, because it would have eliminated all the engineers with expertise in the low end of the product line.

After listening to the CEO, I proposed a two-pronged intervention to guide the integration program. First was a series of one-on-one interviews with members of both companies' leadership teams to achieve the following:

- An assessment of the extent to which key players were or were not on the same page when it came to the purpose and expectations of the acquisition
- Insight into key areas of agreement and disagreement within and between the leadership teams
- Awareness of the dynamics that needed to be addressed to make this integration succeed
- An enhanced sense of how to structure the second part of the initial intervention
- A "heads up" to the CEO on any critical issues that emerged from the interviews
- Establishment of rapport between the consultant and executives from both partners
- The opportunity to explain, one-on-one, to all key executives why this approach was being used to manage the integration

Among other findings, the interviews made it clear that even in the lead company there was not a consistent view of why the acquisition was occurring or what would be required for it to achieve its strategy. This influenced the design of the second part of the intervention. Rather than bring executives from the partners together, I argued that executives from the buying company needed to go away by themselves to build understanding of and support for the acquisition strategy. This runs counter to the advice of some merger consultants, who push to bring the partners together as soon as possible to create the impression of a one-team mind-set. But if the lead team does not have a shared perspective on the reason for the deal and the requirements to make it succeed, then the additional step of working initially with the buying group is warranted.

A one-day off-site meeting was scheduled in which the CEO walked his management team through the rationale for the deal. I then fed back findings from my interviews to alert executives to the potential hindrances to achieving the integration strategy. This put several previously unspoken issues in play and generated an earnest discussion of what the lead company needed to do to prepare for a successful combination. The meeting culminated in the articulation of critical success factors for the integration process. These became the decision-making criteria that were used to assess recommendations for integration. One critical success factor, for example, was to penetrate the low end of the product market. Thus, later, when integration planning teams (including executives from both partner companies) were put together, they were given not just financial targets (for example, cut x number of dollars out of the combined R&D budget) but also strategic decision-making criteria that literally kept the rationale for the deal front and center during integration planning and implementation.

Issue: Pressure to Do a Deal and Hurry Due Diligence

Another factor contributing to failed combinations is the tendency for internal M&A specialists from corporate development and strategic planning to be motivated by the pressure to do a deal, any deal, rather than critically apply strategic, financial, and cultural criteria in assessing targets. At a diversified financial services firm, corporate staff was charged by the company's executive committee to "formulate a growth strategy via acquisition" and "identify targets that fit our criteria." Not bringing forward a recommended target, the staffers figured, would be seen as failure and would be an unacceptable response to the executive committee's command.

Psychological factors contribute to the pressure to do a deal. Few events in corporate life are more exhilarating than making an acquisition. Searching for the right target, stalking it, zeroing in, and then "bagging" it are considerably more exciting and energizing than the relatively mundane work of pushing paper and running numbers back at headquarters. Acquiring is winning: *we* get *them*. It feels good to win, to be on top, and corporate staffers in most firms get caught up in the rush to do a deal.

That rush lasts through the deal-making stage. As excitement over doing a deal escalates, staffers hurry due diligence. Certainly they look for any significant liabilities in the target, but they usually make an inadequate effort at truly digging into the candidate to understand what is being purchased, how well it might fit with the lead company's current businesses, and what pitfalls may lie ahead. Without a close look at the capabilities and characteristics of a partner, it is easy to overestimate synergies and underestimate the costs and headaches involved in integrating businesses.

Intervention: Add the I/O Perspective to the Deal-Making Process

Someone has to counter the momentum that grows as senior executives and corporate staffers select acquisition candidates or merger partners. I/O psychologists, with their arsenal of methods and their orientation toward matters organizational, human, and cultural, can broaden the traditionally narrow financial perspective that guides the search and selection of most combination candidates. I/O psychologists can offer valuable insights, including assessments of competencies in the target organization, investigations of what is motivating the seller to seek a buyer, and comparisons of human resource practices, corporate cultures, and organizational structures.

Importantly, the I/O perspective is not limited to influencing a go–no-go decision in selecting a partner. Rather, the collection, dissemination, and discussion of I/O data may influence the terms of the deal—the price to be paid, the pace at which integration occurs, or the placement of acquired personnel in the lead organization, for example. An early assessment of the capabilities of an acquired leadership team (and of their desire to stay on after the sale) can help a buyer understand the extent to which people from the lead company need to take a hands-on approach in running a new acquisition. Assessments of culture clash and organizational fit can lead to the creation of more realistic integration timetables. And in general, an understanding of the human, cultural, and organizational issues can provide solid content for crafting communication messages at a time when most acquirers claim there is nothing to say.

The addition of the I/O psychology perspective to the precombination process also offers a symbolic value to buyers. When members of the scouting or due diligence teams raise human, cultural, and organizational issues, it signals to the to-be-acquired employees that the lead company is sensitive to these matters. It builds confidence that the buyer will manage the integration process well.

How do I/O psychologists add their perspective in the precombination phase? In some organizations, internal OD and HR professionals are invited to join due diligence teams. One company convenes dual due diligence teams—one team makes a case for buying a particular target and the other makes the case for not going forward with the purchase. As noted earlier, the input of the nay-saying team does not necessarily result in a go–no-go decision, but it alerts senior leadership to dynamics that prompt modifications to purchase prices and integration timetables.

Another intervention for I/O psychologists during the precombination phase is to conduct what I call *cultural due diligence*. I recently did this for an electronic distribution company that sought to make a series of acquisitions in various parts of the world. The CEO contacted me after his internal staff identified several candidates that passed the company's financial and strategic filters. With several candidates in some countries, he wanted to know which potential targets would pose the fewest organizational and cultural challenges in integration. Fortunately, the early negotiations between the buyer and potential targets were extremely friendly. I was able to interview executives and employees, observe meetings, and review archival data. In many other cases, however, the negotiations are decidedly unfriendly and I/O psychologists do not have firsthand access to the potential target. In these cases they should look to secondary sources—such as former employees, financial analysts, and professors who have studied the firms—to develop a study of the prevalent cultural and organizational dynamics. Obviously these data are not as robust as when collected directly in the organization, but they still help leadership attend to integration requirements.

The I/O psychology perspective should not be limited to the buying company. I work with a small but growing number of target organizations to raise awareness of human, cultural, and organizational issues. A particularly in-depth precombination planning session was coordinated by internal organization development professional Ronny Versteenskitse of Seagram Spirits and Wine Group

(SSWG). Soon after acquiring Seagram, French entertainment conglomerate Vivendi announced its intention to retain the target's film and music holdings but divest its liquor and wine businesses. Thus, employees in SSWG were in limbo while their unit was put on the auction block. Versteenskitse went into action, however, and convened a four-day meeting of senior human resource professionals. On the first day of the meeting there was an update on the acquisition and divestiture process and a discussion of the status of major HR initiatives in the company, given the eventual change in ownership. The second day's sessions focused on the fate of employees who would not be retained after the sale and on dealing with the questions and issues of all employees during the transition. The third day addressed surviving employees and began with a presentation, by me, on success factors in mergers and acquisitions and the human and cultural realities of joining forces. There were also activities to prepare attendees for communicating the strengths of the to-be-acquired organization to a potential buyer and to engage them in envisioning what a desired postcombination organization might be like. On the meeting's closing day, executives from BP/Amoco and Chemical Bank/Chase discussed their successful integrations. The meeting concluded with a "taking initiative" activity in which the attendees strategized how to be proactive in dealing with the buyer by sharing the output produced at the meeting and reaching out to form a collaborative relationship with counterparts in the lead organization. There was no assurance that the buyer would be receptive to this activity, yet HR professionals left the conference feeling confident that they were doing the best job possible to prepare themselves, their organization, and their new colleagues for the rigors of integrating previously separate organizations.

Combination Phase

The deal gets announced, receives legal approval, and is celebrated. The optimism that energizes the decision to purchase a target or merge with another firm carries into the combination phase in the form of high hopes and confident expectations. They soon are forgotten, however, as the grueling work of combination planning, the critical mass of personal stress and uncertainty, and the pervasive clash of cultures overwhelm people. Some common problems besiege organizations and their people during this period, when the highs of doing a deal are replaced by the lows of making it work (see Exhibit 3.3).

Issue: Integration as a Distraction from "Real Work"

As responsibilities move from corporate staffers to line executives, reality hits hard. Operating managers see inflated projections and become overwhelmed at how they will meet the numbers. Usually these executives are busy running their current businesses. Their performance evaluations and rewards are based on how well they meet their core business targets, not on how the integration goes. They see integration as a distraction from getting products and services to customers. Thus, what on paper seems like a comprehensive and sophisticated integration program is in practice implemented in a rapid and shallow manner.

Intervention: Prepare and Motivate People
for Managing the Integration Effectively

I/O psychologists have a few leverage points to use in influencing preparedness and motivation for managing the combination well. One is to conduct a realistic merger preview, much like the classic

Exhibit 3.3. Issues and Interventions in the Combination Phase.

Issue	Intervention
Integration is seen as a distraction from "real work."	Prepare and motivate people for managing the integration effectively.
Crisis management approach is adopted, value-added is misunderstood, critical success factors are overlooked.	Design and conduct launch meeting.
There is inadequate attention to human and cultural issues.	Raise awareness of the merger syndrome and how to manage it.
	Put culture in play by conducting culture clarification activities and facilitating the articulation of the desired cultural end state.

realistic job preview. The idea is to alert executives to the common pitfalls in a combination and provide a realistic accounting of all the resources required to integrate previously independent entities. When coupled with collecting internal data that confirm the potential presence of these pitfalls, this intervention is especially powerful in creating a felt need for giving the work of integration management the status and resources it requires.

I/O psychologists may also use rewards. Sometimes these are significant financial rewards. In the merger that created newsprint manufacturer Abitibi-Consolidated, a bonus scheme rewarded transition team members for cost savings identified beyond the baseline established by external analysts. Cost savings that doubled analysts' estimates were identified and participants received a bonus of close to a year's base salary. In most instances, however, rewards are more symbolic. I/O psychologists advise senior executives to drop in on transition team meetings and surprise members with gift certificates and a message to "take your spouses out to dinner since they haven't seen you much during the long grueling months of integration planning." They coach CEOs to clear a path for integration planning by reminding supervisors that transition team members need to be taken off some assignments to fit integration planning into their schedules, and they repeatedly promote the work of integration planning in speeches, informal chats, and priority setting.

Issue: Crisis Management Approach Adopted, Strategic Intent and Critical Success Factors Overlooked

Operating managers who get handed acquisitions frequently misunderstand the value-added potential of a target and ignore or downplay the critical success factors. Corporate strategists may have developed a clever game plan, but it is those at the operational level who have to play the game. Many are less visionary in their outlook and may not appreciate the strategic and political sensitivities in making the combination work. Rather than identify and mine sources of strategic synergy in integration planning, they take shortcuts that save time but result in poor decisions. This works in the short run because managers can get their attention and energy back on what they see as their real work, but in the long run it results in disintegration of the partners and disappointing results.

The transition from two independent organizations to one integrated entity can be a time for enhancing the organization and building a one-team mind-set. It is during this relatively "unfrozen" period that first impressions are made of new partners and practices are adopted for the combined organization. If positive working relations are the rule during the transition period, then individuals will feel confident about the process and comfortable with new colleagues. If, instead, domination and politicking are the norms, then employees will refreeze into separate, combative camps and feel cheated by what they perceive as a flawed integration process.

In almost every integration today, a transition structure is adopted to focus executive time and talent on obtaining the strategic synergies in a combination. A transition structure is a temporary system that usually lasts three to six months but can extend up to a year to provide for coordination and support during implementation. In a typical transition structure, functional integration teams propose integration opportunities to a senior management steering committee. But despite the wide use of transition structures, most mergers and acquisitions fail to achieve their desired financial or strategic results. In fact I recently was asked to conduct four postmortems on disappointing integrations (one each in the high-tech, financial services, health care, and consumer products industries), and the most widely discussed issue in each case was the ineffectiveness of the transition teams. Four specific complaints were made about the transition teams: they did not know their charter, they did not know the decision-making criteria to be used in evaluating their recommendations, they suffered from poor leadership, and they were plagued by dysfunctional group dynamics.

Intervention: Design and Conduct a Transition Team Launch Program

The transition team process makes or breaks integration success. Teams either will identify and lock in synergies or will miss the opportunity to make organizational enhancements and stay with the status quo. Team members either will have positive experiences and report back to the constituencies in their respective organizations that "our new partners really listen to us; we can work with these people" or will have negative experiences and spread the word that "these people don't care what we think and are just dominating us."

Because nearly every integration uses some kind of transition structure and 75 percent of them fail, the challenge is not merely to establish a transition structure but to launch and nurture an *effective* one—one that brings the deal's potential synergies to life and builds positive working relations among the partners. At the high-tech company mentioned earlier that made an acquisition to round out its product offering, I worked with internal I/O psychologists and human resource professionals to design, launch, and nurture an effective transition structure. We addressed each of the four key complaints of transition teams in our intervention.

Articulate charters. Successful transition teams do not begin with a blank sheet of paper. Instead, they are guided by clearly articulated assumptions or biases held by senior leadership (for example, organizational architecture preferences, such as wanting a decentralized versus a centralized organization, or cultural preferences, such as pushing decision making down to the lowest practical levels). A charter designates what a transition team is supposed to do—select among current practices in the combination partners, look for new approaches, develop an implementation plan for a preordained course of action. The charter is essential to transition team success because it directs the team members' energy during a period when people are already stretched between running the core business and managing the transition. Prior to initiating transition teams in the high-tech company, we met with senior leadership to articulate any assumptions, predetermined decisions, or "sacred cows" that would influence the integration process. In staff areas like finance, the lead company CEO mandated that his firm's approach be adopted in the combined organization. So the finance integration team had a charter to "develop a plan for integrating the target company into the lead company's financial systems and procedures." In areas like sales, manufacturing, and R&D, the CEO had no established bias and wanted to use the transition period to identify and lock in best practices. Thus, the charter for these transition teams was to "review current practices in both partner organizations and propose best practices from either current practices or new practices from outside either partner."

Clarify and discuss decision-making criteria. Simply stated, if the transition teams do not know what to look for, they will not find it. If the strategic synergies in a deal are not kept front and center during the combination phase, then the void will be filled by power politics. Rather than identify and lock in ways to achieve the potential synergies in a deal, teams will make decisions based on who yells the loudest or drops the highest-ranking name, or by horse trading. It is also a problem when transition teams work well together and get energized about their proposed recommendations but then get shot down by senior leadership with a message "that's not what we are looking for." Leadership needs to put its cards on the table before managers set off on the difficult work of proposing integration recommendations. At the high-tech company, senior leadership articulated critical success factors (CSFs)—such as to penetrate the low end of the product offering—that supported the strategic rationale for the deal. When transition teams were convened, team members were given a list of CSFs in addition to cost-saving targets. Internal I/O psychologists set up forums in which the team members could ask questions about the decision-making criteria, clarify their intent, address any consistencies between strategic and financial aspirations, and get any hidden agendas or sacred cows out in the open.

Establish team leadership. The knee-jerk reaction of most executives is to appoint function heads as leaders of transition teams. This is fine if the function head is more diplomatic than dominating—that is, is able to give airtime to employees from the acquired company, can lead a group toward consensus and creative decision making, and has a propensity to keep an eye on group process while dealing with high-stakes content. But a successful integration cannot rely on assumptions and trial-and-error learning about the competencies of senior executives. In the high-tech company, internal I/O psychologists drew up a profile of transition team leadership competencies and ranked senior executives against it. They reviewed the assessments with the CEO, who made decisions about team leadership. In some cases, function heads were selected to lead transition teams; in other cases, the CEO dipped down a notch to select someone else to lead the team. In these latter cases, the CEO held a one-on-one conversation with the function head to explain his decision and to make a no-nonsense request that the department head fully support the transition team process. Although not as leaders, these function heads often were placed on the teams. So a delicate working relationship ensued between subordinate team leaders and function heads. To retain the integrity of the team process, I/O psychologists paid special attention to these teams and convened periodic meetings with the team leader and function head to discuss the dynamics.

Strengthen group dynamics. Dysfunctional group dynamics have nothing to do with mergers per se but everything to do with teams. Transition teams must develop positive working relationships in a short period of time. Members are challenged to help build relationships and share information with new colleagues while still conducting their core work activities. Anything that can plague a group's process—too many discussions, unprepared members, hidden agendas, forced decisions—can afflict a merger or acquisition transition team. At the high-tech company we addressed the matter of group dynamics head-on. First, I trained internal I/O psychologists and other professionals to be transition team facilitators. Next, we conducted a training session with team leaders to alert them to the demands of transition teams and raise their awareness of group dynamics. Finally, we designed and conducted a full-day transition team launch meeting in which all participants came together to prepare for their roles. The meeting began with the CEO reiterating the deal's rationale and strategic intent. He used this as an opportunity to review the CSFs and solicit questions about their intent. Then, I gave a brief presentation—"Success Factors in Mergers and Acquisitions"—with particular attention to the role of transition teams. This gave team members an opportunity to ask an outsider some critical questions about the transition process. For example: "Why not just appoint someone the head of the merged function and let them create their desired organization?" "What do we do when the team hits a roadblock?" "To what extent should we involve and communicate with people from our departments who are not team members?" The morning portion of the meeting concluded with the senior internal I/O psychologist delivering a presentation on "Transition Team Member Do's and Don'ts" and the facilitators conducting a humorous role-play of "the transition team from hell," which highlighted many of the process problems that plague most teams. The team members had lunch together and then met in their teams that afternoon. This first meeting had a structured agenda to ensure that the members understood their roles and responsibilities, the context and rationale of the merger, and their expected deliverables. Facilitators led teams through a twelve-item agenda that focused on critical matters that would influence their eventual success or failure. For example: "What questions do you have regarding the team's charter?" "What ground rules should govern team behavior?" "How do team agendas get set?" "What is an excused absence?" and "How will the team make decisions?" The launch meeting concluded with all teams returning to the main meeting room and a final question-and-answer session with the CEO.

Taking the time to clarify charters, articulate decision-making criteria, establish strong leadership, and acknowledge and address group process dynamics paid huge dividends in this integration. Transition teams produced recommendations that were accepted by the senior steering committee, and in several instances identified cost savings greater than initial projections.

Issue: Inadequate Attention to Human and Cultural Issues

Senior executives regularly deny or ignore the human and cultural issues when combining organizations. They issue dictums—"It's business as usual" or "If people are worried about their jobs, maybe they should be." When they announced the merger of AOL and Time Warner, Steve Case and Gerald Levin literally had their arms around each other as they said to the cameras, "There is no culture clash here." I appreciate that these two CEOs have known each other for several years and trust each other, but to suggest that the techies from Virginia and the publishers from New York City would not experience a culture clash in their combination is pure fantasy. Ignoring or denying the realities of employee stress and culture clash only makes matters worse—employees feel that their concerns are not understood and have little confidence that the integration will be well managed. This is why so many talented people jump ship rather than wait to see how things play out in the integration.

Intervention A: Raise Awareness of the Merger Syndrome and How to Manage It

Several years ago, Philip Mirvis and I identified symptoms of what we call *the merger syndrome* as a primary cause of the disappointing outcomes of otherwise well-conceived mergers and acquisitions

(Marks & Mirvis, 1985; Mirvis & Marks, 1986). The syndrome is triggered by the often unavoidably unsettled conditions in the earliest days and months following the announcement of a deal and encompasses stress reactions and development of crisis management in the companies involved. In one of our most striking discoveries, we found that the merger syndrome occurs even when the partners have devised a thoughtful integration designed to minimize upheaval and provide due consideration for its effects on people.

What creates the merger syndrome? For employees, it is a fusion of uncertainty and the likelihood of change, both favorable and unfavorable, that produces stress and ultimately affects perceptions and judgments, interpersonal relationships, and the dynamics of the combination itself. In organizations, the syndrome is manifested by increased centralization and lessened communication so that people are left in the dark about the combination, and rumors and insecurities grow. As a result, employees are distracted from regular duties and become obsessed with the impact of the combination on themselves and their work areas. All of this hampers integration, reduces productivity, and contributes to the turnover of key people.

The culture clash exacerbates the "me issues." By their very nature, mergers and acquisitions produce feelings that it is "us against them," and there is a natural tendency for people to exaggerate the differences rather than find similarities between the two companies. Noted first are differences in the ways the companies do business—maybe their relative emphasis on manufacturing rather than marketing. Then, differences in how the companies are organized—their centralization rather than decentralization, for example—are discerned. Finally, people ascribe these differences to competing values and philosophies, with their company seen as superior and the other as backward, bureaucratic, or just plain bad.

Ironically, a fair amount of diversity in approaching work aids combinations by sparking productive debate and discussion of desired norms in the combined organization. When left unmanaged, however, the clash of cultures pulls the two sides apart rather than joining them together.

I/O psychologists can help manage the merger syndrome by acknowledging that worries about survival of self and culture clashes are common in all combinations. Thus, the point is not to try to eliminate the merger syndrome but to help people manage its sources and symptoms. Doing this begins with raising awareness of the syndrome and its impact on combining organizations and their people and cultures. Soon after Pfizer announced its acquisition of Warner-Lambert, the president of Pfizer's R&D announced that he was using the integration as an opportunity to transform the structure and process through which the pharmaceutical giant discovered and developed new drugs. This sent shock waves through all involved, especially veteran Pfizer employees who had assumed their practices would prevail in the combined organization. I worked closely with senior HR and OD professionals at Pfizer to raise awareness of the human and cultural realities of the transition. To begin, we held a series of workshops on "managing the merger syndrome" to alert employees to the signs of the syndrome and teach them about methods for minimizing the unintended impact of stress, uncertainty, and culture clash. In addition to practical tactics, the overriding message was that people should acknowledge their reaction to the integration but control their emotions rather than have their emotions control them. In the sessions we also discussed the difficulty of merging previously independent complex organizations and urged employees to cut one another and their leadership some slack during this trying time. Feedback showed that employees appreciated that they were being leveled with about the stresses and strains inherent in a combination and gained an understanding of ways to manage their personal stress and build positive relations with new colleagues.

Another intervention used to raise awareness of human and cultural issues in the Pfizer–Warner-Lambert integration was the collection of data to confront senior leadership on the integration process and progress. Various methods were used to conduct employee research: one-on-one interviews, focus group interviews, and questionnaires. Periodically, internal staff and I met with senior executives to feed back and discuss the findings and to make key enhancements in the integration process. Senior leadership in R&D made important midcourse corrections based on the findings and feedback, ranging from strengthening the merger communication process to improving their own style of modeling teamwork at the top of the organization.

Intervention B: Respect and Clarify the Partner Company Cultures

Buying another company sends an implicit message to those in the lead organization that their ways of doing things are superior to those of the target firm. If you add in the self-imposed sense of urgency to move quickly to consolidate gains, you get a tendency by acquirers to dominate the action in the integration process. However, if buyers want to retain key people and realize hoped-for strategic value and financial returns then they had better consider the potential for culture clash in a combination. I/O psychologists can help prevent or minimize immediate incidents—and contribute to the longer-term necessity of building enduring positive relations between the parties—by educating executives about the causes and consequences of culture clash. These educational interventions can be piggybacked onto activities already cited, such as merger syndrome awareness raising or precombination planning sessions.

The primary intervention for minimizing the unintended consequences of culture clash is to foster respect for the partner cultures. This is true even if the ultimate intention is to absorb a company and assimilate its culture. Managers who show consideration for their partner's way of doing things rather than denigrate it are likely to gain a reciprocal sense of respect for their own culture. In cases where one side's culture is going to dominate, respectfulness helps employees see what the lead company is all about and has to offer in the way of structure, processes, and business behavior. And in cases where a new culture is being built—either through transformation or by selecting the best from both organizations—a tone of cross-cultural consideration helps employees open up to different ways of doing things rather than tightly hold onto their ways.

One intervention for I/O psychologists is coaching people from the lead company on how to show respect for the other side's culture. A simple way to do this is to ask people in the acquired company how and why they do things. Most appreciate the chance to describe how they go about their work. It is important to keep in mind that many of the people from the partner organization helped shape its history. Their contribution needs to be honored. Informal and spontaneous opportunities to ask partners about their ways of doing things are both welcome and informative. Naturally, the tone is important here—the question should come off as an honest inquiry, not as a challenge or a little spying.

Although informal questioning and respectful show-and-tells help educate partners on observable behaviors, neither can uncover the deep-rooted values and basic philosophies that underlie those behaviors. To understand a culture, you need to appreciate the why's behind the what's that you observe. Many misunderstandings and communication breakdowns result when managers lack the means to decode, translate, and contextualize the overt messages and publicly available information about their partners. Unless key players from the combining organizations learn to read into the other side's culture, then mutual working relations will always be under threat.

One method to help combining people gain a deep understanding about each organization's culture and ways of doing business is a hands-on "cultural clarification" activity. Its objectives are, first, to raise emerging cultural perceptions and stereotypes between the partners, and second, to initiate dialogue on the desired cultural end state for the combination. The activity is built around each partner group making three lists: how we view our organization's culture, how we view the other side's culture, and how we think the other side views our culture. The rosters include business practices, interpersonal behaviors, and values. Importantly, participants are instructed to include characteristics that either have been experienced firsthand or heard about secondhand. The intention is to unearth all the perceptions and stereotypes that are circulating about the partner.

Exhibit 3.4 shows a sample of the output from this activity conducted with the combining senior executives from an energy industry combination. The two groups had been working together for about two months, so they had plenty of time to form initial impressions. The list shows how both sides tended to describe their own culture positively and be more critical of the other's. For example, company A viewed itself as having a balanced business and technical approach, but regarded company B as being financially driven; the implication here was that company A regarded B's technological expertise as inferior to its own. In its self-description, company B recognized that it put a priority on financial performance but nowhere did it indicate any technical inferiority. Yet executives from company B knew how A felt about their technological capabilities. This was a sore point for them and it surfaced in the ensuing discussion.

Exhibit 3.4. How Two Companies View Each Other's Cultures.

Company A:

How Company A Views its Own Culture	How Company B Views Company A's Culture	How Company A *Thinks* Company B Views A's Culture
Responsive to the customer	Bureaucratic	Bureaucratic
Program management oriented	Managed by consensus	Makes decisions by consensus
Uses collegial decision making	Too polite	Gentlemen's club versus "tough guy" approach
Respectful of people	Unwilling to change	Arrogant
Participative	Offers vertical career path	Layers of management
Civil	1950s-style organization	Respected competitor
Balances business and technical approaches	Makes decisions at the top	Willing to take business and technical risks
Emphasizes ethics and integrity	Big-customer oriented	Overfacilitated
Has structured management	Project oriented	
Has problems with small projects	Workers too serious about themselves	

Company B:

How Company B Views its Own Culture	How Company A Views Company B's Culture	How Company B *Thinks* Company A Views B's Culture
Push back required	In your face	Rude, in your face
Empowered	Processes not documented	Undisciplined
Sets the bar high	Oriented to line of business (not project)	Nontraditional energy company
Has delayered organization and small staff	Decisions don't hold—need to argue and revisit	High risk takers
Has broader career path	Darwinian system	Stubborn
Change oriented	Financially driven	Technological neophyte
Uses minimal oversight		
Gives priority to financial performance		
Has a sense of humor		
Prefers speed and simplicity		

Frequently the two sides agree on their differences. In the energy combination, company B had a behavioral norm of confronting people head-on over disagreements. Executives cited this in their roster as "push back required." Executives from company A described it as "in your face" and "decisions don't hold—need to argue and revisit." Interestingly, executives from company B knew this behavior irritated the "too polite" A group. In their list of how they thought company A viewed them, the B executives unambiguously reported "rude, in your face." The airing of this cultural distinction led to a joint discussion about desired norms for their combined culture. Both sides agreed that company A's style was too reserved and polite—a faster-paced style of decision making and more head-on debate of the issues were required. But company A's executives felt that B went too far in the other direction. Together, the two groups settled on a desired end state of "polite confrontation"—speak up and challenge, but not in a rude manner.

This example shows two of the benefits of the culture clarification process. First, it brings the language being used behind closed doors when one side discusses the other out in the open between the two partners. What company B valued as "push back," A distastefully regarded as rude. Second, this activity engages the two sides in mutually discussing which aspects of the existing cultures should be retained in the combination and which should not be carried forward. Sometimes, as in the "polite–push back" example, the result is a hybrid of the two precombination cultures. Other times, the partners agree that one side's norms are preferable. Still other times the partners agree that a characteristic shared by both sides should not be carried forward.

Postcombination Phase

After months of planning, the postcombination phase arrives with the requirement of implementing the decisions made for integrating organizations, structures, cultures, policies, practices, and people. In cases where combination planning has been more political than productive, the problems of the combination phase bleed over into the new organization. Yet even in cases where combination planning has succeeded in identifying ways to obtain strategic synergies and in designing an organization that is more than the sum of its parts, problems arise (see Exhibit 3.5).

Exhibit 3.5. Issues and Interventions in the Postcombination Phase.

Issue	Intervention
There is functional tunnel vision and lack of cross-unit cooperation.	Enhance cross-functional relations.
Postcombination attitudes and behaviors are reinforced by default rather than by design.	Coach senior leadership to model desired behaviors and attitudes.
	Provide a onetime-only bonus opportunity early in the postcombination phase.

Senior executives often hurry to get on with things and rush through implementation. Time and talent have been directed away from core business requirements during the months of combination planning, and executives grow impatient, wanting to turn their attention back to running their business operations or even to making their next acquisition. The task forces may have identified sound approaches to extracting gains from the integrated organizations, but inattention and sloppy implementation regularly undercut any hopes of realizing their potential.

Meanwhile, people experience renewed stress in the postcombination phase. Up to this point, many were worried about job security. Now they have to contend with new systems, coworkers, leaders, and ways of doing things. This can be an invigorating and creative period; more often than not, however, it is a confusing and chaotic time that further adds to employee stress and organizational ineffectiveness.

Issue: Functional Tunnel Vision and Lack of Cooperation

A whole slew of coordinative issues arise during implementation. Sometimes, coordination problems emerge within units, as when the sales staff in a high-technology acquisition learned of their quotas for selling products and services but had no sales materials ready to assist them. Often, though, implementation problems occur across units. In a hospital merger, a much publicized, new state-of-the-art maternity ward remained empty for months because the legal department had not secured all the required government permits to operate it.

Intervention: Enhance Cross-Functional Relations

One of the ironies of effective integration management—and an example of why these events are so difficult to manage—is that when functional transition teams do well, they tend to develop a functional tunnel vision. Team members dive deeply into the issues and opportunities in their functional area but overlook cross-functional dynamics. A few firms address this by cross-breeding functional transition teams—putting a manufacturing person on the HR transition team or a product development person on the marketing team, for example. Even so, as executives focus on building their departments and teams, fissures between interdependent units commonly develop in the postcombination phase. The responsibility for developing effective cross-unit relationships often falls through the cracks until tension mounts or a crisis occurs. Being proactive about horizontal organization building helps keep a newly combined company aligned and averts conflicts that will require considerably more effort to address later on.

In a multinational pharmaceutical combination, I used an intergroup relations exercise to help headquarters staff build better relations with field business units. One meeting brought together headquarters staff directors with country managers from the field to address roadblocks to an effective working relationship. The goal was to clarify what each group needed from the other, identify any gaps, and agree to cross-unit working arrangements. The process involved breaking the two groups out into separate rooms and having them respond to two questions: What does our group need or want from the other group? And what can the other group expect from us?

The units posted their needs and expectations on flip charts and reconvened in the main meeting room. Country managers presented their cross-unit needs first. They compared their lists of "what country managers need or want from headquarters staff" with the headquarters staff list of "what the country managers can expect from headquarters staff." The two lists had many similarities, but some key differences jumped out.

After working through what was needed from headquarters staff, the focus turned to "what headquarters staff needs from the country managers" and "what country managers say can be expected from them." This meeting increased understanding of what each group needed from the other to accomplish its objectives. It also established in the still-fledging organization a workable process for raising and addressing issues. Before the combination, staff-line relationships in both of the partners were chary at best, and often counterproductive. The cross-unit dialogue here set a new tone and demonstrated how the combination could enhance organizational effectiveness.

Issue: Postcombination Attitudes and Behaviors Reinforced by Default, Not Design

Extremely frustrating to people in the postcombination organization is the sense that they now have targets, goals, and expectations on which their job evaluations, pay increases, and promotional opportunities will be based but do not have all the tools, information, and other resources required to perform well. And scarce time, if any, is allotted to train people in new systems or procedures or to let them experiment with new approaches to getting work done. Compounding such concerns is the desire to make a good impression on a new boss and coworkers. Although learning by trial and error is very common and effective in getting people to adopt new methods, the notion of learning through mistakes is troubling to individuals who want to get out of the blocks quickly and make a good first impression.

Seeking to understand which way the wind is blowing in the postcombination organization, employees from an acquired or merged company look to the behaviors and attitudes that prevailed during the recent months of integration planning. The cultural norms that emerge during the relatively unfrozen combination period get refrozen or reinforced in the postcombination phase. Usually this occurs by default rather than design. Leadership does an inadequate job of articulating a desired new culture, so the norms that employees saw during the combination phases—practices like constricted communications—become solidified in their expectations of life in the postcombination organization. In an acquired manufacturing firm that had enjoyed excellent employee-management relations as an independent company, employees felt abandoned by their leaders, who concentrated on managing relations with their new owners during the combination phase. Morale plummeted and a union drive ensued. Leadership turned its attention back to employees and successfully fought off the unionization effort. The battle required considerable resources, however, and the effort to rebuild leadership credibility, as measured in a biannual employee survey, took several years.

Even in cases where leaders do a good job of articulating the desired culture for the combined organization, their efforts frequently are undercut by reward, information, and other systems that continue to reinforce the ways of the precombination organizations. Executives at merging consumer products companies hoped to use the combination as an opportunity to break traditional hierarchical silos on both sides. Yet no systems were established to speed information across business units, either through the formal MIS systems or informal opportunities for managers to meet and share ideas and insights. People regressed back to their prior behaviors rather than establish connections across business units.

What is in it for people to contribute to a productive combination? The promised long-term benefits of the combination may seem a long ways down the road for individuals contending with the confusion and uncertainty of the developing organization. In the meantime, employees keep their eyes open for direct and indirect cues about which behaviors are being rewarded and which are discouraged in the emerging organization.

Intervention A: Coach Senior Leadership to Model Desired Behaviors and Attitudes

As the postcombination organization begins to jell, it is an opportunity for I/O psychologists to provide feedback to senior executives on the cultural norms that are being reinforced and to establish a course of action for reinforcing the desired culture. The behaviors and attitudes of leaders that prevailed during the transition have a powerful impact on employees during implementation. Through methods including surveys and individual and focus group interviews, the I/O psychologist can conduct employee research to assess employee perceptions of the emerging organization, and in particular the extent to which the desired culture is or is not prevailing. By focusing executive attention on these data, gaps between the culture that employees experience and the culture that leadership envisions can be dealt with early in the postcombination phase. These gaps can be addressed by direct executive action (for example, at the acquired manufacturing firm, I/O psychologists could have coached executives to increase face-to-face contact with an employee population that felt abandoned during the transition process) and by indirect actions (for example, in the consumer products merger compromised by functional silos, senior executives could have been coached to model cross-unit cooperation by inviting staff from other departments to sit in on key meetings that had been restricted to within-department staff in the precombination organization).

Intervention B: Provide a Onetime Bonus Opportunity Early in the Postcombination Phase

Rewards play an obviously important role in shaping the post-combination organization. Part of the work of refreezing desired norms is to design an incentive system suited to the desired post-combination organization. One rule of effective compensation programs is timeliness. Waiting for the annual performance evaluation cycle to kick in is too late—it will take at least two years for newly merged or newly acquired employees to determine what is or is not rewarded. Some short-term performance evaluation and reward helps monitor and shape behavior as the organization moves from the old to the new. Otherwise, the norms and practices that were rewarded in the precombination organization—and are still being measured and reinforced through the precombination performance evaluation system—will prevail, and people will have little incentive to contribute to transition activities or adopt new behaviors. Increasingly, I/O psychologists are helping firms establish special short-term reviews and rewards. In a merged professional services company, onetime-only three- and six-month performance reviews were conducted. I/O psychologists proposed and implemented a scheme in which payouts from these reviews were based on a formula integrating the extent to which individuals followed key operating principles and made progress on their regular performance targets.

Early in the life of the combined organization, as people are sorting out their roles and adjusting to their resources, it is *not* the time for stretch targets or high-stakes rewards. Instead, targets should be attainable and payouts in these onetime bonus opportunities should be more symbolic than substantive—showing people they can "win" in the combined organization and providing timely feedback on the extent to which they are abiding by the desired postcombination culture.

Conclusion

The interventions described here represent but a fraction of those available to I/O psychologists to facilitate successful mergers and acquisitions. Every combination is different, so every one requires a unique set of activities to minimize unintended consequences, like employee distraction and culture clash, and to increase the possibilities for productive transition teams and operational enhancements in the postcombination organization. The interventions described here show that managing a merger or acquisition is not rocket science but requires simple principles of good management—building understanding and support for the integration rationale and critical success factors, raising awareness of potential pitfalls, confronting executives with valid data, leveraging tools like reward systems, clarifying and respecting cultural differences rather than denying their presence, and continually involving and communicating with people. Yet three-quarters of all mergers and acquisitions fail. So the delicacy comes in the execution.

Even when guided by a sound strategy and careful implementation, mergers and acquisitions are incredibly difficult events to manage. The vast scope of change, the huge number of decisions to be made, and the myriad human reactions to change tangle up the combination process and encumber the realization of strategic synergies. I/O psychologists are not immune from the pains of personal uncertainty, culture clash, and the need to contribute to transition while maintaining ongoing business activities. But many of those I have met and worked with in buying and selling companies have shown the value they can add by putting a combination on the course toward achieving financial and strategic objectives and by helping the combined entity become more than the sum of its parts.

References

Elsass, P. M., & Veiga, J. F. (1994). Acculturation in acquired organizations: A force-field perspective. *Human Relations, 47*(4), 431–453.

Hitt, M. A., Hoskisson, R. E., Ireland, R. D., & Harrison, J. S. (1991). Effects of acquisitions on R&D inputs and outputs. *Academy of Management Journal, 34*(4), 693–706.

Management Analysis Center. (1985). *A study of the performance of mergers and acquisitions in the financial services sector.* Cambridge, MA: Management Analysis Center.

Marks, M. L., & Mirvis, P. H. (1985). The merger syndrome: Stress and uncertainty. *Mergers & Acquisitions, 20*(2), 50–55.

Marks, M. L., & Mirvis, P. H. (1998). *Joining forces: Making one plus one equal three in mergers, acquisitions, and alliances.* San Francisco: Jossey-Bass.

Marks, M. L., & Mirvis, P. H. (2001, May). Making mergers and acquisitions work: Strategic and psychological preparation. *Academy of Management Executive, 15*(2), 80–94.

Mirvis, P. H., & Marks, M. L. (1986). The merger syndrome: Managing organizational crises. *Mergers & Acquisitions, 20*(3), 71–77.

Wright, M., Hoskisson, R. E., & Businetz, L. W. (2001). Firm rebirth: Buyouts as facilitators of strategic growth and entrepreneurship. *Academy of Management Executive, 15*(1), 117–128.

CHAPTER 4

Succession Planning

Ben E. Dowell

Succession planning is choosing to plan for and develop the future leadership of an organization. The process is one of the most challenging strategic actions to be taken in today's complex, rapidly changing, talent-starved business environment. One can always choose to recruit from outside an organization to fill key roles when they open up, a process of external succession. However, my own experience and the literature suggest that executives hired directly from outside are almost twice as likely to fail as those promoted from within (Ciampa & Watkins, 1999). In times of dramatic change, external succession can be desirable. And if not well designed, internal succession can impede organizational changes needed to cope effectively with a changing business environment. The purpose of succession planning is not necessarily to ensure that all positions are filled from inside the organization but rather to be systematic in assessing the organization's requirements and to determine in a disciplined way the actions needed to ensure the availability of future leadership.

This chapter explores the decisions and the consequences of the decisions that should be made to design and implement a succession planning system to increase the probability of success of the future leaders. Figure 4.1 describes the process of implementing succession planning across a period of one year. At each stage alternatives are possible and decisions need to be made to ensure that the system matches the requirements of the organization.

Figure 4.1. The Annual Cycle of Succession Planning.

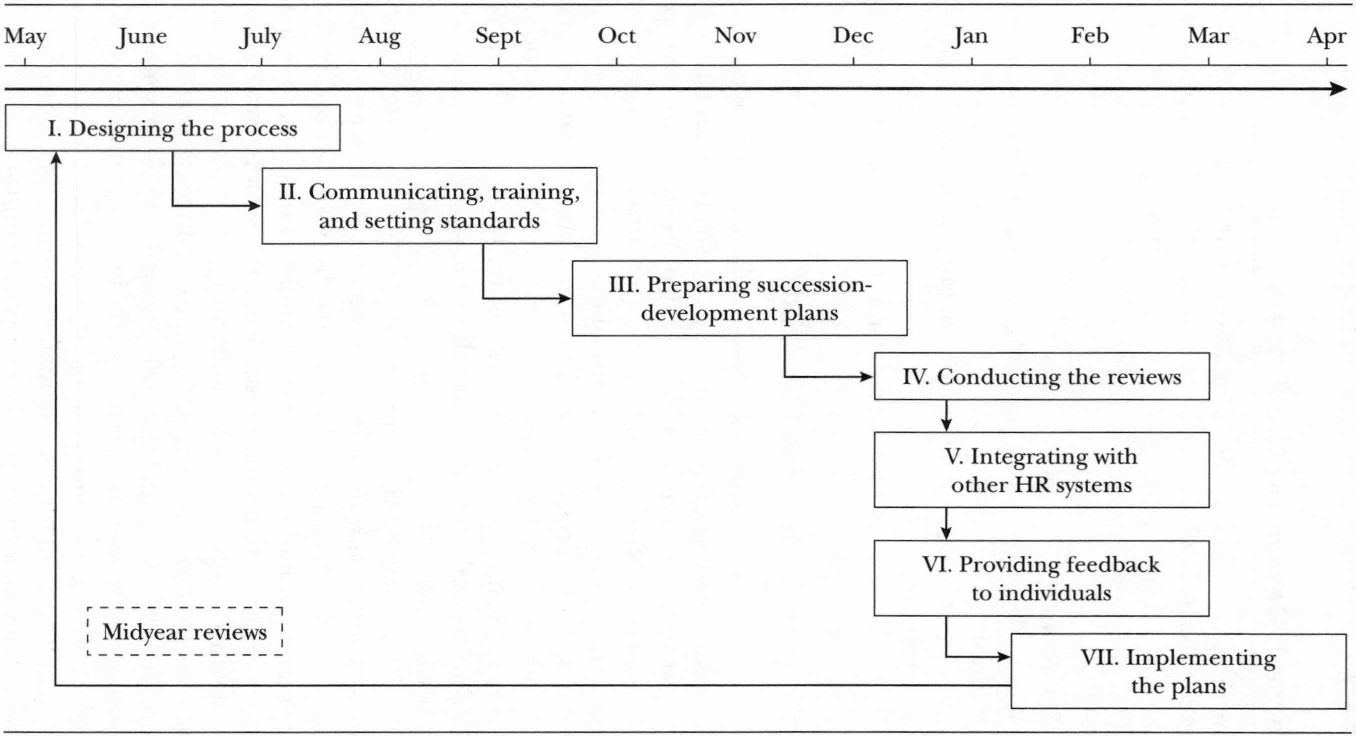

Phase I: Designing the Process

The design phase lays the foundation for the succession planning process. As with all change interventions, the design phase is critical to the ultimate success of the system. During this phase several initial questions need to be addressed:

- Do senior leaders see the need?
- Where does succession planning belong in the annual cycle of business processes?
- Do we adopt a position-based, pool-based, or combination system?
- Which positions or persons should be included in the plan?

Do Senior Leaders See the Need?

The first step in building a succession planning system is to ensure that senior leaders understand the necessity for it and are not just going through the motions. When key retirements are anticipated, the issue may be obvious. But at other times the need is not as clear. Managers often say, "Our management team is young. If everyone had successors, the successors wouldn't have anyplace to go. They would just get frustrated and leave. What is the point?" If this view prevails, a succession planning system may be designed that looks good on paper but will not have a meaningful impact on the business.

History may be the simplest way to demonstrate the importance of succession planning. "How many of the senior leaders of the organization assumed their current positions within the last five years?" should be the first question asked. Then, to help paint a picture of future requirements, candid assessments of the senior leadership should be made concerning, first, their ability to continue to grow to meet increasing performance standards, and second, the likelihood that they will stay with the organization. Such assessments frequently lead to insights into the importance of comprehensive succession planning.

Leaders often do not adequately consider the impact of an organization's growth in scale or complexity on the performance demands made on its leaders. Yet this growth can put extraordinary emphasis on the ability of leaders to continue to grow and adapt. Some leaders will be able to reinvent themselves continuously and adapt to the changing demands of the business; others will not.

Historically, companies have compensated for ineffective succession planning by recruiting successors from outside the organization. But the talent available to lead companies in today's complex business climate is becoming more and more limited. The supply of future executives is decreasing just as the demand is increasing. McKinsey & Co. (Chambers, Foulon, Handfield-Jones, Hankin, & Michaels, 1998) coined the phrase "the war for talent" to describe the increasing difficulty of attracting and retaining superior talent. It is challenging to build smooth internal succession, but this effort diminishes the threat to the future success and continuity of the business that results from placing individuals from outside the organization directly into key roles (Ciampa & Watkins, 1999).

Early in the design phase of the succession planning process, it is important to ensure that the senior leaders agree on its objectives and the measures of success. Without this understanding the process may not deliver the desired insights into the depth of talent in the organization.

Where Does Succession Planning Belong in the Annual Cycle of Business Processes?

The typical succession planning process has a cycle of twelve months. Usually a decision is made on which time of year to review the plan, and then other elements of the process are timed accordingly.

Organizations have predetermined times during the year when they focus on various business processes. Most businesses do budget planning during one part of the year and strategic planning during another. My experience suggests that succession planning should not compete with these reviews; a time should be selected when senior leadership can focus on it. Ideally, succession planning is positioned between strategic planning, when long-term strategic needs of the business are identified, and budget planning, when near-term initiatives are funded.

Do We Adopt a Position-Based, Pool-Based, or Combination System?

If an organization is relatively stable or if the focus is on senior leadership positions, then a position-based system is probably the best approach to choose. A position-based approach generally takes the form of identifying the key positions in an organization and identifying those individuals who have the potential to move into those positions. For many organizations these key positions are the senior leadership positions. A typical form used to gather position-based succession planning information is presented in Exhibit 4.1.

Including only senior leadership positions in the succession planning process may address only a part of the succession challenges of an organization. A better approach is to identify all the positions that are critical to the future success of the organization based on the strategic plan. A rule of thumb is to select those positions that reflect a core competency of the organization and would be difficult to replace from outside if they suddenly became open. Incumbents for these strategic positions may be in current posts in which they have irreplaceable customer relationships or technical knowledge; if they moved up, it could pose a threat to the organization. Thus, succession planning for these positions may be as critical to the continuing success of an organization as planning at the senior level.

When taking a position-based approach, there are a number of potential issues to consider. First, will the positions planned for even be in existence by the end of the planning period? The CEO position usually continues. But below the CEO level, positions may evolve at a rapid pace to stay abreast of the changing environment the organization faces. The challenge arises when key roles in the organization change qualitatively. For example, the structure may change from a functional to a general management organization; if not anticipated this will render prior succession planning less than useful. Including an organizational analysis component early in the succession planning process linked closely to the strategic plan can reduce the likelihood of a disconnect between the succession plan and the organization's future requirements.

The second issue is simply the constant rise in performance standards. As Figure 4.2 illustrates, succession planning occurs

Exhibit 4.1. A Typical Form Used in Position-Based Succession Planning.

Key Position Succession Plan

Division:			Organization:		
Key position			**Potential successor(s)**		
Title (grade level)	**Incumbent (date moved to present position)**	**When position is expected to be open**	**Ready next 12 months**	**1–3 years**	**4–5 years**
VP Marketing (22)	Jan Jones (3/1/2001)	Q2 / 2005	Jean Cristi Pat Tumeri	Chris Toms	Sean Adria

Date: _____

Completed by: _____

Approved by: _____

against a moving background. Frequently those who assess potential do not recognize that as individuals develop over two or three years to qualify for a position, so too do the positions. They will grow more complex and may require significantly greater capability than when the plan was developed. Thus, individuals may be developing toward positions that exist only in title, because the requirements for them have changed. Being successful in succession planning might be likened to being successful in hockey. When Hall of Famer Wayne Gretzky was asked to what he attributed his outstanding performance in hockey, he replied that he skated to where the puck was going to be, not to where it was (Bennis, 1989). This is also the challenge in succession planning: accurately forecasting the future needs of the organization and taking the necessary actions today to prepare the leaders for tomorrow.

A third issue is relying on a small number of high-potential individuals as successors. Identifying two or three very high-potential individuals to be the successors for many key positions may provide

Figure 4.2. Implication of Changes in the Business on Standards and Performance Capabilities.

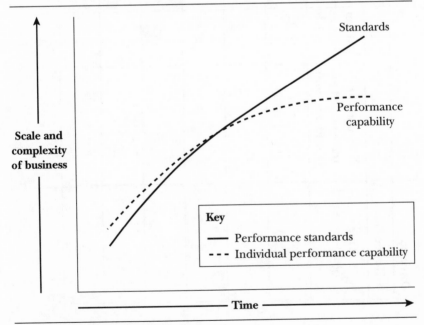

the organization with a false sense of security. This practice can quickly come back to haunt the organization if a couple of successors are promoted and the third one leaves. A final issue associated with position-based succession planning is when managers merely want to fill in the blank—that is, include individuals on the plan who would not be selected if an opening actually occurred. Unless there is a thorough and frank discussion to uncover these issues, these last two practices can mask serious gaps in succession planning.

In organizations that are changing dramatically to cope with an evolving business climate, pool-based planning may be the best option for succession planning. In a pool-based system, the organization seeks to optimize the future capabilities of high-potential individuals. The expectation is that if a pool of talent with sufficient depth and breadth is created, the organization will have enough successors for key positions regardless of the direction in which it evolves. This approach may provide the leadership to allow an organization to take advantage of unexpected strategic opportunities that a position-based system might not.

Pool-based systems generally involve identifying high-potential talent in the organization, assessing strengths and developmental needs, and then creating development plans to enhance the individuals' capacity for the future. Exhibit 4.2 presents an example of a form for collecting this type of information.

There are a number of potential problems with pool-based succession planning. Managers often underestimate the size of the pool of high-potentials that must be created. Growth in the business, turnover, retirements, timing of openings, and breadth of competencies required all influence the size of the pool needed. In a high-growth business it is not unusual for 40 to 50 percent of the managers to need to have the capability to move to higher levels in the organization.

A second issue is the diversity of talent in the pool. As the challenges faced by an organization change, the core competencies required to compete may change as well. These competencies may not be resident in the organization, and therefore the pool-based approach will fall short. As part of strategic planning, an organization should review the core competencies it will need in the future, translate these into talent requirements, and take the actions needed to build these competencies by infusing talent at multiple levels in the organization.

**Exhibit 4.2. A Typical Form
Used in Pool-Based Succession.**

Name:

| **Position:** | **Position date:** |

Career aspirations: What are the individual's career aspirations?

Strengths: Describe the areas of competence, skills, and behaviors demonstrated by this individual that will most contribute to this individual's future success.

-
-
-

Developmental needs: Describe the areas of competence, skills, and behaviors that most need to be developed to enhance future success.

-
-
-

Possible derailers: Describe characteristics of the individual which if not corrected may prevent the individual from achieving his or her potential (e.g., arrogance, micromanaging, failure to build a team, etc.).

-
-

Key developmental question: What question do we most need to answer to determine how far the individual can go in the future?

Developmental actions: Identify guided on-the-job developmental experiences and other experiences, such as task forces or formal development-training programs.

**Exhibit 4.2. A Typical Form
Used in Pool-Based Succession, Cont'd.**

Action/assignment:

•
•
•

Career plan: What are the most likely next career steps for this
individual assuming he or she develops according to expectations?

Position: **Quarter/year:**

•
•
•

Possibly the most effective approach to succession planning is
to combine position-based and pool-based planning. This approach
incorporates individual assessments of potential for all managers
and the identification of specific successors for the most critical
roles. In my experience, building broad talent pools enhances the
organization's flexibility and ability to take advantage of unexpected opportunities. Position-based planning that targets a few
key positions will ensure that critical gaps in succession can be
identified and filled.

Which Positions or Persons
Should Be Included in the Plan?

The depth of the planning depends on the strategic issues faced
by the organization, the approach taken, and where the organization is in the implementation process. The position-based approach works best at senior levels of the organization and for select
key positions. If a position-based approach is taken down to lower
organizational levels where there are many incumbent positions,
the diversity of positions and volume of successors will overwhelm
the planning process. If the senior leader wishes to press past the

top two or three levels, it is advisable to adopt a pool-based succession for these lower levels. Organizations facing the prospect of rapid growth should move pool-based planning down in the organization as quickly as possible.

Succession planning implementation works best in a top-down manner, with the most senior leaders modeling the desired behaviors. If succession planning is not in place in the organization, the designer should consider implementation over several years, taking the process down a level each year until all levels of management are covered. An alternative approach is to focus on critical organizational areas—units representing core business competencies—and provide in-depth training to all levels at once. For example, in the beginning stages of implementation in a consumer products company, a designer might focus on an area critical to the business, such as marketing. The assessment of where the key succession issues exist should drive the choice of approach.

Phase II: Communicating, Training, and Setting Standards

The quality of the initial implementation of a succession planning system cannot rely solely on the support of the senior leaders in the organization. All managers need to understand the purpose and be trained both to complete the assessments and to review the results of the planning at lower levels of the organization. The key questions to address at this phase are these:

• What is the purpose?
• How do we communicate succession planning to the organization?
• How do we train managers to prepare plans?
• What standards do we use to assess gaps and planning?

What Is the Purpose?

Fundamental to this phase is the decision on the purpose of the planning. Expectations of managers in the organization should be clear, or they may become cynical. In some succession planning systems the purpose is simply to complete an audit of the depth of talent in the organization. Often these systems emphasize assessing talent rather than developing it, and few visible follow-up actions besides recruiting external talent ensue. If communications have not been clear and managers expect more pervasive development actions to be taken as a result of the planning process, they may quickly begin to question its value and resist future implementation cycles.

In most succession planning systems the purpose is to develop a plan of action to address identified gaps at both the organizational and the individual levels. In addition to communicating how the planning is to be done, it is important to emphasize that implementation will be scrutinized. The planning process can consume an organization's energy with little remaining for the most critical component—implementing the plans. An overemphasis in the communications process on forms, structure, and presentation formats for reviews can make succession planning look more like a mechanical exercise than an integral part of business planning.

How Do We Communicate Succession Planning to the Organization?

Decisions made earlier in the design process greatly define the extent of communications. If position-based planning is selected for senior-level positions only, then communications may extend to only a few key executives at the top of the organization and be best handled on a one-on-one basis. Once a decision to look more deeply into the organization is made, however, a much more comprehensive communication plan must be developed. Communications should openly describe the purpose, process design, and expected outcomes. Another consequence of the decision to look deeply into the organization is that managers will expect to receive feedback after assessments of their potential. Openly communicating what type of feedback a manager should expect during this phase of implementation will serve to set an appropriate standard for follow-up communications.

How Do We Train Managers to Prepare Plans?

Training managers in the mechanics of the process is just the beginning. Perhaps the most challenging element of the process is educating managers on the standards and the organization's philosophy concerning development of individuals. When succession plans are made that follow the strategic planning process of the organization, it helps set the stage for a better understanding of the future needs of the business. If the organization does not communicate the strategic shifts in competencies that will be required of future leaders then the succession plans will not meet expectations. The organization will be planning for the past, not the future. As a senior leader put it following a particularly disappointing review, "I realize now that I was expecting them to read my mind."

One of the more effective ways to help managers understand the organization's philosophy on management development and the consequences of failing to plan effectively is to conduct discussions of short cases. An example of such a "caselette" is presented in Exhibit 4.3. It is drawn from a program titled Building a Pipeline of Talent, used by Bristol-Myers Squibb to teach its leaders about leadership development. In this program, which is led by the senior leaders of the company, short cases like the one pre-

---

**Exhibit 4.3. Bristol-Myers Squibb Company
Caselette Used to Teach Succession Planning.**

Two Much of a Good Thing?

With retirement coming Jon Smith had focused significant efforts on developing a successor. In fact, two individuals were widely acknowledged to have the talent to follow in Smith's footsteps. Although Jones and Brown were not equal in every respect, they had complementary skills and were assessed as being quality successors. Both had indicated that they were not at all interested in moving out of the function but enjoyed working in a variety of roles in the function. In fact, recently the two had switched positions to broaden their experience and both were equally successful in their new roles. Smith's retirement, effective at the end of the year, was announced last week.

- *The business can afford to lose neither Jones nor Brown, what do you recommend be done?*
- *How do we know Jones and Brown are both qualified successors?*
- *Could this problem with choosing a successor have been prevented? If so, how?*

---

sented are used to help leaders understand the consequences of failing to project future standards and plan effectively.

What Standards Do We Use to Assess Gaps and Planning?

As discussed earlier, standards for positions evolve over time to keep pace with the demands of the business environment. Effective succession planning, whether position-based or pool-based, requires the organization to project future standards and the developmental experiences that prepare an individual for a future role. Bristol-Myers Squibb's position profiling system provides an example. Inside the company, position profiles have been created for all key positions, from chairman down to financial analyst. These profiles are aspirational; that is, they are focused on future requirements. They cover five areas:

- *Areas of competence:* What an individual in the role is expected to accomplish
- *Leader behaviors:* How the individual is expected to accomplish goals
- *Experiences desired:* Experiences an individual should have prior to moving into the position (not a listing of jobs)
- *Knowledge desired:* Knowledge needed to perform in the role (not a listing of degrees)
- *Developmental value:* Learning opportunities, experience, and knowledge to be gained in the position

Because roles in the organization continue to change, these profiles are updated at least once every two years. When position profiles are used, the gaps in a successor's experience and knowledge can be assessed by comparing that individual's background with the experiences and knowledge identified in the profile of the target position. Intermediate developmental positions can be identified for the individual based on their learning value.

The foundation for successful succession planning is having standards that accurately reflect the future of the organization to guide the assessment and development process. Exhibit 4.4 illustrates a position profile for a senior leader at Bristol-Myers Squibb.

Exhibit 4.4. A Position Profile: Bristol-Myers Squibb Company.

Position profile: President, Worldwide Medicines

Expected areas of competence:

• Able to synthesize large amounts of input, see novel relationships, and think ahead in nonincremental ways that enable the development of superior competitive strategy. Able to add value to areas beyond own expertise by asking questions to stimulate innovative thought.

• Able to select and develop a team of individuals with the capacity and personal accountability necessary to achieve competitive superiority. Able to guide the leadership development process, ensuring ongoing succession for key positions.

Leader behaviors:

• Delivers results, drives for continuous improvement. Sets high performance expectations and holds others accountable for the results expected. Acts with a sense of urgency.

• Demonstrates principled leadership and sound business ethics; shows consistency in principles, values, and behaviors.

Experiences desired:

• Demonstrated ability to grow a pharmaceutical business, participated in the successful development and commercialization of major products.

• Demonstrated ability to deal effectively with regulatory authorities, government officials, major customers, and the investment community.

Knowledge desired:

• Knowledge of the medicines business, including the science, products (BMS and competitors), disease states, the research and commercialization process, manufacturing, marketing, and sales.

Developmental value:

• Gain a board-level perspective of what is required to run the total enterprise, including the nonmedicines segments of the business.

• External development, including alliances, licensing, and acquisitions.

Note: Exhibit shows selected items from a position profile.

Phase III: Preparing Succession-Development Plans

Preparing plans can be a highly structured process, complete with detailed forms and elaborate presentations, or it can be very informal. The following are the key questions the designer should consider during this phase:

- Will input be sought from the individuals involved?
- How will assessments of potential be made?
- What sources of information will be made available to assess potential?
- Who owns the assessment of potential?
- What are the legal considerations?

Will Input Be Sought from the Individuals Involved?

An often-overlooked but critical element in the succession planning process is seeking employee input. To make a realistic succession plan it is important to understand employees' career aspirations and desires for work-life balance. With dual-career families and the increasing value placed on life outside of work today, it cannot be assumed that the career desires of high-potentials will match the desires of the organization. To address these issues, organizations are being increasingly creative in finding development alternatives. For example, instead of two- to three-year assignments abroad, organizations are more frequently providing short-term tours of duty—six months or less—to accommodate the employee's personal desires while still providing needed international experience.

Although career aspirations may be aligned with the organizational expectations, the developmental price that an individual is willing to pay may not be. Often high-potential individuals exhibit "career path myopia"—not seeing the need to make any moves other than straight up the organizational ladder. Open communication and honest career feedback is the only cure for this disease.

The simplest way to learn about an employee's desires and limitations is to ask that individual. However, organizational culture will influence the accuracy of these dialogues. If individuals feel that being candid about their desires will severely limit their opportunities or rewards, they are unlikely to be candid. The best way to address this issue is to demonstrate to employees that the organization will be flexible when balancing employee desires with succession and development plans.

How Will Assessments of Potential Be Made?

There are myriad ways to identify successors and assess potential. In some systems, only individuals perceived as having the potential to move to a more senior level are assessed. See again Exhibit 4.1, which illustrates an approach where individuals are identified who can succeed to key positions.

In pool-based systems, assessments may be limited to those whom leaders perceive have the potential to move up in the organization, or all managers may be assessed. In some pool-based systems ratings are made of how many levels an individual is capable of being promoted, although specific positions may not be named. To be effective, these assessments of potential should be combined with likely career paths to ensure that appropriate standards are applied to the assessments.

In other systems, categorical assessments are made of all managers. The ratings range from categories such as "high potential" or "solid performer" to "marginal performer," referring to various combinations of performance and potential. Categorical ratings such as these pose problems, however. The critical question is always "High potential for what?" Anchoring assessments with a target position or role is usually the only way to be sure that they are based on appropriate standards. In addition, employees can become fixated on the label and not focus on their development. Even "solid performers" must continue to develop to meet increasingly difficult performance standards. Finally, managers may feel that communicating the category label to an employee provides sufficient feedback, thereby avoiding an in-depth dialogue of career and developmental opportunities.

A variety of assessments may be made during the succession planning process. Performance ratings are frequently made during the succession planning process as are assessments of culture fit. Generally these additional assessments are gathered to reinforce various organizational messages, such as the importance of achieving results in a manner consistent with the desired corporate culture.

One constant challenge is to help managers differentiate between performance and potential. In most cases, performance at one level of the organization does not reflect the ability to perform at more senior levels. One solution is to ask managers to rank individuals' performance and potential separately on a grid. Exhibit 4.5 presents an example. Comparing rankings of performance and potential can help managers differentiate between the two and guide allocation of scarce developmental resources.

Exhibit 4.5. Assessment of Performance and Potential.

		LOW		HIGH
P O T E N T I A L	**H I G H**	Enhance investment in development for current role	Accelerate development for current and next role	Increase investment in development Accelerate movement to next role
R A N K		Monitor performance closely Develop in role	Continue to monitor performance and potential closely Develop in role	Invest in development Ready to move to next role
	L O W	Monitor performance closely Questionable potential	Monitor potential closely Develop in role	Ensure appropriate awards and recognition Develop in role

LOW HIGH

PERFORMANCE RANK

Note: Placement on grid is determined by ranking of performance juxtaposed to ranking of potential.

What Sources of Information Will Be Made Available to Assess Potential?

Ultimately, assessments of potential are judgments made by senior managers. The sources of information that contribute to this judgment can range from simple assessments made by immediate managers to reviews of work history, 360-degree survey assessments, 360-degree interview assessments, assessment centers, personality assessment, and in-depth assessments by psychologists. Although a thorough review of assessment methodologies is beyond the scope of this chapter, designers may want to keep in mind the following principles:

- *Multiple sources and methods enhance assessment accuracy.* Combining an assessment from an individual's direct manager with 360-degree assessment data and the individual's prior track record in a variety of work settings is likely to produce a more accurate prediction of the future than relying on an assessment by the individual's immediate manager alone.
- *Given the changing demands on managers, early career assessments of potential are better based on assessment of ability to learn from experience and adapt than on assessment of current competencies.* Van Velsor and Guthrie (1998) provide a summary of factors that contribute to the ability to learn from experience.
- *Often overlooked is assessment of factors that might derail an individual.* Strengths and sources of early success can ultimately lead to failure as an individual progresses in his or her career if competencies important for early-career success actually detract from success in later years (McCall, 1998). Failure may be more related to having undesirable qualities than lacking desirable ones (Hogan & Hogan, 2001).

Who Owns the Assessment of Potential?

One critical design decision that must be made is who will ultimately assess the potential. Unlike performance assessment, where an individual's manager is probably his most accurate assessor because she can frequently see how he performs against job standards, assessment of potential requires a perspective that immediate managers may not have. Most managers are not adept at projecting individuals into their own position or further. Although immediate managers may have input into the potential-assessment process, the one-over manager is likely to have a better perspective on the future position requirements and the individual. As potential assessments are reviewed up the organization, there are usually frequent changes. The system for data capture, which is an element in all succession planning systems, must be easily updated to minimize the administrative burden of these changes.

What Are the Legal Considerations?

Succession planning is done in the same legal context as all human resource processes. The types of decisions made during the reviews will determine the steps required to ensure that actions taken are consistent with laws and statutes. The legal implications of succession planning vary depending on the nature of the process—which may range from discussions of strengths and development needs, to planning for developmental experiences, to creating candidate slates for future openings, to deciding on specific job assignments. If a designer has a question, he or she should review the process with an individual familiar with statutory and legal requirements.

Phase IV: Conducting the Reviews

How to review the plans presents a host of decisions for the designer. The operating culture of the organization and what senior leaders want to review are both important determinants of the options available for this phase. Do senior leaders just want to discuss the people in the succession plan or do they want to see a strategic plan for developing talent throughout the organization? The more leaders want a strategic talent plan, the greater the likelihood that there will be elaborate preparations for the reviews. Here are the questions to be addressed in this phase:

- Who is present and what is discussed?
- What is the style of the reviews?
- How are reviewers prepared?

Who Is Present and What Is Discussed?

Reviews are critical to ensuring an even application of standards across groups or the entire organization. Usually, succession planning systems start by managers reviewing their subordinates with their immediate managers and human resources. Over time, many organizations learn the value of having the managers' peers present during the reviews so that multiple perspectives of individuals can be discussed with the one-over manager. This approach greatly enhances the accuracy of assessments of potential.

Position-based succession planning discussions generally focus on those individuals who have been identified as having the capability to move into selected key positions. In pool-based systems, individuals identified as high potential are discussed. If there is an organizational assessment component to the review, then all the managers at senior levels may be discussed. In this approach the assessment of leadership in the organization will identify those who have the potential to grow in the organization and those who are not performing and should leave. It may be just as important to discuss this pruning process as to identify high-potentials. A more comprehensive review tends to lead to a more strategic plan. An example of a talent review agenda incorporating position-based and pool-based succession planning is shown in Exhibit 4.6.

As the exhibit shows, it takes time to do a thorough review—at least a full day in this example. In the early stages of implementing a new succession planning system there is a tendency to underestimate the time required. As a result, there will be only a cursory review of the talent in the organization, few specific plans, and a dissatisfied senior management group. Reducing the scope of the review to match the time available is a much more desirable approach. The scope can be reduced by starting with a review of only key individuals; this is better than starting with a strategic plan for the development of talent or limiting the review to a few key areas of the organization. The appetite for more in-depth or extensive reviews will grow once senior management understands the value of the sessions.

What Is the Style of the Reviews?

The formal aspects of a succession planning system, particularly the forms or presentation guidelines, can overwhelm the process and get in the way of what is probably the most valuable element: the dialogue between levels of management. Organizational culture and style of communication can determine whether the re-

Exhibit 4.6. Talent Review Agenda.

Time Required	Agenda Item
15 minutes	**Overview of agenda and objectives for review**
4 hours	**Review of leadership team:** A review of all key executives within two levels of the division president. This review should include a discussion of strengths, development needs, key developmental questions, and possible derailment factors (approximately 7–10 minutes per person).
1 hour	**Leadership assessment:** As a summary, performance and potential of all key executives should be rank ordered and presented in the 3 × 3 chart (Exhibit 4.5).
1 hour	**Succession planning:** Succession charts for all positions within two levels of the division president.
30 minutes	**High potential pool:** Identification of very high potential managers who will be recommended for inclusion in high potential pools.
30 minutes	**Building depth:** External executives and managers to be recruited to the organization to fill succession gaps. Ports of entry should be specified for each person to be recruited.
30 minutes	**Retention:** A discussion of individuals at risk and plans to enhance the retention of key talent in the organization.
30 minutes	**Wrap-up:** Review of action items.

views are made as formal presentations or in informal conversation. Formal presentations tend not to produce the level of candid, open dialogue that is required to address tough succession and people issues. Engineering an informal dialogue with the presenters telling the "story" of their people and organization, focusing on actions to build leadership and depth, will be seen as a productive use of time. If the tough questions are not addressed and appropriate challenges to the assessments not made, the entire succession planning process runs the risk of being perceived as just another bureaucratic exercise.

How Are Reviewers Prepared?

The simplest way to prepare reviewers is to let them know what types of questions they should ask. Senior managers are generally very comfortable reviewing financial and other operational plans and know the kinds of questions to ask to probe beneath the obvious. This may not be the case when launching a new succession planning system. Exhibit 4.7 presents the kinds of questions a designer might list for leaders conducting their first reviews.

Phase V: Integrating with Other HR Systems

Succession-leadership development planning is unlikely to have the desired impact on organizational effectiveness unless it is appropriately linked with other human resource systems. Here are some of the questions that should be addressed during this phase:

- What should the link with compensation be?
- What should the impact on training and development be?
- What is the link with internal and external staffing?

What Should the Link with Compensation Be?

Almost all organizations want to make sure that their highest-potential managers are given financial incentives to stay with the organization. The arguments for directly linking rewards, pay, and options to assessments of potential are seductive; however, the unintended consequences can subvert an otherwise well-designed system. One consequence relates to managerial assessments of potential. Feeling the need to reward their staffs, managers tend to enhance their assessments of potential to deliver those rewards. As a result, there is an overestimate of organizational depth. Another consequence relates to individuals who are high performers but are not seen as high potential. Directly linking rewards to assessments of potential may disenfranchise these high performers and threaten the credibility of a pay-for-performance philosophy.

That said, differentially providing rewards to those identified as high potential is necessary to ensure retention of the individuals most likely to become the organization's future leaders. The problems

Exhibit 4.7. Sample Questions for Reviewers.

Key position succession plan:

- Why have you identified this person as a successor? How will the position change over the next five years? What are you doing to ensure he will be ready for the position?
- What are his career interests? Do they match your plans?
- What does he need in order to be ready for that position? How could you accelerate his development?
- What will be happening in the next five years that couldn't be done from a developmental perspective in the next two years? (This question should be asked if the person is noted as a long-term successor.)

High potential assessments:

- When will he be ready for promotion? Into what kind of role would he be promotable? If he were promoted, would he be stronger than the current incumbent? What does he need in order to be ready?
- Does the timing of his projected movement coincide with succession needs? If not, what are the plans to accelerate his development in the next six to nine months? How will we keep him challenged if he will be ready before the position becomes open?
- If you promoted this person would you be building for the future or just filling a job?
- Could you find someone stronger if you went outside?
- Do we have any retention issues? Why does he stay with the organization? Does he have a mentor?

General follow-up questions:

- What behaviors have you seen to support your potential assessment? (Challenge the reviewer in terms of all aspects of the assessment—i.e., demonstrating organizational values, developing others, achieving results, etc.)
- Compare and contrast the behaviors of two individuals (selecting one individual that you know as a benchmark helps to clarify standards).
- Who is the most talented (least talented) person in your organization? Why do you say that?

Note: The pronoun "he" has been used for space purposes only; the candidate will of course be male or female.

generally arise when there is a qualitative difference in the rewards that are available to those who have high potential and those who are high performers, such as stock option grants for the former only.

Providing differential access to extraordinary developmental opportunities is a far better solution. Differential access to development should result in higher performance and capability to move to higher levels in the organization. Both performance and actual promotion are perceived as more objective and acceptable bases for reward than subjective assessments of potential.

What Should the Impact on Training and Development Be?

Training and development systems should be directly linked to succession planning. Systematic analysis of development needs for all managers assessed can lead to insights into the types of formal training and developmental experiences that should be provided broadly in the organization. Although training programs play a role in building functional skills and networks inside the organization, job experiences are probably the most critical developmental tools available for the very high potential individuals identified in a succession plan. "Who gets the job" is the most important developmental decision leaders make.

There is significant evidence that experience is the best teacher and that carefully crafting job experiences is the best way to develop high-potentials (McCall, 1998). There is a tendency to move high potential individuals quickly through a number of roles to close the experience gaps identified in succession planning. This may provide a great deal of exposure to the organization, but the rapid movement does not necessarily produce the most effective learning experiences. Combining early identification of high potential talent with a thoughtful analysis of the key experiences required to prepare for succession—as in Bristol-Myers Squibb's position profiling system described earlier—creates the opportunity to sequence an appropriate series of meaningful job experiences.

Job experiences are meaningful when they meet the following criteria:

- *Relevancy:* The individual gains skills needed to perform effectively in a future role. Often high potential managers do not understand what they are expected to learn from a developmental role and miss that value. Letting people know what they are supposed to learn, providing feedback and coaching, and helping them reflect on their learning are all key to enhancing the developmental experience, whether it is in a job or in another, shorter development action.

- *Magnitude:* The developmental experience is sufficiently different from prior experiences to move the individual beyond her current range of comfort and confidence.
- *Duration:* Sufficient time is available for the individual to experience two performance cycles. Performance cycles are not of uniform length for all positions. Generally, positions that are lower in the organization have shorter performance cycles. A performance cycle begins with a plan of action and ends when the plan's results can be observed. In the first cycle, the individual observes the results and develops hypotheses about how to enhance performance; in the second she tests those hypotheses. In contrast, if she experiences only one performance cycle, she will be unlikely to test ideas, learn, and get the most development out of the experience.

Because performance cycles are generally longer the higher the position, the opportunity to provide a sequence of meaningful experiences depends heavily on early identification of potential successors. Often the least attention is paid to the assessment of the longer-term successors identified in a plan because of the perceived inaccuracy of these long-term assessments. But when possible successors are identified early, the organization has the greatest freedom to act to close gaps in experience and capabilities.

What Is the Link with Internal and External Staffing?

Ensuring that individuals identified as successors to key positions are given priority when filling jobs internally is a critical follow-up to succession planning. This might seem obvious, but often a choice must be made to select an individual who might perform best in a specific role in the short term rather than one who should have the experience to progress in the organization in the long term. Frequently a senior leader, someone with the long-term health of the organization in mind, must intervene to assure the right developmental assignments are being made available to the right people.

Effective succession planning can also provide an early warning for external recruiting. Closing near-term gaps in succession by external recruiting presents the greatest likelihood of organizational discontinuity and failure of the individual (Bennis & O'Toole, 2000). Identifying gaps in succession early, recruiting potential successors—usually more than one—into lower-level roles, and providing them with developmental experiences significantly raises the probability of success.

Phase VI: Providing Feedback to Individuals

The decisions made about feedback on assessments and plans are among the most critical in implementing a succession planning system. Individuals in the organization will judge the quality of the process based on the feedback they receive. The questions that need to be addressed are these:

- How is feedback provided?
- What feedback is provided?
- Is the emphasis on assessment or development?

How Is Feedback Provided?

Once succession plans have been reviewed and finalized, feedback must be provided down through the organization. Two issues must be addressed: feedback to managers who made the assessments and feedback to those individuals whose potential was assessed.

Managers who made assessments that were changed need feedback and coaching so that their assessments may improve in the future. These feedback sessions provide an opportunity for managers who are lower in the organization to gain greater perspective on the standards being set for roles in the organization and how position requirements will evolve over time. Failure to provide this feedback will perpetuate inaccurate assessments and feedback to the individuals assessed. Individuals who were assessed in the process will expect feedback on what was discussed about them. Many organizations struggle with what to communicate and the anticipated consequences of this feedback. Philosophically, the organization must decide who owns an individual's career—the individual or the organization. If the decision is that individuals' own their careers, then as a matter of organizational justice individuals should be given honest feedback so that they can make the appropriate decisions for themselves about their careers.

What Feedback Is Provided?

For high-potentials, the questions about feedback generally include this one: Do we provide feedback on future moves and their expected timing? Telling individuals about expected career paths provides the opportunity to align their expectations with those of the organization. But communicating the specific timing of moves can cause them to focus on their next move prematurely, or it may lead to disappointment if a move is delayed.

When the feedback is inconsistent with an individual's self-perceptions, it should be emphasized that the assessment is temporal and may change as the individual develops. In addition, if the specific gaps that led to the assessment can be identified and what the individual needs to do differently is explained, then disappointment should not lead to frustration and possible departure. In my experience, providing honest feedback does not result in increased turnover and actually has the effect of building greater trust among employees.

Is the Emphasis on Assessment or Development?

Having clear standards for what is expected of individuals in more senior roles supports feedback that is developmental rather than evaluative. Telling individuals that they are "high potential" does little to help them prepare for future roles. Instead, explaining that "these are the competencies you need to demonstrate and these are the experiences you should acquire" tends to keep individuals focused on what they should do developmentally to achieve their potential.

Phase VII: Implementing the Plans

Follow-up during the year is critical to ensure that plans are acted on. Immediately after a review, a specific list of the most critical follow-up actions should be documented and distributed to those who participated in it. The following questions should be addressed at this phase:

- When should the follow-up reviews be conducted?
- What should the format of these reviews be?
- What did we learn about the process itself?

When Should the Follow-Up Reviews Be Conducted?

Quarterly follow-up on action plans is the optimal scheduling. Following up more frequently does not allow sufficient time to take actions; less frequent follow-up generally results in a loss of momentum. Aligning follow-up sessions with other business reviews serves to communicate that succession management is a core segment of the normal business planning process, not something apart, and simplifies logistics.

What Should the Format of These Reviews Be?

The format of the follow-up reviews is far less important than that they take place at all. Some organizations prefer a brief written submission addressing progress on the critical items and follow-up discussion on exceptional items. Others prefer a formal review that looks at progress and adjustments to the annual plan.

Some organizations identify high potential pools of talent during the annual review and then allocate time during the year to complete in-depth development plan discussions of those individuals. These reviews usually focus on the individuals' developmental progress and actions taken to accelerate their development. Byham, Smith, and Paese (2000) discuss in detail an approach to managing these high potential pools.

What Did We Learn About the Process Itself?

Succession planning is always evolving. Metrics should be established in the beginning to measure the effectiveness of the succession planning process. The designer should plan a midyear review of the process itself with key stakeholders, discussing how well the process met its objectives, what went well, and what could have been better.

Metrics can be both soft and hard measures. Soft measures are gained by answering questions such as these: Did presenters feel the sessions were long enough to communicate their point of view, and was the tone of the sessions conducive to discussing issues openly? Did the reviewer feel the assessments and plans were objective, and did the reviewer believe the presenters were candid and revealing in discussing their staff?

Frequently changing the succession planning process limits the ability of the organization to learn and improve the process. Once the process is designed, only changes that will substantially enhance the results should be made. This need to maintain continuity reinforces how important it is to make the right design decisions originally.

Hard measures can be made in the short and long term. In the short term, possibly the best measure is this: What percentage of the plans that were presented were actually implemented? In the long-term, two metrics are these: Were the individuals identified as successors actually promoted into those positions when they became open? Are the numbers of successors identified for key positions increasing over time?

It is important to be cautious when looking at the numbers of successors identified. As the process becomes more disciplined, the numbers of successors identified may actually decrease because of its rigor.

Conclusion

This chapter explored the implementation of succession planning systems by discussing the decisions to be made at each phase of the process. A review of lessons learned over the last twenty years may help guide the design of a succession planning system that will successfully identify and develop an organization's future leaders. Here are some lessons learned:

- Managers throughout the organization must see the need for succession planning.
- Succession planning should be linked to other business processes; succession planning reviews are best conducted after strategic planning and before annual budget planning.

- There is no one best way; both position-based and pool-based planning work depending on the dynamics and culture of the organization.
- Implementation should begin at the senior levels and then cascade down through the organization during successive cycles.
- Realistic expectations should be created throughout the organization by clearly communicating the intent of the system.
- Projecting future standards for key roles in the organization is fundamental to effective planning.
- Labeling individuals as "high potential" or "solid performers" can subvert the assessment process.
- Understanding employees' wishes when it comes to career and work-life balance is essential.
- Open, candid discussions of potential are required to create realistic plans. One-over managers should make the final call on potential.
- Linking succession planning and assessment of potential with compensation will undermine a well-designed system.
- Early identification of successors or the need to recruit externally are the most valuable outcomes of succession planning.
- The time required for effective reviews should not be underestimated; the scope of the reviews should be tailored to fit the time available. Support for more extensive reviews will build as their value is demonstrated.
- Employees will expect honest feedback on what is said about them during reviews.
- Disciplined implementation of plans are key to the credibility of the system.
- The dialogue is far more important than the forms or elaborate presentations.

In summary, a succession planning system is a key strategic element in building an effective organization. The challenge is to ensure that the process is developing leaders for the future—not for the past.

References
Bennis, W. (1989). *On becoming a leader.* Cambridge, MA: Perseus.
Bennis, W., & O'Toole, J. (2000, May-June). Don't hire the wrong CEO. *Harvard Business Review*, pp. 171–176.

Byham, W. C., Smith, A. B., & Paese, M. J. (2000). *Grow your own leaders.* Pittsburgh, PA: DDI Press.

Chambers, E. G., Foulon, M., Handfield-Jones, H., Hankin, S. M., & Michaels, E. G. III. (1998). The war for talent. *McKinsey Quarterly, 3,* 44–57.

Ciampa, E., & Watkins, M. (1999). *Right from the start: Taking charge in a new leadership role.* Boston: Harvard Business School Press.

Hogan, R., & Hogan, J. (2001). Assessing leadership: A view from the dark side. *International Journal of Selection & Assessment, 9,* 1–21.

McCall, M. (1998). *High flyers.* Boston: Harvard Business School Press.

Van Velsor, E., & Guthrie, V. A. (1998). Enhancing the ability to learn from experience. In C. D. McCauley, R. S. Moxley, & E. Van Velsor (Eds.), *Center for Creative Leadership handbook of leadership development.* San Francisco: Jossey-Bass.

CHAPTER 5

Information Technology

David W. Dorsey

If you were to sit down and spend some time with your favorite Internet search engine and conduct a search on "implementing information technology," you would find a long and quite diverse list of links and topics ranging from "implementing LDAP on Sun Solaris platforms" to "the seven deadly hazards of scope creep." Even if you constrained the domain of interest to implementing information technology (IT) relevant to human resources or human capital, the panoply of topics and information might still be overwhelming. This said, deploying information technology (IT) successfully is a real facet of modern organizational effectiveness. Organizational consultants, researchers, and practitioners should have at least a basic understanding of the "what" and "how" of implementing organizational IT systems because almost every intervention, program, or system seems to be touched by technology in the modern business age. This chapter is intended to provide such a basic understanding. The focus will be on practical implementation guidance for project managers, implementation team members, researchers, and non-IT professionals interested in ensuring successful IT implementation. A couple of themes that will emerge throughout this chapter are that implementing IT cuts across technological, human, and organizational-management subsystems, and that customer-focused, human-centered approaches to developing and implementing IT are critical.

Because IT systems can affect so many facets of an organization, the complexity of implementation should not be underestimated. To drive this point home, I will share with you the simple fact that many (if not most) IT projects fail. The *Wall Street Journal* has estimated that approximately 42 percent of all technology projects launched in the United States are abandoned before completion, with more than 50 percent of IT projects exceeding original cost or schedule estimates by 150 percent (Kapur, 1999). When analyzing the underlying reasons for these findings, a number of salient factors usually emerge (Lientz & Rea, 2000), as shown in Exhibit 5.1.

A review of these factors highlights the importance of various organizational subsystems (for example, people, technology, management). These factors are treated throughout the chapter as targets for serious consideration and strategic intervention.

From PC to ERP: An Overview of Organizational IT

Before discussing implementation, it is worthwhile first to consider briefly the state of organizational IT. One way to think about it is in terms of three phases of evolution. First came the personal computer (PC) revolution, which facilitated desktop access to "killer" office applications such as spreadsheets, word processing, databases, and so on. Because of redundancy in using, maintaining, and upgrading systems, in the second phase client-server–based technologies were ushered in, with networks facilitating remote access and distributed functionality. The third and current phase of organizational IT can be characterized as the Internet phase, where IT solutions internal to an organization are based on the same software, hardware protocols, and platforms that have made the Internet

Exhibit 5.1. Factors Related to IT Project Failure.

- Lack of top management commitment
- Failure to gain user commitment
- Lack of user involvement
- Misunderstanding of requirements
- Changing scope and objectives
- Lack of required skills and knowledge in implementation team
- New technology (IT infrastructure compatibility issues)

what it is today. It is this third phase that serves as the context for Web-based recruiting, on-line assessment, IT-enabled performance management, on-line surveys, e-learning, decision support tools, employee self-service applications, knowledge management, and various types of corporate communication.

Besides changes in IT infrastructure, another important trend has been the emergence of omnibus enterprise resource planning (ERP) systems (Kumar & Hillegersberg, 2000). These systems attempt to integrate a vast number of business functions, including inventory control, sales, production, purchasing, finance, human resources, and more. With vendors such as PeopleSoft, Oracle, and SAP leading the charge, human resource management systems (HRMS) have been developed within the ERP framework, integrating various HR functions such as recruitment, training, compensation, and so on. The cost and complexity of implementing these systems can be exorbitant, with the potential payoff being an integrated approach to capturing, using, and disseminating critical enterprise data. The ERP revolution has challenged the traditional notion that software development and implementation should reflect the desired business processes and requirements defined by the customer. Instead, it has proven in many cases to be more cost-effective for companies simply to change their business processes to reflect ERP technology than to try to customize ERP software modules. Reference models embedded in ERP systems presumably reflect best practices in business models, underlying data structures, and organizational structures (Kumar & Hillegersberg, 2000). However, there can be considerable mismatches between these models and a specific company's actual practices. This raises a "chicken-and-egg" problem: Do customer requirements drive technology or does technology drive customer requirements? Especially in the HR arena, as ERP vendors move toward more strategic functions rather than purely transactional functions (for example, payroll processing), it may become even more important to anticipate and manage this technology-requirement tension.

With so many technologies, tools, and platforms available today, a general implementation strategy can be discussed only by overlooking differences in various types of IT implementations. Few would argue that implementing a data warehousing system might pose different challenges and obstacles than an e-commerce project, for example. But many issues and challenges can be anticipated with any IT implementation, and in the following sections of the chapter a broad implementation road map is presented along with suggested steps and strategies.

Implementation Road Map

Figure 5.1 presents a model, or road map, for IT implementation. Before reviewing the details of this model, let me make a few general comments. First, the model to some extent merges the concepts of IT planning, development, and implementation. Any one of these concepts could, and do, have entire chapters and even books devoted to them. In merging these concepts, I hope to provide an overview of implementation—from creating a vision of the IT solution all the way to evaluating implementation success. In presenting such a model, I try to communicate a lesson learned from professional experience: that so much of the IT implementation challenge is won or lost in the initial conceptual phases of a project. Without planning and explicit agreement on vision and goals up front, ambiguity of purpose often comes back to haunt IT projects in implementation. Of course, this model should not be viewed as a panacea for all IT implementation problems. Instead it should serve to highlight important considerations and point out ways to avoid common obstacles. It should be evident, given the failure rates noted earlier, that the bulletproof IT implementation model has yet to be developed.

The model in Figure 5.1 begins with establishing a vision, goals, and strategy for implementing the IT system. This should be done in partnership with senior organizational management. Remembering that lack of top management commitment has been cited as a factor in the demise of IT projects, gaining this commitment at the beginning is crucial. To gain and sustain management commitment, it is a good idea to give management a clear picture of several things: the old versus new IT-enabled business process, projected savings (using specific examples or scenarios if available), anticipated system requirements and potential "work-arounds," a cost-benefit summary, and the sequence of steps anticipated for implementation (Lientz & Rea, 2000). Commitment will need to be sustained, not just attained. Therefore, clear communication

Figure 5.1. Implementation Model.

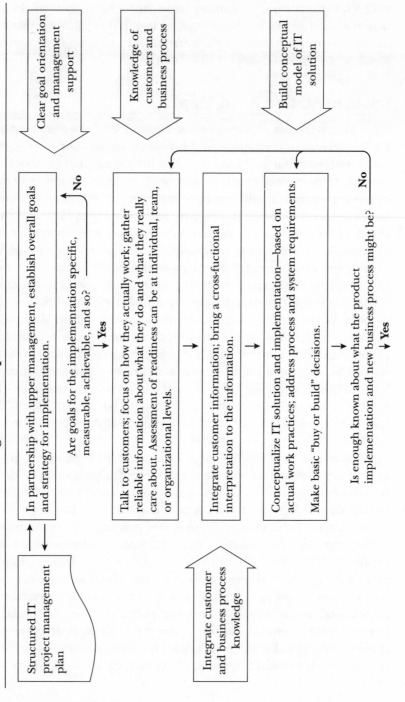

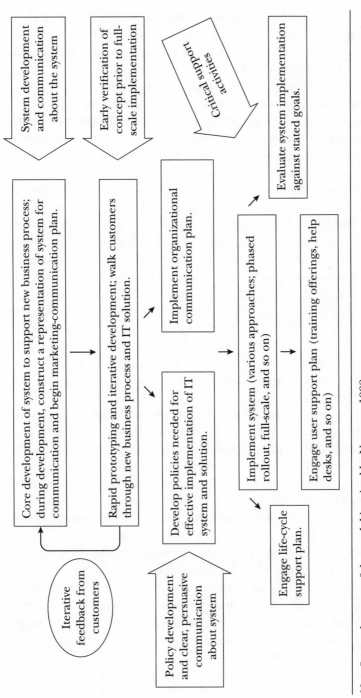

System development and communication about the system

Early verification of concept prior to full-scale implementation

Critical support activities

Core development of system to support new business process; during development, construct a representation of system for communication and begin marketing-communication plan.

Rapid prototyping and iterative development; walk customers through new business process and IT solution.

Iterative feedback from customers

Implement organizational communication plan.

Develop policies needed for effective implementation of IT system and solution.

Policy development and clear, persuasive communication about system

Implement system (various approaches; phased rollout, full-scale, and so on)

Engage life-cycle support plan.

Engage user support plan (training offerings, help desks, and so on)

Evaluate system implementation against stated goals.

Note: Some elements of the model inspired by Norman, 1998.

channels with senior management should be established. The goals and strategy derived during these initial steps should be translated into a structured IT project management plan, complete with steps, roles and responsibilities, schedule, and so on. This working plan should be kept up-to-date and changed as needed.

To reinforce the importance of gaining commitment for a specific IT strategy and set of plans, consider the following situation. During project planning efforts with a large organization, a set of options for building a customized Web-based performance management system was presented to key project stakeholders. Essentially, the client organization in this case had to choose one software development package, where the optional packages represented increasing numbers of features and capabilities. Because of varying priorities among the different stakeholders (that is, budget versus infrastructure versus functionality), they had a difficult time achieving consensus around the right package for their organization. In essence, this led during later project stages to difficult rounds of requirements negotiation, eventually leading to expenditures that exceeded original projections. In hindsight, organizational members realized that even more up-front consensus building around choosing a certain development approach was required than had been conducted. The ambiguity in this case literally translated into increased project costs.

The next steps in the implementation model start with gaining reliable information about the customers (that is, the end users and stakeholders) and business processes affected by the IT implementation. In line with the themes cited earlier, an up-front understanding of customers and business processes, instead of a narrow focus on potential IT, is critical. A recent report issued by the CIO Council reinforces this idea. In a review of best practices in the federal government, the CIO Council found that successful IT programs had a heightened attentiveness to customers, including clearly identifying who the customers were and monitoring their satisfaction after implementation (CIO Council and Industry Advisory Council, 1997). Business processes that need to be understood may include work flow-operational steps; systems and technologies; jobs, roles, and tasks; the functions of organizational units; and guiding policies.

One element in understanding the customer base is assessing organizational readiness for IT implementation. This can range from informal discussions with customers to formal assessments involving data collection methods such as surveys. The formality and the comprehensiveness of the assessment (for example, assessing readiness at multiple organizational levels) should be matched to the complexity of the implementation and the need to assess readiness accurately. Usually, informal interviews focusing on how people actually work and what they really care about are sufficient to gain an initial understanding of the effects of the IT solution on customers and business processes. The key concept here is to go beyond the IT product itself to understand the full-systems context of the IT implementation (Norman, 1998). One important reason to understand the full context ahead of time is that people often create informal "shadow systems"—side processes or systems to handle exceptions not handled by the formal systems or processes (Lientz & Rea, 2000). Without understanding such systems ahead of time, a conceptualized IT solution may fail to fit in with how people actually work.

The information gained through this up-front assessment should be integrated and interpreted from a cross-functional perspective, with project team members who understand the technology that may be involved, marketing and organizational communication, the functional requirements (for example, training experts for a training-related IT system), and the end user groups. Others have echoed the need to overcome organizational boundaries and pursue a multidisciplinary approach to implementing IT (for example, Mondragon, 1999).

The implementation model in Figure 5.1 contains a feedback loop. After assessing customers, business processes, and organizational readiness, it is important to reflect back on the vision, goals, and strategy established to guide the project. Based on the knowledge acquired, are the goals for the implementation specific enough, measurable, and achievable, or should changes to these goals be made based on the realities of the customer base and current business processes?

The next step in the implementation model is to develop a conceptual model of the IT solution. Specifically, the project team should try to create an image of the technology components that will be required to meet the stated goals; the organizational and business process changes that will be affected by implementation; and related roles, responsibilities, and policies that will make the implementation a success. Once the foundational conceptual model is developed, the basic decision to buy or build can be made (Lientz & Rea, 2000). That is, based on the envisioned new business process and conceptual IT solution, the fundamental decision of whether to develop an IT solution in-house or acquire commercially available products and software must be made.

Making buy-or-build decisions can be incredibly complex. Some organizations tend to build IT solutions in-house when these solutions are part of their core business or mission. Thus, you will hear heuristics such as, "Build what you need to be best at and buy everything else in a box" (Andrews, 1999). In reality, a number of factors must be considered in making these decisions, including the current capabilities and availability of in-house IT staff and the availability, capabilities, and costs of outside vendors and consultants. Often an environmental scan can be conducted efficiently by purchasing an evaluation guide of a given market segment (for example, compensation software). These guides are available from both commercial organizations (for example, the Gartner Group) and professional associations (for example, the International Association for Human Resource Information Management [IHRIM]). When estimating costs associated with buying or building, it is important to realize that *cost* here is a multidimensional concept. Cost estimates can change dramatically based on a number of factors. Exhibit 5.2 presents a snapshot of some of these factors.

Exhibit 5.2. Factors in Evaluating IT Solution Costs.

- "Bundled" software versus individual module pricing strategies
- Multiproduct discounts
- Licensing based on number of users or "seats" versus unlimited users
- IT infrastructure upgrades (databases, software versions, hardware, and so on)
- Installation costs
- Customization, programming, development costs
- Implementation team costs (for example, training)
- Maintenance fees
- Possible consulting fees

A review of recent buy-or-build trends shows that there has been an emphasis on buying commercial off-the-shelf (COTS) software. In addition, there has been increased outsourcing of both IT infrastructure maintenance and upgrade services, along with the actual outsourcing of software applications. This last type of outsourcing currently goes by the term *application service provider* or ASP. Usually with an ASP you pay a monthly rental fee for the use of a particular software program or suite of programs. Potential cost savings stem from the fact that you are avoiding up-front purchasing costs, and ASP fees generally cover implementing and maintaining these systems over time. Human resource applications are currently an active area in ASP vendor offerings. Human resource ASP providers are now covering functions such as recruiting, benefits, training, and compensation. A number of Web sites are available that list ASP providers (for example, www.apps.com). In addition, professional associations such as the Information Technology Association of America (ITAA; www.itaa.org/asp) provide a number of resources for learning about ASP vendors, agreements, and the state of the marketplace.

Turning back to the implementation road map, assuming that an initial conceptual model of the IT solution is developed, Figure 5.1 at this point contains another feedback loop. This loop denotes that finding the "right" solution—one that integrates with the new desired business process and the customer base—may be an iterative process.

The next major step in the model is the core development of the IT solution. Keeping to the scope of this chapter, I will not delve into the details of development; development is often driven by various competing (and often complex) professional software engineering models and methods. Instead, I would like to discuss two elements of development that I believe are worth mentioning (also highlighted in Figure 5.1). First is the idea of constructing a representation of an IT system or solution in order to communicate about the system and for marketing. Here, I echo the sentiment of Norman (1998), who noted that technology change is easy whereas organizational change is hard. Early communication about a system concept can alert relevant stakeholders to potential change, facilitating discussion and feedback about the system before full-scale implementation. This idea is a simple extension of all viable organizational change models, which emphasize the crucial role of communication.

A second concept related to development is the idea of prototyping and iterative design—ideas from the school of user-centered or human-centered development (Norman, 1998). Essentially, a software prototype is a product that to some extent actually works (and so is usually not just an idea or drawing), has a limited purpose or lifetime, and is built quickly and cheaply (Preece et al., 1994). The idea of prototyping is to build a limited-fidelity, working model of the envisioned IT solution quickly and take this to customers to gauge their reactions to its basic functionality, operation sequences, user support needs, and required representations and to the look and feel of the interface (Preece et al., 1994). Through the use of prototypes, iterative development can take place using the customers as design assistants. Comments and concerns about an initial prototype can quickly and inexpensively be turned into a "next version" prototype prior to full-scale system development.

Critics of a prototyping approach would say that standard software interfaces are currently used (so there is not much variation in interface design to test) and that getting rounds of user feedback would increase time to market. In the Web-based world of development, the prevailing idea is that speed to market is everything, and the "theory of mud-throwing" should hold (Nielsen, 2000b). That is, you "throw it at the wall and see if it sticks," and if the initial design has weaknesses, they will be addressed in redesign. But as usability guru Jakob Nielsen (2000b) has pointed out, the problem with the mud-throwing approach is that it can be very hard to get a user to come back after a bad experience, and you may deprive yourself of your best customers—those eager to use your system or service and visit it as soon as they hear about it. Obviously, with COTS software, prototyping and early user feedback and involvement may not be as applicable. Moreover, there are projects where speed to deployment is a serious constraint. However, remembering again the factors related to IT project failure—including failure to gain user commitment, lack of user involvement, and misunderstanding requirements—prototyping and iterative design can often help get an IT development effort on the right track.

I can relate from personal experience the power of prototypes. As a team member on a large customized software development effort reaching out to literally thousands of users, I arrived on the project just as an initial version of the software was literally being pulled back from deployment. Outcry from end users was so strong (in the negative sense) and politically damaging that the project leadership decided to recall the software product and redesign it. In hindsight, it seemed that much of the problem with the development stemmed from backroom engineering. That is, a relatively talented programmer had worked in isolation developing the software with little or no user involvement. To remedy the situation, we brought in a professional usability group who built several rough prototypes, based on usability testing, for possible new designs. These initial prototypes led to a restructured interface that received a much warmer response from end users. As one senior executive in this organization later noted: some organizations (and people) are not good at specifying what they want until they see it.

After core development of the system, the next steps in the Figure 5.1 model point to the importance of two activities before actual implementation: developing policies and implementing an organizational communication plan. The first of these is often overlooked and is especially important with human resource and human capital IT systems. Policies are often needed to guide and define appropriate access and use of an IT system. Moreover, policies governing an existing business process or system may not translate well (or easily) to a new process and IT system. For example, having worked on a number of performance management projects involving IT, I can say that many policies on access to appraisal information, certifying appraisal results (that is, signatures), and routing appraisal information among stakeholders have serious consequences for the IT implementation. Often, it is a good idea to form policy guidelines well before implementation, early in the conceptual design of the IT system, so that policy-driven IT requirements (for example, digital signatures, work flow management, and security structures) can be adequately understood.

A second activity occurring before implementation is employing an organizational communication plan. This plan should lay out and clarify how to communicate objectives, scope, progress, and plans for implementation and training so that all stakeholders understand. The representations of the new IT system and related business processes developed during earlier phases may be used in the communication plan to explain its features, functions, and benefits. A number of media and vehicles for organizational communication can be used, from formal presentations and newsletters to a centralized intranet project site and more. A critical lesson learned in communication is that you are really striving to achieve two kinds of user commitment: commitment to the project itself and commitment to the change required to implement the new system successfully (Ginzberg, 1981).

So, you have successfully negotiated development, formed and implemented the necessary policy, communication, and training plans, and now you arrive at the point in Figure 5.1 where the actual system is deployed. There are several ways to go "live" with the new system, ranging from an all-out Big Bang deployment to a phased rollout (Markus, Tanis, & Fenema, 2000). The implementation approach to choose depends on numerous situational factors, including the business need for the new system and process, organizational member readiness, and the importance of piloting the system versus stretching out implementation. Such decisions must be made on a case-by-case basis. It should be noted that a phased rollout approach can mean either implementing the system in only one division or unit in the organization or going live with only a subset of system processes or functions.

In the last stages of the implementation model, Figure 5.1 shows a number of critical support activities that should occur at the time of actual implementation. First, IT systems have a life span or life cycle. The stakeholders interested in keeping the system viable must have a support plan to deal with both maintenance issues and requested upgrades or enhancements. In conceiving such a plan, which IT staff will be available to perform such activities, how maintenance and enhancement activities will be budgeted and paid for, and how the variety of enhancement requests will be prioritized and handled should all be considered. Also, upgrades and maintenance can be a significant resource drain. As part of the plan for handling these issues, the resources spent should be tracked and reported to ensure awareness of maintenance and enhancement costs.

A second critical support activity is developing and using a plan to support IT system users. To the degree that users have been involved in the earlier stages leading to implementation, the project team should have a good idea of the types and level of support they need. Recent trends have been to use minimal documentation and embed much of the help available to users in the system itself. In addition, quick reference guides or so-called cheat sheets are often employed as working aids. For more complex systems, or systems requiring extensive organizational change, a help desk may be needed. At a help desk, assigned individuals respond to users' questions and problems. Establishing an adequate help desk can take time and obviously involves staff and other organizational resources. In the course of running a help desk, a database of frequently asked questions is often developed.

Training is often added to help customers adapt to new business processes and a new IT system. Because extensive treatments on effective training methods are readily available, I will not dwell on the subject. However, consistent with the themes of this chapter, I will note that training needs to address both the business process and the IT system. Because systems are generally embedded in processes, users often benefit from a training approach that provides a context for system use. Developing such omnibus training requires input from both IT and business process staff.

Finally, the project team should be prepared to revisit the goals established for implementation and evaluate their success against these goals. Obviously, the types of evaluation measures used will be influenced by the nature of the stated implementation goals and the types of benefits expected from the system. Going back to the idea of multiple subsystems, it is important to evaluate the system along multiple organizational facets, such as behavioral and attitudinal change, technical success, process measures (for example, administrative burden, activity-based accounting), and productivity measures. For example, consider an IT-enabled performance management system. Stated goals and subsequent evaluation measures might center on the quality of obtained performance ratings, the perceived quality of employee involvement and participation in the performance management system, and the time spent and administrative burden associated with the IT system and process. It is also a good idea to compile and reflect on lessons learned. For no matter how smoothly an implementation goes, there will be lessons learned.

Critical Success Factors, Lessons Learned, and Practical Advice

Having reviewed the implementation road map, let us take a step back and reflect on some of the elements linked either directly or indirectly to a successful implementation. Following the themes cited earlier, we will review these items in terms of people, technology, and organizations.

People

I have been told by friends who are professional information technologists that IT system implementation would be easy if people were not involved. The underlying idea is that end users do have preferences, likes and dislikes, and individual differences. As I stated at the beginning of the chapter, failure to get user commitment or to involve users is a common reason for implementation failure. Ultimately, user commitment is heavily affected by the usability of the system. With any IT system involving a design component, I strongly advise that some type of usability testing take place to gauge user reactions to the interfaces, operations, and processes. A common reaction to the idea of usability testing is that it is too costly and too complex and should be reserved for only the largest projects. This is a serious misconception. As pointed out by usability experts, beneficial results can be obtained by testing no more than five users and running as many small tests as can be afforded (Nielsen, 2000a). The idea behind running several small tests is to improve the design (as with prototyping) and not just document its deficiencies, which is what many projects end up doing. There are many excellent guides and consulting resources for those interested in usability testing (for example, Nielsen, 1995).

An important aspect of the whole usability question is that many IT system designers are not typical users. A designer's mental model and conceptualization of a system may be drastically different from the user's mental model, which develops to explain the operation of a system (Norman, 1988). Designer and user mental models will only converge if the designer communicates through the actual system design and system image how the system is intended to function. This is why good designers use conceptual models that are meaningful to IT system users and use common, everyday knowledge. For example, Intuit's Quicken, the popular financial management application, uses an interface that fits a checkbook mental model (Craiger, 1999). The checkbook metaphor is an interface device to help even inexperienced users quickly ascertain how to enter financial information, as they would when writing a paper check or entering information into a paper checkbook registry.

Individual differences may also affect customers' reactions and their use of the IT system. For example, recent research has documented that age is an important influence on technology adoption and sustained use decisions (Morris & Venkatesh, 2000). Some researchers have suggested that these findings should have an impact on practical elements of implementation such as training. For example, Morris and Venkatesh, based on their research findings, suggest that younger workers may react more positively to an emphasis on instrumentality (for example, productivity benefits), whereas older workers may be influenced to adopt technology with a training approach that emphasizes ease of use. More definitive research is needed on these issues.

IT implementers should also be sensitive to the needs of communities such as disabled individuals. Assistive technologies may be available and required for these users. As a side note, an interesting ongoing legal debate concerns whether the Americans with Disabilities Act (ADA) applies to the Internet and Web sites in general (Isenberg, 2001). At this point what is clear is that the ADA *does* apply to the Internet world. However, who the "covered entities" are is a matter for legal definition outside the scope of this chapter. At the time this chapter was written, the World Wide Web Consortium (W3C), an international body responsible for establishing many different Web standards, had developed the Web Accessibility Initiative (WAI; http://www.w3.org/WAI). This may be a very useful resource for those who want to learn more about accessibility issues and legal matters, such as ADA compliance.

Another emerging issue is "e-loaded" adverse impact (Sharf, 2000). This pertains to the presumed digital divide between various demographic groups (rich and poor, white and minority) who have different access to and experience with digital technologies. With applications such as on-line Internet-based recruiting, this might have serious consequences for an organization pursuing certain diversity or recruiting goals.

Another important set of people factors come into play when building the actual IT project implementation team. As noted earlier in the list of factors related to project failure, it is critical to have the right knowledge and skills on the implementation team. The competencies and roles that will make the implementation team a success are multiple. Exhibit 5.3 lists just some of the competencies to consider.

The last item shown on the list—project champion—is actually not a competency, but it is shown because implementation success will be influenced heavily by having a committed and powerful organizational sponsor. A project champion is an individual associated with the project who can ensure sustained buy-in, resolve important policy obstacles, ensure that resources are allocated, fight political battles, influence key stakeholders, communicate the vision, and generally keep people motivated (Kapur, 1999). Obviously, such an individual must have political power or at least an influence in the organization. Indeed, this is such a key role that this chapter on implementation would not be complete if I did not offer the following advice: if you do not have a project champion,

Exhibit 5.3. Implementation Team Competencies.

- Marketing-organizational communication
- Requirements analysis
- Systems analysis-integration
- Business process knowledge
- Prototyping
- Development-programming
- Specific product knowledge (for commercial software)
- Testing (operational and usability)
- Technical writing (documentation)
- Policy development
- Training-user support
- Project champion

go and get one. A recent study by the Center for Project Management involving a survey of senior IT managers showed that only about 17 percent of projects receive solid sponsorship (Kapur, 1999). This probably goes a long way in explaining the IT project failure rates cited earlier.

Another approach to maintaining sponsorship is to use an executive steering committee. Such a committee can facilitate a cross-functional view of IT system development and implementation and may be helpful in (re)assessing business goals as the project progresses.

Technology

Traditionally, a fundamental building block for IT solutions has been requirements gathering. This normally means some type of interview process with IT system project sponsors and customers that is aimed at defining the key functions, capabilities, and so on to be built into the system. Currently, methods have evolved to capture both business process requirements and system-technology requirements (Lientz & Rea, 2000). These approaches involve customers playing a collaborative role in requirements development. If process and technology requirements are addressed at the same time, key questions will emerge. For example, consider an organization where certain documents must have multiple rounds of review and multiple signatures in order to be approved. Work flow software can be used to automate this process, but the real question may be why several rounds of review and signatures are needed (CIO Council and Industry Advisory Council, 1997).

Whatever the methods used, requirements specification can affect implementation in a number of critical ways. First, requirements for software are almost never complete and change constantly over time (Lientz & Rea, 2000). Thus, prioritization of system features becomes a critical part not only of development but also of implementation and postimplementation management. Individuals in the organization will have their own "pet" features and will argue vigorously for their inclusion in the system. Such incrementalism in adding features during an IT development inevitably leads to "scope creep," where the scope of the project quickly exceeds earlier expectations and resources. One of the scariest aspects of IT development is that the true complexity of the effort may not be known ahead of time. For example, in one organization's recent IT implementation the presumably simple requirement for a spell-checker in a Web application was not adequately articulated and assessed. This ended up causing a great deal of consternation on the part of project stakeholders when it became apparent that this required capability was not only missing but also relatively complex to add after core development.

Second, because it is usually not feasible to capture all possible requirements or to build to all requirements, project stakeholders should know their tolerances ahead of time for implementing a 90 percent or 80 percent solution. You will find expert advice that suggests that at least 80 percent of original business requirements should be met initially and that applications should be flexible enough to adapt quickly to changes (Radosevich, 1999). Even though you might prefer to fix all problems prior to implementation, a more realistic approach is to assume some level of incremental development.

This incremental development aspect of IT implementation may quite possibly be the most consistently overlooked aspect of the process. Many organizations and their members expect an IT solution to meet 100 percent of expectations, working flawlessly out of the box. Unless there is adequate communication to build more realistic expectations, many implementations will not meet expectations. The real danger of such "expectation gaps" is that negative perceptions of the IT solution can spill over, creating an overall negative impression of the larger organizational change elements of a project. Thus, potential remedies once again include not only effective, early discussion of expectations but also explicit prioritization of system features.

Another lesson learned is for the project team to understand clearly the IT infrastructure that the IT solution will depend on. I can recall a number of examples from professional experience where the presumed "right" IT solution met with serious implementation obstacles because of limitations in the IT infrastructure. This infrastructure can include a number of elements—hardware platforms, networking components, software versions, and so on. Even something as simple as an e-mail or Web-based survey tool can fail to work in certain situations if there is a basic incompatibility with e-mail servers, Web browsers, or other IT components. One way to avoid such problems is for the implementers to have access to individuals who understand an organization's infrastructure while they are conceptualizing the IT solution.

Organizations

The relationship between IT and organizations is incredibly complex. One way to conceive of the relationship is as a two-way, mutual influence (Laudon & Laudon, 2000). On the one hand, IT systems and capabilities must be configured in a way to fit with organizational interests, needs, and priorities. On the other hand, organizations for competitive reasons must be open to the influences of innovation and waves of emerging technology. Factors thought to mediate the relationships between organizations and IT include environment, culture, structure, standards procedures, business processes, politics, and management decisions (Laudon & Laudon, 2000). Indeed, this list reads like an inventory of all the defining elements of an organization. So, what are the practical implications of this obviously complex interdependency?

First, executives and managers will build systems that match their interpretation of the organization's needs. Thus, to sell an implementation, designers have to know and understand their perspectives, goals, and priorities. The importance of aligning the goals of IT implementation with leadership directions, programs, and goals should not be underestimated. A primary reason for my emphasis in this chapter on focusing on both business processes and IT is that such a focus establishes a basis to communicate with executives and managers about key organizational processes, rather than just about the technology itself.

Second, standard operating procedures and cultural norms can drastically affect the look and feel of IT systems. For example, I have worked with organizations where information security was of primary concern, and companywide limitations in usability and design for security purposes were routinely accepted. Tolerance for risk also varies with organizational culture and environment. Some organizations value high-risk, high-payoff technology investments, whereas others prefer the "late adopter" model, using tried-and-true technologies. During implementation planning, IT project teams should attempt to identify, assess, and be prepared to communicate the risks involved with a given IT solution.

Laudon and Laudon (2000) provide a good example of how environment and culture affect an organization's approach to IT adoption and implementation. These authors discuss the variation in IT use by utility companies as a function of deregulation. The culture of traditional power companies was influenced by a stable market and a lack of competition. Their IT profile shows that IT systems are implemented around functions such as billing and collecting from customers and maintaining capital assets. In contrast, deregulated companies, which face a highly competitive marketplace, have deployed more strategic systems. Large database and data warehousing systems are used to collect and track extensive information on customers and potential customers. Advanced systems dedicated to the repair of outages and downed lines have become essential, because quality of service now stands as a competitive advantage. These companies also use IT systems to monitor and control costs, and advanced Internet and e-commerce systems to locate and purchase available power. Given this dramatic contrast in how IT systems may be used to support organizational functioning, it is easy to see how the organizational environment (both internal and external) and culture drive IT system development and implementation.

Conclusion

We began this chapter with an overview of the current organizational IT landscape and a review of some of the critical factors associated with IT project success and failure. We then examined an implementation model or road map, which highlighted important activities and approaches. This model was then elaborated in terms of critical success factors and lessons learned about people, technology, and organizations. A couple of key themes that appeared consistently throughout the chapter were that implementing IT cuts across technological, human, and organizational-management subsystems, and that customer-focused, human-centered approaches to developing and implementing IT are critical.

Having reviewed these ideas and concepts, you might wonder if IT implementation is so complex that all implementation efforts are likely to fail. I suggest that the answer is no. As this chapter's discussion showed, IT implementation is obviously multifaceted, but many of the factors that account for the "runaway" IT project horror stories reported in the business, IT, and popular press are fairly well known.

It is obvious that a large part of the IT implementation equation involves human elements. Therefore, information technologists and IT managers should not be viewed as the sole source for either IT project success or failure. In fact, in looking at the public sector, a federal CIO group inquired, rather comically, if a constant stream of failed IT projects recently reported in the press had created false impressions, such as "most federal IT managers couldn't run a roadside watermelon stand if you spotted them the watermelons and had the highway patrol flag down the cars" (CIO Council and Industry Advisory Council, 1997). Ultimately, to create successful IT solutions, those of us who work as internal and external consultants on the functional or business-process side of IT projects must act as informed consumers, ensuring that the many facets of implementation (people, technology, organizations, and so on) are addressed. When we address these factors, IT implementation takes on a different character and can be viewed more as a kind of organizational change effort and less as a single technical element of organizational functioning.

References

Andrews, W. (1999, August 1). In commerce, it's build vs. buy. *Internet World.* [http://www.findarticles.com/cf_1/m0DXS/26_5/55723842/print.jhtml].

CIO Council and Industry Advisory Council. (1997, October). Best IT practices in the federal government. [http://www.cio.gove/docs/iac.htm].

Craiger, P. (1999, July). Traveling in cyberspace: The psychology of software design. Part I. *Industrial/Organizational Psychologist, 37*(1), 113–122.

Ginzberg, M. J. (1981). Key recurrent issues in the MIS implementation process. *MIS Quarterly 20*(3), 47–59.

Isenberg, D. (2001, February 2). Web access for all. *Internet World Magazine.* [http://www.internetworld.com/020101/02.01.01policy.jsp].

Kapur, G. K. (1999, March 22). Bad management is to blame for IT skills crunch. *Computerworld.* [http://www.computerworld.com/cwi/story/0,1199,NAV47_STO34998,00.html].

Kumar, K., & Hillegersberg, J. (2000). ERP experiences and evolution. *Communications of the ACM, 43*(4), 23–26.

Laudon, K. C., & Laudon, J. P. (2000). *Management information systems.* Englewood Cliffs, NJ: Prentice Hall.

Lientz, B. P., & Rea, K. P. (2000). *On time technology implementation.* Orlando: Academic Press.

Markus, M. L., Tanis, C., & Fenema, P. C. (2000). Multisite ERP implementations. *Communications of the ACM, 43*(4), 42–46.

Mondragon, N. J. (1999, July). Should we be driving technology solutions or just be passengers on the wild ride? A positive look at our field and technology. *Industrial/Organizational Psychologist, 37*(1), 42–55.

Morris, M. G., & Venkatesh, V. (2000). Age differences in technology adoption decisions: Implications for a changing workforce. *Personnel Psychology, 53,* 375–403.

Nielsen, J. (1995). *Usability engineering.* New York: Morgan Kaufmann.

Nielsen, J. (2000a, March 19). Test with five users. *Alertbox.* [http://www.zdnet.com/devhead/alertbox/20000319.html].

Nielsen, J. (2000b, April 2). Mud-throwing theory of usability. *Alertbox.* [http://www.zdnet.com/devhead/alertbox/20000402.html].

Norman, D. A. (1988). *The design of everyday things.* New York: Doubleday.

Norman, D. A. (1998). *The invisible computer.* Cambridge, MA: MIT Press.

Preece, J., Rogers, Y., Sharp, H., Benyon, D., Holland, S., & Carey, T. (1994). *Human-computer interaction.* Reading, MA: Addison-Wesley.

Radosevich, L. (1999). A lean, mean IT machine. *Infoworld.* [http://www.infoworld.com/cgi-bin/displayArchive.pl?/99/30/z01-30.64.htm].

Sharf, J. C. (2000, October). As if "g-loaded" adverse impact isn't bad enough, Internet recruiters can expect to be accused of "e-loaded" impact. *Industrial/Organizational Psychologist, 38*(2), 156.

CHAPTER 6

Implementing Reward Systems

Paul W. Mulvey
Gerald E. Ledford Jr.

Reward systems are powerful management tools for attracting, motivating, and retaining employees and aligning employee behavior with a firm's business strategy. By *reward system* we mean not only compensation and benefits but also all other inducements offered by the organization to reinforce behavior and performance and lead employees to join it and remain a part of it. Training opportunities, interesting work, employment stability, positive supervisor and coworker relationships, a pleasant work environment, and the potential for advancement are examples of nonmonetary rewards.

Although our primary emphasis is on monetary rewards, it is useful to place compensation into a broader context. We will do so by discussing compensation in a "rewards of work" framework, which makes the assumption that several types of rewards, including compensation, are important for attracting, motivating, and retaining employees.

We focus on compensation rewards in this chapter in order to keep the discussion to a manageable length and center on the dominant topic in the field of rewards. The chapter describes the key issues, challenges, and steps in designing and implementing effective compensation systems. Our discussion has two parts. First, we identify critical management challenges in successfully implementing compensation systems. Second, we describe a step-by-step approach for designing and implementing these systems.

The chapter makes two assumptions. First, although we acknowledge that compensation systems are usually the domain of the compensation function in a human resource department we maintain that they need to be consistent in their goals and effects across human resource functions. Consistency in the compensation, staffing, training, and performance management functions is particularly important to attract, motivate, and retain employees. Thus, to be effective, compensation systems need to be implemented in such a way that they are integrated with other human resource systems. If a firm wishes to implement a compensation system that emphasizes employee innovation on the job, for example, this change should also be reflected in the characteristics of the selection, training and development, succession planning, and performance management systems.

Second, implementation of effective compensation systems should be aligned with broad corporate and human resource strategies (Barney & Wright, 1998). That is, they should embody a firm's strategic focus. Furthermore, a firm's strategy (or strategies) ideally should influence human resource and reward strategies and ultimately the design and implementation of the compensation system. We discuss this issue further in the second section of the chapter.

Management Challenges in Implementing Compensation Systems

Compensation managers and teams who design and implement reward systems face numerous challenges. In our experience, several challenges need to be addressed before design and implementation—fundamental issues that corporate leaders must face, implicitly or explicitly, when they propose new or modified compensation systems.

Although implementation of any significant organizational change presents challenges, changes in the compensation system often face particular resistance and controversy. No other organizational system is as laden with unexplained assumptions, values, and emotions, is as transparent to employees, or is as subject to politicking. Redesign or implementation of new compensation systems usually raises the ire of employees who do less well under the new system, because they usually feel the change is inequitable.

Conversely, firms that are slow to change find employees fleeing to other firms with more innovative, equitable, and effective reward systems. In this section, we discuss the motivational impact of money, compensation and human capital strategies, the employee value proposition and total rewards strategies, the elements of compensation systems, the fundamental areas of compensation practice, employee satisfaction, and the link between pay and performance.

Does Money Motivate?

An important question is whether compensation motivates performance and other changes in employee behavior. If it did not, then the task of designing compensation systems would be much simpler. Managers would need to worry about paying wages adequate to attract and retain employees and would be concerned about administering pay fairly, but they could avoid troublesome issues in designing and implementing systems that link pay and performance.

The question "Does money motivate?" was answered long ago with academic research and is no longer debated in those circles. Summaries of existing academic research demonstrate convincingly that money can motivate performance and other changes in behavior (see Gupta & Shaw, 1998, and Jenkins, Mitra, Gupta, & Shaw, 1998, for summaries). Unfortunately, the question of the motivating potential of money remains an issue with some managers, and the debate has reopened several times in practitioner-oriented compensation journals and magazines.

Having established the motivating potential of money, it is prudent to note that providing compensation or incentives to employees will not always motivate the desired behavior or performance for several reasons. First, at any given time compensation may not be as valued as other rewards, and other factors may take precedence over money. For example, employees with families who value an equitable work-life balance may prefer time off rather than the money that comes with working harder or more hours. Second, several factors may hinder the desired level of performance. Personal factors such as lack of training, skills, and competencies may prevent employees from achieving it. Situational factors such as lack of equipment or other resources may also act as constraints on individual performance. If employees realize that achieving the requisite performance level is not possible and thus that the compensation will not be received, they may not engage in the desired behaviors. Third, managers may fail to measure employee performance accurately or measure the wrong things. Employees may not be motivated by a system that measures performance poorly, feeling there is "no way to win." Alternatively, a system may encourage employees to engage in the wrong behaviors—for example, by emphasizing cost controls at the expense of quality.

Compensation system designers and implementers need to be aware of these limitations to the motivating potential of compensation.

Compensation and Human Capital Strategies

The key questions to address here are these: "Are employees treated as a cost or as an investment?" and "To what degree?" These questions can be answered by examining the goals of a firm's human capital strategy, which can emphasize talent, motivation, or cost, as shown in Figure 6.1.

Although no firm can ignore any of these goals, certain types of firms pursue some goals with more vigor than others. For example, big-market professional sports teams and entertainment firms such as movie studios usually do not emphasize costs but

Figure 6.1. Possible Goals of a Human Capital Strategy.

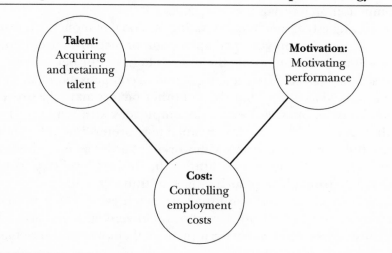

rather focus on acquiring talent. Even though the cost of acquiring talent has skyrocketed in recent years, the profit associated with a hit movie or a world championship is used to justify such decisions.

In contrast, a typical retail or manufacturing organization will emphasize cost control primarily because profit margins are invariably thin. For firms in these categories, costs need to be controlled to make money. Even high-end retailers such as Macy's, Lord & Taylor, and Filene's focus on controlling labor costs. Finally, high-technology organizations generally emphasize motivation more than cost control or talent acquisition. These firms are constantly looking for creative professionals to invent or develop new products. Start-ups usually offer cash incentives in exchange for the hard, sustained work needed to succeed in the business. Consequently, these firms need to be able to hire and retain these kinds of employees.

Each of the three reward goals implies somewhat different reward practices. Statements of corporate philosophy or human resource strategy often provide clues about which of the three goals is emphasized, but these broad statements do not always filter down to compensation system practices. The real compensation system goals can be readily inferred by looking at these practices. Exhibit 6.1 illustrates the link between each of these goals and the implications for base pay and incentives. The human capital goal of acquiring and retaining talent is usually linked with high levels of base pay that push the high end of the market (a market leader position). Additional incentives are possible to an already high base pay level. The motivation-of-performance goal is often connected with a market match or market lag base pay policy. Below-market to market wages are supplemented with heavy incentive pay programs. The objective is to receive a return on the investment in the incentive programs. These kinds of firms have implemented a wide range of programs, such as individual, group, or organizationwide incentives. One high-technology firm, for example, uses performance-based incentives such as stock options, profit sharing, and a management by objective (MBO) system to motivate high levels of performance. Finally, the cost-control goal is often paired with market lag base pay policies. Manufacturing firms often target base pay as low as possible in a given labor market—that is, base pay will fluctuate with the labor market rates. Incentive techniques are possible but often are capped to control costs.

**Exhibit 6.1. Links Between Human Capital Goals,
Base Pay, and Incentive Implications.**

Human Capital Goal	Base Pay Implications	Incentive Implications
Acquiring and retaining talent	Tends to push the market	Incentives possible as additions to already high base pay
Motivation of performance	At or below market levels	Heavy emphasis on incentives
Cost control	As low as possible given labor market	Incentives useful but must be carefully designed (for example, capped payouts and modest incentive levels)

Although the links between these three human capital management strategies and base pay and incentive systems are ideal, the disconnect between philosophy or policy and actual practice has been noted by many authors (see Kerr, 1975). Furthermore, there are trade-offs in these three goals. An incentive plan could be cost-effective, but if it works badly it will cost much more than if it is not used. Furthermore, there are some inconsistencies among the three goals. For example, overpaying helps to attract and retain talent, but it hurts cost control. Offering heavy compensation for top performance may motivate many employees but make it more difficult to attract and retain average performers who do not like the culture. And cutting employment costs may sap motivation and morale.

Employee Value Proposition and Total Reward Strategies

The effectiveness and fairness of total reward systems are embodied in the employee value proposition (EVP). The EVP is the "deal"—the monetary and nonmonetary rewards that the organization offers to induce employees to join, remain, and perform well. Before entering an employment relationship, applicants evaluate what they and the potential employer bring to the exchange. Research from a variety of literatures has consistently demonstrated that both applicants and employees often contemplate the value proposition, and that the EVP influences decisions to join, perform, and remain with an employer (see Cappelli, 1999; Milkovich & Stevens, 2000).

Total reward strategies are necessary to change the EVP positively and must be taken into account during compensation system implementations in the current business environment. Firms can no longer focus on one reward or set of rewards without regard to the others they provide to employees. The basic premise behind a total reward strategy is that rewards and systems should be broadly viewed and no single reward should be looked at in isolation. Therefore, all aspects of what employees find rewarding need to be considered when designing and implementing compensation systems. For example, perhaps a firm that offers lower market wages than other potential employers offers stock options, good career potential, interesting work, or generous benefits.

Many total reward models in the literature are similar in that they have separate designations for direct (compensation) and indirect (benefits) compensation. Direct compensation usually specifies base pay, such as salary or hourly wage, short-term incentives, long-term incentives, premium pay, and cash recognition. Indirect compensation, or benefits, includes voluntary benefits such as health care, retirement, welfare benefits, paid time off, and perquisites. One total reward model developed by Nextera's Sibson Consulting Group is called the rewards of work model. It is illustrated in Figure 6.2.

The rewards of work model is composed of five factors—direct financial, indirect financial, affiliation, career, and work content—which capture the critical reward element relevant to the employee value proposition and represent the primary components of a total reward strategy. Although each one is intended to be independent of the others, some overlap is unavoidable. For example, an employee's relationship with his or her supervisor may be associated with several categories, because a supervisor may be responsible for giving that employee feedback (work content), raises (direct financial), and training opportunities (career). Also, it is important to note that each reward category will have an influence on the EVP.

Figure 6.2. Rewards of Work Model.

Affiliation
- Organization commitment
- Organization support
- Work environment
- Organization citizenship
- Title

Direct financial
- Base salary
- Incentives
- Ownership
- Cash recognition
- Premium pay
- Pay process

Work content
- Variety
- Challenge
- Autonomy
- Meaningfulness
- Feedback

Employee value proposition (EVP)

Indirect financial
- Benefits
- Noncash recognition
- Perquisites

Career
- Advancement
- Personal growth
- Training
- Employment security

Source: Nextera's Sibson Consulting Group.

Basic Elements of a Compensation System

The remainder of the chapter focuses more narrowly on direct compensation. Base pay, pay for performance, and incentive pay are the three primary elements of most compensation systems. *Base pay* is what employees earn on a regular basis for performing their jobs. They receive base pay either in the form of an hourly wage rate or a fixed salary. *Pay for performance,* or merit pay, includes monetary rewards determined by merit. This is distinguished from other types of incentives by being permanently added to the previous year's base pay, with the level of increase determined by the assessed performance. *Incentive pay* refers to onetime bonuses that are usually not permanent additions to base pay but are determined by individual, team, unit, or corporate performance. Each type of incentive pay is described briefly as follows:

- *Individual incentives* are a onetime payment for individual performance. Examples are piecework plans, management incentive plans, behavioral encouragement plans, sales bonuses, employee referral plans, and reduction-in-error bonuses.
- *Team incentives* reward a work group, project team, or other small group for its performance.
- *Unit incentives* reward a plant, division, or other large group for its performance. A unit incentive is usually a bonus paid for the performance (productivity, cost reduction, quality improvement, safety, and so on) of a plant, department, business unit, or other organization below company level. Unit incentives include gain sharing, goal sharing, win sharing, plant performance bonuses, Improshare, Scanlon plans, and Rucker plans.
- *Corporate incentives* are profit sharing or other bonuses for an entire organization's performance. These plans are usually based on company profits, cost containment, market share, or sales revenue.

Other elements that may be included in a pay system are these:

- *Overtime pay* (or time-and-a-half) is given to employees who are not exempt (nonexempt) from the Fair Labor Standards Act of 1938 provisions. Professionals and supervisors used to be given overtime, but currently this practice is very limited.
- *Cost-of-living increases* (or COLA) are additions to base pay given to all employees based on an economic index such as the consumer price index. This practice too is less common today than it once was.
- *Seniority and longevity increases* are raises to base pay for employees who have been with the firm for a specified period or have reached the top of their pay range.
- *Promotion increases* are raises to base pay for employees who have received a promotion. They are often associated with a move to a higher pay grade.

- *Stock options or stock grants* are opportunities to buy shares of stock in the future at a preset price or an award of shares of company stock.

Obviously, a firm has many options from which to choose. For reasons of brevity, not all are listed here. However, recent research has demonstrated that employees usually prefer compensation options that they can control, such as merit pay and overtime, rather than those over which they have less control over, such as team and unit incentives (see Ledford, Mulvey, & LeBlanc, 2000).

Fundamental Areas of Compensation Practice

Compensation is managed in most organizations through three distinct areas of practice. Although many of the issues are consistent in all three, the actual design, implementation, and practices for each will be different. The three areas of compensation practice are core employees, executives, and sales employees. Exhibit 6.2 describes the main differences between the three areas when it comes to compensation decisions, emphasis of compensation mix, and criteria for performance.

Exhibit 6.2. Areas of Compensation Practice.

Area of Compensation Practice	Organizational Group Responsible for Compensation Decisions	Emphasis of Compensation Mix	Criteria for Performance-Based Pay
Core employees	Compensation department	Base pay with some individual or unit incentives	Individual or unit performance
Executive employees	Compensation committee on board of directors	Long-term compensation	Business performance of company
Sales employees	Marketing or sales department	Cash incentives	Revenue

Human resource or compensation specialists handle compensation decisions for most core employees. In contrast, members of the compensation committee on the board of directors, aided by executive compensation consultants, are responsible for executive compensation decisions. The marketing or sales departments usually handle sales compensation decisions. Compared with employee compensation, executive compensation is heavily oriented toward the long term. In sales compensation, there is generally a much higher emphasis on contingent cash rewards. Executive compensation and sales compensation systems are areas of specialized practice that go beyond the scope of this chapter.

Employee Satisfaction

Although at some level employee satisfaction is a desirable organizational outcome, effective compensation systems never will satisfy all employees. Effective compensation systems discriminate based on some measure of individual, group, or organizational performance. Not every employee will receive the same merit raise, individual or group bonus, stock options, and so on. Those who receive less will tend to be dissatisfied no matter which method is used to assess performance. In short, it is both impossible and undesirable to satisfy all employees all the time.

But when employees are dissatisfied many managers become concerned. Unhappy employees can cause conflict and take a manager's attention away from pressing issues. Managers' concerns also stem from an enduring myth about compensation systems—that "happy workers are productive workers." Ledford and Hawk (2000) note that because of this myth, managers focus on making the workplace employee-centered, and thus happier, while ignoring costly and complicated reward system issues. Those responsible for design and implementation should be aware that they cannot escape making the hard choices that effective compensation systems require and that there will have to be trade-offs.

Link Between Pay and Performance

Apart from the fundamental reward issues noted earlier, there are some management issues from an organizational perspective. The most important is the link between pay and performance. If this issue is not addressed properly it too can hamper the effective implementation of a compensation system.

Assuming that the revised or new compensation system includes some form of contingent pay, one obstacle to overcome is ensuring the perception of a link between pay and performance. Pay for performance is an appealing concept in theory, but in practice has been much harder to implement successfully (see Heneman, 1992, for a review of merit pay systems). If there is not an effective performance management system it will seriously hamper attempts to implement an effective pay-for-performance system. For example, we are familiar with a major food processing plant that wanted to increase its product quality by reducing the number of insect parts found in its canned foods. Management decided to measure and incentivize performance by the number of insect parts workers removed from the canned products. Although the system created accurately measured insect parts, it did not necessarily improve quality. Why? The employees realized that their pay would increase significantly if they brought insect parts to the plant, added them to the food mix, and then removed them immediately.

In summary, management faces numerous challenges when implementing compensation systems. These challenges should be explicitly discussed as part of the design and implementation process. We turn now to some prescriptive guidance for developing and implementing a compensation system.

Steps in the Design and Implementation of Compensation Systems

The remainder of this chapter outlines five specific steps in designing and implementing compensation systems that will allow an organization to achieve both compensation system goals and human resource and strategic organizational goals. The five steps are *laying the foundation, establishing the pay philosophy, designing the pay, creating supporting infrastructure,* and *implementing and evaluating the new system.* Figure 6.3 illustrates the five-step process.

Step 1: Lay the Foundation

The first step, laying the foundation, will set the stage for the remaining steps and thus cannot be skipped. There are several key tasks in this phase: presenting the business case for change, iden-

Figure 6.3. Steps in Designing and Implementing a Compensation System.

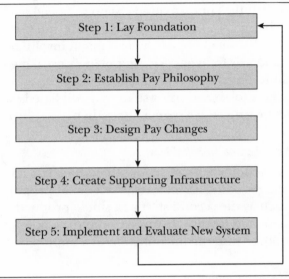

Step 1: Lay Foundation

Step 2: Establish Pay Philosophy

Step 3: Design Pay Changes

Step 4: Create Supporting Infrastructure

Step 5: Implement and Evaluate New System

tifying the scope of change, identifying the relevant stakeholders, creating a steering committee to manage the implementation, chartering the steering committee, and supporting the committee.

Present the Business Case for Change

The business case for change needs to be made before any compensation system implementation should proceed. If compensation systems are originally designed to attract, motivate, and retain employees and to align employee behavior with a firm's business strategy, then the business case should identify which of these goals is not currently being met. For example, a manufacturing plant may find that it is losing key employees to local competitors. A cost analysis may further show that these defections are substantially affecting the bottom line indirectly through delays in shipping the product and longer than normal shutdowns on production lines. In essence, the business case demonstrates that the return on investment would be sufficient to redesign and implement a revised compensation system to increase retention of key employees.

Identify the Scope of Change

An important step during this foundation stage is identifying the extent to which the compensation system will need to change. The required change could be relatively minor, quite extensive, or something in between. Minor changes might involve resetting production standards for a gain-sharing plan or tweaking the level of individual incentives in the pay mix. Extensive changes may involve moving from a job-based pay system to a skill-based pay system or adopting a new incentive system altogether.

Identify the Relevant Stakeholders

Relevant stakeholders must be identified too. The compensation system changes could affect a relatively small proportion of employees, such as the second shift in a single production plant. Or the change could involve the entire employee population of the organization, as with the introduction of a merit pay system.

Create a Steering Committee

A steering committee can be useful in managing the design and implementation phases. The steering committee should include representatives from the population of relevant stakeholders in both line and staff functions. Steering committees may shepherd along system design, implementation, or both, and different groups may be used for the two phases. If there is little membership overlap between the two committees, or none at all, then those responsible for the implementation of the compensation system will find it harder to understand the true intentions of those responsible for the design. The obvious solution is to have some overlap between the compensation design and implementation committees or simply have only one steering committee.

Charter the Steering Committee

Executives need to establish a charter for the steering committee to provide a focus for their task, to provide boundaries within which to operate, and to demonstrate their commitment to the work. Without such a charter the steering committee may waste time on tangential issues or recommend actions that executives are not willing or able to endorse.

Provide the Steering Committee with Support and Resources

Steering committees need sufficient resources to accomplish the task set out in their charter. Their members will need to be able to attend most if not all of the committee's meetings. Thus, a travel budget may be needed if members are geographically dispersed, or teleconferencing or videoconferencing capabilities may be provided. Steering committee members may need training in the compensation issues involved, consulting help, and access to other resources. Furthermore, executives will need to inform the committee members' managers of the importance of this activity and the expectation that they will make appropriate accommodations for the committee members to participate.

Step 2: Establish a Pay Philosophy

Corporate philosophy and strategy should influence the development and implementation of all human resource systems, including the compensation philosophy and strategy. The compensation philosophy and strategy in turn affect the type of compensation programs designed, which then influence compensation policies and practices. Let us reiterate that the compensation system is just one of several systems that make up human resource strategy and practice. Consequently, pay philosophy and strategy are also partly influenced by how well they fit with other human resource systems.

Examine the Compensation Philosophy

Many books have been written about compensation strategy and philosophy in the last decade (see Schuster & Zingheim, 1992, for a helpful overview). It is important to establish whether the organization's existing pay philosophy is clear. A clear pay philosophy provides a guide to decisions about specific pay practices and methods of pay administration. It provides a specific statement that helps design groups determine what is permissible and what is not. It indicates, for example, where the company wishes to price jobs in the market context, how it wishes to pay for performance, and who makes decisions about pay innovations. Many organizations today have a pay philosophy statement that serves the purposes outlined here. If one exists, the job of the design group is to verify that the philosophy still serves as a guide for the organization's decisions and to clarify any ambiguities. If a pay philosophy does not exist, it is often desirable to create one as a starting point for pay changes. The more complex, important, and far-reaching the potential changes, the more helpful a philosophy statement is. Pay mix and pay openness, which are indicators of a company's pay philosophy, are discussed next.

Pay mix. Pay mix is the combination of base pay, variable pay (individual and group bonuses), stock options, and benefits provided in the compensation system. Pay mix can represent broad compensation policies and company values (Milkovich & Newman, 2002). If higher percentages are devoted to base pay and benefits, this conveys a value on security and work-life balance. Introducing incentives and stock options to the pay mix and reducing base pay adds risk in exchange for greater potential earnings. A performance-driven mix might place 50 percent or less of total compensation in base pay.

Pay secrecy, pay openness. There is a lot of variation in what compensation information is communicated to employees. Compensation systems run the gamut from totally open to completely closed. At the closed end of the spectrum, many firms have implemented pay secrecy policies in which only the employees know their own salary or hourly wage. When such policies are in place, there are also often threats of severe punishment, such as dismissal, for their violation. (Most such employers do not appear to appreciate that it is a violation of federal labor law to punish an employee for disclosing his or her pay to others.) However, some employee discussion does occur even when complete secrecy is the official policy.

At the open end of the spectrum, almost all information on pay levels, raises, and pay ranges is known by the employees. Public universities are typical examples of an open compensation system. Employee salaries must be made public, and consequently employees can learn the compensation of everyone in the organization, from the chancellor to the janitor. However, even here the process to determine employee pay may not be fully known.

There are advantages to both open and closed compensation systems, and which an organization chooses tends to reflect values and biases more than hard evidence that one way works best for the organization.

Up until the mid-1990s, organizations could much more easily withhold pay information. But over the last few years, the Internet has greatly increased the amount of publicly available information on compensation and compensation systems. For example, Vault.com (http://www.vault.com) provides insider information about organizations, including their pay philosophy and practices, at no cost, and allows users to post and answer questions about a variety of issues, including starting salaries and pay programs. Other Web sites provide some compensation salary data to anyone who accesses them. The quality of the information may be suspect, but employees have a tendency to believe pay information that is favorable to their own position. Thus, the availability of information on the Web—however misleading—puts pressure on organizations to provide accurate information and explain its choices and positioning compared with labor market competitors.

It would seem prudent to offer information about the compensation system in a manner that is consistent with broader information-sharing policies. That is, does the firm value open communication or does it operate on a need-to-know basis? Although we have a bias for a more open compensation system, there are at least two reasons why an organization would not desire such a system. First, an open compensation system may run counter to the organization's desired culture. After senior management has identified its goals and the type of culture it is trying to create, the compensation system becomes an influential tool to help reinforce that culture. If the organization does not value open communication and high employee involvement, it may not want to share compensation information any more freely than other types of information. Second, if an organization knows that it suffers from severe equity problems—both internally with pay compression and inversion and externally with low market rates—it may not want to share compensation information until it has addressed these issues. Sharing compensation information freely at this stage would only add fuel to the existing fire.

Step 3: Design Pay Changes

Once a firm decides on corporate, human resource, and compensation strategies, the specific compensation programs designated in the steering committee charter need to be designed or redesigned.

As noted earlier, compensation programs usually include some of the following: base pay, merit pay, individual incentives, group incentives, and stock options. In large organizations each program may be directed by separate individuals and have different schedules, eligibility and implementation rules, and payouts. Each compensation program has associated specific practices and policies. In this section we will review the predominant practices and policies of each.

Base Pay Options

Two factors define base pay options. The first is the basis for pay; an organization can choose either to base the pay on the job or on employee skill, knowledge, or competencies. The second is the architecture of the pay system; the choice here is between having a traditional structure or a banding system.

Basis for pay (job or skill). Base pay programs have gone through fundamental changes over the last two decades. From the early 1900s to the 1970s, base pay was determined almost exclusively by the worth of the job. Wage and salary surveys, job evaluation, or both, were used to determine base pay or pay level. Wage and salary surveys help determine external competitiveness or equity, whereas job evaluation determines internal competitiveness or equity. However, during the 1980s there was a gradual shift from position-based pay to person-based pay, including skill, knowledge, or competency-based plans (see Jenkins, Ledford, Gupta, & Doty, 1992, for more complete coverage of skill-based pay plans). Ledford, Mulvey, and LeBlanc (2000) found that approximately 10 percent of American workers reported being compensated by such plans.

Whether the plan is job-based or person-based, information is collected to determine what to value, then a value is assessed, and finally that value is translated into a base-pay structure. In job-based plans, job analyses are conducted, followed by job evaluation that is transferred to a base-pay structure. In skill-based plans, information is collected through a skill analysis from which skill blocks are determined. Employees, usually blue-collar, are then required to enter into a certification process to determine their value. In competency-based plans, core competencies are determined and formed into competency sets. Here employees, usually white-collar, are assessed against the competency sets.

Compensation system architecture (traditional pay grades or broad banding). An alternative to traditional pay grades (within job-based pay designs) that is currently receiving widespread attention is broad banding. Broad-banding systems greatly simplify job-grading systems by revising the overall architecture of the pay system. This system is oriented toward motivating employees to focus on long-term development, and not necessarily on performance.

Large organizations usually develop elaborate pay grade systems over time. This permits them to offer relatively frequent promotions to higher grades, to create pay distinctions that mirror the hierarchical and status distinctions in the organization, and to control salary inflation within each grade. In large companies there are often dozens of pay grades between the lowest paid employee and the top executives.

In contrast, broad banding often radically reduces the number of grades in the organization (see Abosch & Hand, 1998, for a review of broad banding). As grades are combined, the spread between the bottom and the top of the range increases from perhaps 35 to 50 percent to as much as 300 percent. In addition, firms using broad banding usually eliminate traditional pay tools, such as point factor job evaluation and range controls. Some firms that adopt broad banding expect most employees to remain in one band, such as an engineering band or middle-manager band, for their entire careers. For example, one organization with annual sales of nearly $1 billion collapsed its complex grade structure into just three bands (one each for executives, lower and middle managers, and nonmanagers).

Broad banding fits the strategy, structure, and culture of many firms. A company that has radically delayered in favor of flexible, lateral, team-oriented structures may find numerous grades to be anachronistic. Broadening bands can have a positive impact on motivation because it can give managers more flexibility in rewarding employee performance within a very broad band. It also encourages employees to focus on developing skills that make them more valuable, rather than chasing job evaluation points and grades. Broad banding may reduce incidents where employees are reluctant to take assignments that do not offer opportunities for promotion to another pay grade. Companies adopting broad banding also often hope to reduce the time, effort, and energy needed to manage their complex pay grade systems.

However, broad banding may create a variety of problems. Once more familiar methods of cost control are abandoned, it may not be clear how pay costs will be controlled and pay equity will be maintained. Line managers usually assume a critical role in controlling compensation costs in broad banding, and they may need to be evaluated partly on the basis of the effectiveness with which they perform this role. Extensive communication is needed to help employees understand how the new system works and how they can advance in it. Finally, broad banding is incompatible with hierarchical, bureaucratic company cultures.

Pay-for-Performance Options

In addition to base pay decisions there are several pay-for-performance options. Paying for performance is a critical and complex issue. The starting point for any such system needs to be an analysis of the business strategy, organizational structure, and organizational culture. This will indicate the types of performance the organization needs to reward and the level of analysis at which rewards should be located (individual, team, unit, or corporation). We will focus first on merit pay and individual incentives, and then on variable pay options, such as team, unit, and corporate incentives.

Merit pay programs. Merit pay programs are among the oldest and most frequently used pay programs. Merit is usually assessed through a performance management system. Unlike individual and group incentives, merit pay increases are usually added to an employee's base pay. Employee performance is assessed on an annual basis, although semiannual or quarterly assessments are also possible. Decisions about base pay increases are either made on a percentage or dollar value basis. During the corporate budgeting process merit pay pools are established and merit pay is delivered either on an anniversary or a common review date.

Adding merit increases to base pay involves a number of administrative complications and practical considerations, and it tempers the association between pay and performance. Those high in their salary range, for example, usually receive small increases or no increases. This stops salaries for a given position from going "out of range." It also makes it possible to give an average performer who is low in his salary range (and thus eligible for a full increase) a higher percentage increase than someone who is high in the range (and thus ineligible for a full increase). In addition, the size of the increase is usually tied to labor market wage inflation and the firm's financial fortunes. Employees whose performance is high during the most favorable periods will receive far more benefit than the unlucky employees whose performance is high during bad times for the firm and low wage inflation in the economy.

Individual incentives. There are a variety of individual incentive plans, including piecework plans, management incentive plans, behavioral encouragement plans, and referral plans. These plans are most useful when work is performed independently and requires little interdependence with other employees.

Piecework incentive plans such as those that reward employees for meeting or exceeding a production standard per hour are common in manufacturing plants. They are also often used when a unit of production is completed in a relatively short time. MBO systems frequently use management incentive plans. These incentive plans offer bonuses to managers who meet or exceed performance goals. Other incentive plans reward employees for exhibiting specific types of measurable behaviors, such as attendance or safety, and recruiting or referring acquaintances to the firm.

Variable pay options. Variable pay is the most common way to tie pay to performance. There are many forms of variable pay, and variable pay plans have many names: gain sharing, profit sharing, team bonuses, Scanlon plans, and so on. The variable pay plans we discuss here have two key characteristics. They pay for performance through bonuses that are given near the time that the performance occurs, and they pay for the performance of groups rather than individuals. The bonus money that employees potentially can make in a variable pay plan represents "pay at risk," meaning that it is not guaranteed. Pay varies with performance, so that the organization pays out more when it can afford to and less when performance does not justify high payment. A high level of pay at risk can create an entrepreneurial culture.

Many large U.S. firms use gain sharing and profit sharing. Gain sharing has greatly increased in popularity, whereas use of profit sharing has not grown much over the last decade. We make no sharp distinction between plans at the team and organizational levels here. The design issues are the same. The primary caution when considering team bonuses is that an inappropriate plan may create competition among teams that need to cooperate.

The two key elements in variable pay plans that lead to increased organizational effectiveness are a *formula* by which employees share monetarily in the performance gains of the organization, and *structures and processes* by which employees share in the creation of organizational performance gains. If only the first element is present, the plan will not motivate improved performance because there will be no line of sight—that is, no clear connection between behavior and reward. The plan will be simply a fringe benefit that pays some times but not others. The second element is the means by which employees help create improved performance, generating a pool of money in which they share. Without it, employees will not be motivated because they will have no way to influence the size of their bonuses.

Two contrasting examples highlight the differences. When an electronics firm won a contract to install a billion-dollar air defense system for a Middle Eastern country, it lived up to its reputation of providing great technology late, and thus was in danger of losing a $50 million bonus for completing the project on time. The CEO offered the nine hundred engineers involved in the project 40 percent of the $50 million bonus to split among themselves if they completed it on time. They came from a year behind schedule to on-time installation, and each team member earned an average of $22,000. This bonus was motivating because it was high enough to be meaningful to everyone involved, was tied to a clear but challenging goal, and included a small enough group of people that project members could influence the payout. In contrast, the CEO of an airline company offered every employee below senior management a $65 bonus during any month that the airline placed among the top five airlines in on-time arrival rankings. This plan had the advantage of offering a clear goal and it communicated an important company objective to employees. But the amount of money offered was modest and there was little chance for any individual employee to influence the payout.

Variable pay plans have a relatively high success rate. Reviews of the literature and large-scale studies suggest that they frequently result in increased organizational performance (for example, Welbourne & Gomez-Mejia, 1995). Typical benefits reported are increased productivity, better quality, lower costs, lower absenteeism and turnover, and more favorable employee attitudes. Cost-benefit analyses indicate that there is a good positive return to the organization for the increased compensation costs.

In order for the plan to succeed in improving performance, it must change patterns of behavior that can in turn lead to better performance. Better performance may result if employees make more suggestions for improvement, make a greater effort, solve problems better and more persistently, cooperate better in their groups and with other groups in the organization; if there are greater demands on management for improved performance; and if relations between management and employees improve.

Of course, many variable pay plans fail. They fail either because the formula is poorly designed or because the gain-producing structures are inadequate. A plan may be designed to reward the wrong behaviors, or it may not cover all the relevant behaviors and metrics. For example, a formula that only rewards increased labor productivity may lead employees to work harder but also increase scrap and waste materials and supplies. Or payouts may be too infrequent. Frequent payouts are desirable from a motivational point of view, although this may not be practical for an organization's accounting system or performance cycles. Omitting key groups from the plan can also create problems. For example, if the plan covers only direct labor employees, support employees such as maintenance workers and material handlers may resist changing their behavior in order to make it possible for others to earn a bonus. Finally, the formula may be too inflexible. If the formula is tailored to a particular context, it may need to change as circumstances change.

Designing variable pay plan formulas is complex and has been the subject of numerous books. We highlight here only some of the most important principles of variable pay design. First, such plans usually are designed to be *self-funding*, so that the money paid out in bonuses is derived from savings that the plan itself generates. Another principle is *line of sight*. There are many ways of increasing line of sight in variable pay plans, thereby increasing their motivational power. Simpler measures and formulas tend to produce greater line of sight, as do more frequent payouts. Paying out to smaller units (such as teams) creates greater line of sight than paying out in a large plant (say, a thousand employees) or an entire company. Support processes can be critical to creating line of sight. A simple formula and team-level bonuses may be inappropriate, so considerable training and information sharing must help employees understand a plan that is not obvious to them.

Many different performance measures can be used as the basis for a variable pay formula, ranging from very concrete behavioral measures (accidents, absenteeism, safety inspection ratings, and so on), to measures of unit performance (productivity, cost, quality, on-time delivery, cycle time), to measures of financial performance (return on sales or investment, profit, economic value-added).

Nevertheless, there is a clear trend in the United States toward using plans tied to the financial performance of the corporation. The Big Three automakers, for example, all offer profit-sharing bonuses, which have varied greatly in payouts depending on company performance in recent years. In evaluating these plans, we must recognize that they have limited motivational value, lucrative as they are, because there is no line of sight between payouts and individual behavior. But the plans may have other advantages. They give companies a way to pay employees well when they can afford to do so, and they help increase employee identification with the company and its success.

Unit performance metrics are in the middle on the motivation versus ability-to-pay criteria. Employees can influence them more easily than financial performance measures but not as easily as behavioral measures. An organization that shows good performance on productivity tends to make a higher rate of return over the long run. These metrics are most often recommended in the gain-sharing literature.

Many organizations attempt to realize the best of both worlds by combining different types of metrics in the same formula. For example, there may be a requirement that the organization make a profit before it makes payouts on unit performance or behavioral measures. These and other options protect against payouts during bad times, but at the risk of making the plan more complex and difficult to understand. The plan also may inadvertently include so many safeguards that it cannot pay out.

Another design choice is whether to pay out when the organization does better than in the past (gain sharing when performance exceeds historical levels) rather than when the organization reaches targets defined by management (goal sharing). Gain sharing based on historical performance usually seems fair to employees. It also avoids employee fears of a speedup, a common problem in individual incentive plans such as piecework. Goal sharing is attractive because it takes advantage of the motivational power of specific, challenging goals. In contrast, management-set targets are very flexible and can change annually to reflect new business directions and emphases.

Managers can determine the suitability of any particular formula only through an organizational needs analysis. Different plans are appropriate for different settings. Also, we again emphasize that the support processes and structures are probably more important to success than the specifics of the formula.

Stock. There are two primary ways in which companies offer opportunities for equity participation: employee stock ownership plans (ESOPs) and stock options. These plans have many of the same advantages and motivational problems as corporate profit sharing, but they are even more complex from the individual employee's standpoint. Because ESOPs are deferred compensation, we will focus on stock options.

During the past few years there has been an explosion in the use of broad-based stock options. The plans have become a standard part of pay packages in the high-technology sector, and indeed U.S. subsidiaries of foreign high-technology firms often have serious recruitment and retention problems if they cannot offer stock options. The rewards for these plans can be spectacular in successful companies. Microsoft offers below-market base pay but offers stock options so lucrative that fully half of the workforce—and virtually all employees with more than five years tenure—own over $1 million in company stock. Currently, most of the Fortune 1000 firms use stock options, and some cover more than half of their workforce.

Appealing as stock options plans may be from the standpoint of employees who have been made wealthy by such plans, they have questionable motivational value. None of Microsoft's twenty-eight thousand employees below the executive level can have a significant effect on the firm's stock performance. Thus, there is not only low line of sight to company performance but no line of sight to the macroeconomic, international, financial, and market forces far beyond the company's boundaries that influence stock prices. In addition, employees often find it difficult to understand how to use these plans. An administrative employee at a leading biotechnology firm allowed $750,000 in stock options to expire because she did not understand how the plan worked. Once this happened, the company was legally powerless to correct the problem.

Market Change Pricing

One final assessment at this point is to determine if the firm is on target with its compensation policies. The firm may wish to be competitive but not too generous. Both job-based and person-based systems require some collection of market data—usually purchased wage or salary surveys—to determine how a company's pay matches up with the labor and product or service market competition. Most organizations purchase a salary survey for specific job families to determine their market position. The same should be true for other forms of compensation; such surveys can be purchased from professional associations and consulting firms. WorldatWork's Total Salary Increase Budget Survey (2001), for example, presents actual and projected salary budget increase and salary structure adjustments for public and private organizations in North America.

Step 4: Create an Infrastructure That Supports Compensation Changes

Creating an infrastructure that supports pay changes is a crucial but often ignored step in the process of implementing compensation systems. Invariably, organizations use the existing infrastructure to support compensation system changes. Yet the existing infrastructure may have contributed to the reason why change was needed in the first place. Several tasks are important in successfully navigating this step. A communication campaign for the compensation system change is needed, followed by ongoing communications. Once the communication campaign has successfully raised awareness of the impending change, several types of training are needed to increase knowledge and understanding of the new system and to affect values.

Compensation System Communication

Except in the smallest organizations, not every employee and manager will be able to get involved in the compensation design and implementation process. Usually only in union environments are employee compensation interests formally represented and negotiated for every member of the bargaining unit. In nonunion working environments, employee and manager involvement at some level is important to the success of the process.

The importance of communication is supported by one conclusion in the rewards of work study (see Ledford, Mulvey, & LeBlanc, 2000, for the complete findings). Ledford and his colleagues found sharp differences in employee satisfaction depending on how much they received in base pay and how that base pay was determined. We believe that satisfaction with the compensation process represents, in part, the quality of compensation implementation, and in particular, the communication of the process. The researchers found that employees often have strong opinions about the pay process. In short, satisfaction with the pay process was significantly lower than with the pay level. A little less than 75 percent of respondents were satisfied or very satisfied with the overall level of their pay. In contrast, only about 50 percent were satisfied with the pay process, or about 25 percent fewer. More important, the researchers found that satisfaction with pay process is a more important predictor of intention to leave the organization than satisfaction with pay level (see also Miceli & Mulvey, 2000).

One interpretation of these findings is that employees want more information about how their pay is determined. Overall, these findings underscore how important it is to communicate about compensation and compensation systems; such communication should begin before those systems are first designed and implemented. Specifically, two phases are necessary: an initial communication campaign and ongoing communication.

Initial campaign. The initial campaign creates awareness and understanding of the system. It would be prudent to include but also build on the organization's existing communication media. One organization we have worked with used a Web site that was constantly updated with information. Existing media in the organization directed employees to the Web site, as did posters and organizational trinkets such as pens, post-it notes, and the like.

Ongoing communication. Ongoing communication informs employees and managers about performance levels, reward opportunities, and how the two are linked. This kind of communication should not be taken lightly. In our experience the single best predictor of whether a gain-sharing plan works is whether the plant manager can effectively communicate it to employees. The communication should mention how the business is doing overall, how the business is doing based on performance metrics that are part of the plan, what that means for the payout of the individual, and the behaviors necessary to change the metrics included in the plan. If the plant manager can effectively communicate these points, the plan will work. If the plant manager fails in this regard, it will not.

Two caveats. First, the organization should be aware of information overload. Those organizations in which employees have access to a computer will likely use their e-mail and corporate intranet to communicate aggressively with employees. But a common problem with e-mail is that employees are usually overwhelmed by the information and have little time to focus on new issues. Although it is easy and cost-efficient to use e-mail to communicate change, the message may be lost among the numerous e-mails that employees receive each day. Furthermore, we have found that many of the messages that employees receive are irrelevant to them. Thus the compensation system change message, often coming from an unknown sender, may even be deleted before it is read. If the implementation is large enough, a formal meeting to announce the change and answer employee and manager questions may be warranted. In these meetings it is crucial that the message be carefully crafted and that the presenter be well rehearsed.

The second issue is trust in management. A certain level of trust in management by a significant group of affected employees is a prerequisite for a compensation system to work effectively. Lack of trust will lead to suspicion of any new compensation effort—maybe enough to thwart its success. In essence, trust is the foundation on which all implementations are built. Unfortunately, trust in management in many North American organizations is currently low (Ledford, Mulvey, & LeBlanc, 2000). In this kind of environment employees often believe little, if anything, that management says. Pay changes require trust at many levels—that the philosophical decisions were right, that the level of pay employees will receive is fair, and that the process used to make pay decisions is appropriate.

Communications about the change in the compensation system should make employees aware of, understand, and believe in the change. But providing this kind of effective communication is not an easy task, and it is often made more difficult because the systems are kept secret and thus shrouded in mystery. Historically, managers and employees often misunderstood the philosophy, policies, and practices of compensation systems, as the rewards of work study demonstrated. To a large extent this mystery is the legacy of the pay secrecy policies of many firms, which often stem from a cultural belief that pay is a private matter not to be openly discussed. Even if that organizational practice has been discontinued, the compensation process may remain murky because managers and compensation professionals are not given enough training in how to communicate the information.

Training

Although we know of little evidence to support this idea, we suspect that managers and employees need to know more about the compensation systems they use. Before a new or revised compensation system is implemented we suggest that four training phases should be planned to help close this knowledge gap.

Initial training. Before the new compensation system is implemented, all employees and managers should be given information on the system, what its goals are, what behaviors or results are necessary to achieve the compensation levels, and how these behaviors or results will be measured. A step-by-step sequence, for example, outlining the phases of a new merit pay system is often useful to give managers and employees an overview of how the system works.

Refresher training. Even if the initial training is effective, employees and managers will likely forget some of the information that was provided. Refresher training will be necessary on a regular basis—yearly, for example—until information on the compensation system is interwoven into the fabric of the firm's culture.

Ongoing new-hire training. Ongoing new-hire training will prevent new employees from "slipping through the cracks." The training segment on the new compensation system should be provided during the new hire's orientation period.

Special training for managers to help them administer the system. If the new compensation system requires managerial input, training should be provided to managers on how to administer the system.

In addition to training, if a pay-for-performance system is created, a performance monitoring system should be established to determine if the performance goals are being met. For example, if an individual incentive plan is implemented to reduce scrap, then reports of scrap reduction should be monitored to ensure that it is being reduced but not at the expense of quality and quantity of production.

A relatively new development in incentives are software systems that let the organization know the value of its compensation. For example, if managers want to know the value of their stock options, all they need to do is plug in some assumptions and stock data and the software will generate tangible and specific feedback. Similar software programs also explain what employees might do to influence the incentive to be given.

In sum, there are several ways to provide training that ensure that employees and managers are aware of and understand the compensation system, ranging from the interactive software tools just described, to white boards on production floors where costs and profits are tracked, to team meetings and company newsletters, to desktop Web portal information. As more and more employees have access to the Web or an intranet, the latter method will become more popular as a cost-efficient way to deliver information and training.

Step 5: Implement and Evaluate a New System

Installing a system to measure success both during and after the implementation will increase the implementation's chances of success. In addition, the feedback provided by the measurement system should guide the revision efforts for the new compensation plan.

There is currently a movement among corporate compensation departments to demand evaluation of new compensation systems. For example, one forest products company's corporate compensation department now requires systematic evaluation of any newly implemented compensation systems at the local level.

There are several key tasks during this phase. Data must be collected about the implementation success and the outcomes achieved. Because outcomes achieved are the predominant focus of evaluation, implementation success is often ignored. Yet measures of implementation success can act as an early warning system and substantially increase the chances of success later on. And mechanisms for using the data collected also need to be installed. These mechanisms draw conclusions about whether to continue using the system or make midcourse corrections and major revisions.

Collect Implementation Success Data

During the implementation, data can be collected to gauge its success. It is here that implementers will discover how successful the prior design and implementation steps have been. Focus groups and surveys can be used to collect data; anecdotal information may also prove important.

Collect Outcome Data

The degree to which a compensation system is effective will ultimately be determined by collecting appropriate outcome data. For example, if a new merit pay plan was implemented to improve customer service, it is necessary to collect measures of employee behavior from internal raters and ratings of customer service from customers.

Establish Mechanisms for Using the Data to Draw Conclusions

Even though these data are necessary, it is not sufficient to collect implementation success and outcome data. In our experience, a common practice in organizations is to collect survey data and then not act on the data. Mechanisms for using the data to draw conclusions and take actions are necessary as well.

Continue Using the Evaluation System

Once the data have been collected and analyzed, it is usually helpful to continue to use the evaluation system periodically. However, we realize that even if evaluation systems are used, many are not continued past the initial phase. This is unfortunate, because problems may not appear until after the first evaluation is completed.

Make Midcourse Corrections as Needed

It may be necessary to make corrections during the course of the compensation process as data are compiled. Although firms should not make significant revisions at this time, tweaking the system should be allowed. For example, if the phone system is down and calls cannot be rerouted, a call center's individual incentive goal could be readjusted downward because its individual performance was affected by circumstances beyond its control. That is, the performance goal could be adjusted to reflect the circumstances. This will allow the motivational effect of the compensation system to continue uninterrupted.

Make Major Revisions

At the end of each performance period, the data collected throughout the period should be compiled and analyzed. Are any major revisions determined to be necessary? If so, the five-step process outlined here should begin again. Major revisions should not be proposed or implemented more frequently than once a year or every two years; doing so will likely lead to resistance toward or decreased confidence in the system by employees and managers.

Increasingly, the evaluation of new compensation systems is becoming a separate role in organizations for two reasons: to make sure that the evaluation process is done well and to ensure the firm receives corporatewide learning, not just local learning where the implementation is occurring. Although some companies are tightening restrictions on implementing compensation systems while others are loosening them, more companies are insisting on centralized evaluation tools to foster corporatewide learning. If it is true that there is usually little money for the implementation processes (compared with the amount spent on designing the system), there is even less for formal evaluation. But formal evaluation of the implementation of a compensation system, as described here, is the only true way to know how well the system is operating and its likely impact. One current trend may be of help in this regard. Most firms require a business case to be made before going forward with any compensation system implementation. When the business case is developed, it is also critical to plan for a formal system evaluation. The formal evaluation need not be expensive or time consuming.

Conclusion

The many types and complexity of existing reward systems put overwhelming pressure on the implementation process. If this were not the case, it would be easy to provide a series of steps that organizations could follow like a recipe for implementation. Unfortunately, there are many compensation options to choose from, preventing a simple cookbook or best-practice approach. When a change is made to any organizational system and it fails, fingers often point to those responsible for the design or to those responsible for the implementation. The age-old argument of why organizational changes are not effective is as applicable to compensation systems as any other type of organizational change. We take a position in this debate. Based on our experience, we believe that effective implementation of compensation systems is more important than their design, and that effective implementation can overcome poor designs. In contrast, terrific compensation designs cannot overcome poor implementation.

References

Abosch, K. S., & Hand, J. S. (1998). *Life with broad bands*. Scottsdale, AZ: American Compensation Association.

Barney, J. B., & Wright, P. M. (1998). On becoming a strategic partner: The role of human resources in gaining competitive advantage. *Human Resource Management, 37*(1), 31–46.

Cappelli, P. (1999). *The New Deal at work: Managing the market-driven workforce*. Boston: Harvard Business School Press.

Gupta, N., & Shaw, J. D. (1998). Let the evidence speak: Financial incentives are effective! *Compensation and Benefits Review, 30*(2), 26–31.

Heneman, R. L. (1992). *Merit pay: Linking pay increases to performance ratings*. Reading, MA: Addison-Wesley.

Jenkins, G. D. Jr., Ledford, G. E. Jr., Gupta, N., & Doty, H. D. (1992). *Skill-based pay*. Scottsdale, AZ: American Compensation Association.

Jenkins, G. D. Jr., Mitra, A., Gupta, N., & Shaw, J. D. (1998). Are financial incentives related to performance? A meta-analytic review of empirical research. *Journal of Applied Psychology, 83*(5), 777–787.

Kerr, S. (1975). On the folly of rewarding A while hoping for B. *Academy of Management Journal, 18,* 769–783.

Ledford, G. E. Jr., & Hawk, E. J. (2000). Compensation strategy: A guide for senior managers. *ACA Journal, 9*(1), 28–38.

Ledford, G. E. Jr., Mulvey, P. W., & LeBlanc, P. V. (2000). *The rewards of work: What employees value.* Scottsdale, AZ: WorldatWork.

Miceli, M. P., & Mulvey, P. W. (2000). Consequences of satisfaction with pay systems: Two field studies. *Industrial Relations, 39*(1), 62–87.

Milkovich, G. T., & Newman, J. M. (2002). *Compensation.* New York: McGraw-Hill.

Milkovich, G. T., & Stevens, J. (2000). From pay to rewards: One hundred years of change. *ACA Journal, 9*(1), 6–18.

Schuster, J. R., & Zingheim, P. K. (1992). *The new pay: Linking employee and organizational performance.* San Francisco: Jossey-Bass.

Welbourne, T., & Gomez-Mejia, L. (1995). Gainsharing: A critical review and a future research agenda. *Journal of Management, 21*(3), 559–610.

WorldatWork. (2001). *Report on the 2001–2002 total salary increase budget survey.* Scottsdale, AZ: WorldatWork.

CHAPTER 7

Performance Management

Nancy L. Rotchford

Effective performance is key to productive, high-quality work groups and organizations, and performance management is an excellent tool for maintaining and strengthening performance. It allows an organization to obtain the highest quality work from employees, and allows employees to understand their performance and what they can do to improve it. Performance management facilitates and focuses communication of performance information between managers and employees, and provides a method of assessing performance. This chapter discusses developing and implementing practical, usable performance management systems that fit the culture and business needs of the organization.

For clarity, distinctions need to be made between performance appraisal, performance development, and performance management. In this chapter, *performance appraisal* refers to the process of assessing performance in order to make decisions (for example, about pay increases). The focus is on assessment only; feedback about how the employee may improve performance may or may not be provided. *Performance development* refers to assessment of performance with the end goal of providing feedback to facilitate improved performance. The focus is on providing information that employees need to develop their skills, abilities, competencies, or behaviors in order to perform well in a current or future position. *Performance management* refers to a process that incorporates appraisal and feedback to make performance-based decisions and help employees improve their skills, abilities, competencies, or behaviors. When methods for monitoring the effectiveness of performance management (for example, tracking completion of steps required in the process) are added, the result is a performance management system that supports increased productivity and a quality orientation.

Gathering Input and Disseminating Information

It is essential to gather input and disseminate information from the very start of performance management system development through implementation. Input must be gathered to ensure that the system matches the organizational culture and business needs. The system needs to match the level of support for performance management in the organization, the extent of managerial experience with and expertise in performance management, and time frame constraints. Information about the system must be disseminated on an ongoing basis to ensure that there are no surprises regarding organization compatibility with decisions made during development of the system.

Project Teams and Team Responsibilities

If the performance management system is being developed for a relatively large organization, a team including representatives from each major function should be formed. If the organization is geographically dispersed, then team members should represent the various geographic locations. On-line meeting tools can be used to allow team members to participate without frequent national or international travel.

Each team member must be a strong participant so that the project may be completed with as small a team as possible. The larger the team, the more difficult logistics become. Team members should be selected based on their problem-solving ability, ability to communicate effectively, willingness to work with the team, and ability to take on three important responsibilities: provide input that represents their functional and geographic areas, disseminate information to and collect input from key stakeholders in their respective functional and geographic areas, and serve as champions of the performance management system. Each of these responsibilities is discussed in more detail in the following paragraphs.

Providing Input

First, team members must provide input that represents their functional and geographic areas. They should meet with executives, managers, and employees to determine the business needs and significant issues of their constituents and the feasibility of the primary components of the system. These must be addressed to ensure that the system is useful to, and therefore used by, these constituents.

A performance development system created for a large manufacturing organization with facilities across the United States offers a good example of how team members can gather information to determine needs, issues, and feasibility. The system was designed to provide performance development feedback to managers using confidential rating forms distributed electronically to the managers' manager, direct reports, peers, and customers.

Team members representing each of the functions and geographic areas initially gathered information from groups of managers and employees. Separate meetings were conducted with each group because each had different perspectives on the needs for, and issues associated with, a managerial performance development system. The information they provided allowed the team to address constituents' needs and issues in the system itself and in communications throughout the development and implementation phases.

Similarly, team members reviewed a draft rating form with constituent executives, managers, and employees to make sure it was readable and understandable. Changes were made based on their input, and the final rating form was again reviewed with constituents. Team members continued to gather information from constituents at each major step in the development and implementation process, including pretesting the delivery of the electronic rating form with managers and employees.

Disseminating Information

Second, team members need to inform key stakeholders in their respective functional or geographic areas of decisions made about the performance management system during its development.

Team members must also operate as intelligence officers, assessing and reporting back to the team the constituents' reactions to those decisions. This iterative process—initially collecting information on performance management needs and issues from constituents and then disseminating information to, and gathering reactions from, them—keeps the system in line with the organization's needs and issues and helps ensure that the end product supports the organizational culture. Without such ongoing information dissemination and gathering of reactions, unresolved issues stemming from decisions made during development of the performance management system could reduce the feasibility of the system or result in costly rework.

Another example taken from the managerial performance development system created for the large manufacturing organization illustrates the importance of disseminating information and continuing to gather reactions about a system's feasibility. Government agencies make up a substantial part of this organization's customer base. Team members from departments that have government customers found out and quickly reported back to the team that it was not appropriate to ask government agency representatives to complete the rating form. This information was obtained in time to make adjustments to the electronic system being designed to generate and process the rating forms.

Serving as Champions

Third, team members should serve as champions of the performance management system. They need to market the system to their constituents and find key stakeholders in their functional or geographic areas who will do the same. Champions are individuals who are respected in the organization and whose opinions are listened to. They are particularly important if an organization does not have a culture that strongly supports performance management. The champions' role is to communicate the value of the system to their peers, stressing how users will benefit from it and how obstacles to performance management are being addressed. One of these champions' key challenges is to win over antagonists and skeptics, so that even if these people do not become overtly enthusiastic about the system, they will at least keep an open mind about what can be gained from its effective use. If there are no such champions, it will be much more difficult to get managers to use the system.

Project Leaders and Their Responsibilities

In a relatively small organization, the person responsible for developing and implementing the system can gather the input and disseminate information about the system on an ongoing basis to key stakeholders. Regardless of whether this is done by a team or an individual, input from and ongoing communication to those who will use the system are necessary to meet the culture and business needs of the organization.

Making Key Decisions in Development and Implementation

The remainder of this chapter will provide practical guidance, based on lessons learned in business organizations, about key decision points in the development and implementation of performance management systems. A number of decisions have to be made during the process:

- Use of the performance information
- Frequency and timing of performance management activities
- Source of performance information
- Type of information collected
- Type of rating scale and form
- Calibration of performance ratings
- Type and frequency of performance feedback
- Mechanisms to ensure proper use of the system
- Monitoring of system effectiveness

Use of the Performance Information

The first step in developing and implementing a new performance management system, or in redesigning one, is to determine the primary use of the information obtained from it. Performance appraisal and performance development are both important. However, in many cases one system cannot support both equally well and still meet the organization's time and budget constraints. Therefore, it is important to determine the primary use of the information and emphasize it in the system. If this is not done, the system may turn out to be so cumbersome that either performance appraisal or performance development will be emphasized by default, or the system may simply collapse under its own weight.

A large, fast-paced, high-tech organization that tightly links performance to rewards provides a good example of why the two uses of performance information usually cannot be emphasized equally without overburdening the system. The organization has a strong performance-based culture, and a lot of time is given to appraising performance and ensuring that pay increases and stock option awards match it. Performance is appraised twice per year, and ratings for relatively large groups are required to meet a specified distribution. Managers assign a numerical performance rating to each of their employees and then meet with their peers and their own manager to calibrate ratings across managers and meet the required rating distribution. This process frequently takes several meetings, and hence a lot of time.

Managers then meet with each employee to discuss performance and how it links to that individual's pay increase and stock option grant. Performance development is important in this organization too, and during the meeting employees are supposed to get feedback on how they can improve performance and develop additional skills, abilities, and competencies. The range of percent increase and stock options is large, thereby allowing managers to link performance with rewards effectively. With so much at stake, most of the meeting is usually taken up with justification of the rewards allocated rather than a discussion of how the employee could develop. The climate of the meeting is not conducive to giving and receiving feedback, and therefore the development discussion is usually not effective unless conducted separately. Yet because managers have already spent so much time on the appraisal process, only rarely do they have separate development discussions. Thus, even in the strong performance-based culture of this organization one aspect of performance is, by default, given more emphasis.

If one system cannot support performance appraisal and performance development equally well, which use of the information should be emphasized? The answer is that the use most important to or most needed in the organization should be emphasized. For example, if it is important to link performance to rewards such as pay increases, then appraisal needs to be emphasized. Without an effective appraisal process, higher levels of performance cannot be linked to higher pay increases to provide performance-based pay. However, this does not mean that performance feedback must be overlooked. An organization emphasizing appraisal can supplement this emphasis with the clear expectation that managers must provide ongoing performance feedback.

In another organization, performance development may be more important. For example, if an organization's exit interviews reveal that a frequently cited reason for voluntary termination is lack of development opportunities, and if turnover needs to be decreased, it may be more important to emphasize performance development. A system could be implemented to increase feedback and facilitate development opportunities. Of course, this system needs to be supported by classroom, on-line, or on-the-job training opportunities.

It is critical to decide at the very beginning whether performance information will be used primarily for appraisal or for development. Exhibits 7.1 and 7.2 show how decisions about each component in the performance management process should be based on the intended use of the information. Exhibit 7.1 shows possible steps involved in developing and implementing a system that emphasizes appraisal for use in allocating rewards. Exhibit 7.2 shows possible steps in a system that emphasizes performance development. (The notion of appraisal purpose has been discussed at length in the literature, and interested readers are referred to Borman, 1991, and Murphy & Cleveland, 1995.)

Key decision makers and those responsible for developing a performance management system need to understand that the decision about the intended use of the information, and hence decisions about the components of the system, can become turning points not easily changed once development begins. The performance development process at the large manufacturing company mentioned earlier shows the importance of understanding the constraints imposed by the primary intended use of the performance information.

Exhibit 7.1. Performance Management System That Emphasizes Allocation of Rewards.

Frequency and timing of performance management activities: Appraisals completed in close proximity to reward allocation.

Source of performance information: Manager and self (overall performance, including performance to goals), direct reports (management behaviors), peers (teamwork), customers (customer service). Requires controlled information source.

Type of information collected: Metrics and judgment-based ratings, with behavioral examples to aid understanding.

Type of rating scale and form: Behaviorally anchored rating scales or 5-point scale with use of behavior standards. Short, user-friendly forms and accompanying materials.

Calibration of performance ratings: Very important to achieve accuracy and consistency.

Type and frequency of performance feedback: Throughout rating period, ongoing feedback using specific behavioral examples; weekly or biweekly, project update and performance discussions; end of rating period, performance discussion that includes examples of effective or ineffective behavior tied to reward allocation.

The executive management team's initial request was to create a performance development system for managers. The system was ready to be rolled out when the executive team changed the requirements, specifying that the performance information was to be used as one component of pay increase and succession planning decisions. A number of key decisions made during the system's creation were based on using the information for performance development, not appraisal. These decision points had to be revisited and the system substantially revised.

For example, it had been decided that managers would distribute the rating forms to their manager, direct reports, peers, and customers (if appropriate). This was less costly than creating an electronic list for the system to use to distribute the forms. Because the feedback was to be used by managers in their own development, they would have little motivation to "cheat the system" by distributing rating forms only to those who would give the most

**Exhibit 7.2. Performance Management System
That Emphasizes Development.**

Frequency and timing of performance management activities:
Performance development discussions conducted throughout year.

Source of performance information: Manager and self (overall
performance, including performance to goals), direct reports
(management behaviors), peers (teamwork), customers (customer
service). Control of information source of minimal importance.

Type of information collected: Written narrative description with
specific behavioral examples and judgment-based ratings to anchor
description.

Type of rating scale and form: Behaviorally anchored rating scales or
5-point scale with use of behavior standards. Short, user-friendly forms
and accompanying materials.

Calibration of performance ratings: Helpful but not essential.

Type and frequency of performance feedback: Throughout rating
period, ongoing feedback using specific behavioral examples; annually or biannually, development discussion that includes examples of
effective or ineffective performance and offers improvement and
developmental resource suggestions.

---

positive ratings. Further, because the performance information was
not to be used in making decisions, legal defensibility was not an
issue. But this distribution process had to be revised to meet performance appraisal requirements. This meant substantial repro-
gramming so that electronic lists, which were first approved by the
manager of the manager being rated, would distribute the rating
forms directly from the vendor to raters.

Frequency and Timing of Performance
Management Activities

The frequency and timing of performance management activities
should also be based on the planned use of the information. For
example, if emphasis will be given to performance appraisal and
performance will be linked with rewards, then appraisals should
be scheduled with the same frequency as reward allocation. The

appraisals need to be made in as close proximity to reward allocation as possible to reflect performance accurately and link it closely
to rewards. For example, if a pay increase is given once per year,
then appraisals need to be conducted once per year just prior to
the increase. If pay increases for all employees are given at the same
time throughout the organization, then all appraisals will have to
be completed in a relatively short period of time, putting a heavy
burden on managers with a large number of employees reporting
to them. Strong support of the performance management system
will be needed from top management down through all management levels. If the support is not there, it is unlikely the managers
will take enough time away from their other responsibilities to do
an effective job on the appraisals, which means that pay increases
may not be closely linked to performance.

If performance development will be emphasized, then development discussion meetings can be conducted throughout the
year. For example, development discussions could be held after an
employee has been in the organization (or position) for one year,
and then annually thereafter. Or they could be held following a
schedule based on the first letter of the employee's last name. This
kind of system spreads the discussions out throughout the year and
considerably lessens the burden on managers who have a large
number of employees reporting to them. However, a system will be
needed to remind managers when each employee is due for a development discussion to ensure that all occur in a timely manner.

Source of Performance Information: Managers, Direct Reports, Peers, and Customers

The source of performance information and how controlled the
input will be depend on both the intended use of the information
and the dimension of performance being rated. If the system will
be used for performance development, then control over information sources is relatively unimportant and information can be obtained from the manager, direct reports, peers, and customers of
the individual being rated. This type of data is particularly useful
for facilitating development of competencies and behaviors needed
to be successful in a given position. Because the performance information will be used by the individual who is being developed,

there is little motivation to "cheat" with selective input and little need to exercise control over the performance information source.

The performance dimension being rated affects the most appropriate source of information too. For example, peers and customers usually do not have sufficient information to provide accurate ratings of management behaviors such as goal setting or providing ongoing feedback to employees. The manager's direct reports are generally a more accurate source for this type of information. Similarly, direct reports and peers usually would not have sufficient information to provide an accurate rating of whether the manager met profitability and budget goals; the manager's manager is generally a good source for this.

If the system emphasis is on appraisal to be used in allocating rewards such as pay increases or stock option grants, then the individual's manager is usually the best source of overall performance information and the only accurate source of information about meeting goals. However, the manager can be encouraged to solicit input from other credible sources. For example, direct reports can provide information about management behaviors, peers can provide information about teamwork, and customers can provide information about customer service. In all cases, the manager should judge the credibility of information obtained from other sources. Multisource feedback provided by direct reports, peers, and customers can also be used, assuming collection of this information is controlled to prevent "cheating the system" with selective input. (For more information on multisource feedback see, for example, Bracken, Timmreck, & Church, 2000.)

Another source of performance information is input from the employee himself or herself. Employee input, or self-evaluation, has been used effectively in many large organizations and is particularly helpful when the emphasis is on appraisal. For appraisal, the input is probably best provided as statements of key accomplishments, then given to the manager who rates the employee's performance and comments on it. In one large organization, employees provide a written narrative of their most meritorious accomplishments and then managers review their narrative, verify its accuracy, and provide an overall rating. In another organization, managers simply edit employee narratives to reflect any changes they think are needed. In yet another organization managers verify whether they agree with the employee input and write a separate statement if they do not agree or want to add information.

Employee input usually has a number of positive results. First, it involves employees in the performance management process, which usually gives them a greater sense of ownership and increases their acceptance of the process. Second, it helps ensure that managers rate and discuss all key accomplishments made during the review period. Employee input helps avoid the unfortunate situation in which busy managers, who most likely do not take notes throughout the rating period, neglect to include a significant accomplishment simply because it occurred early in the rating period and they have forgotten about it. Third, employee input generally helps reduce the amount of writing managers have to do, minimizing the amount of time they have to spend on appraisal. The burden is spread out, making the overall appraisal process more manageable. Fourth, using employee input increases communication and discussion. In the examples just described, before employees' accomplishment statements become final, the manager and employee are encouraged to discuss them. This generally results in a better understanding of what the employee should work on and fewer disagreements between the manager's and employee's perception of the employee's performance. (For more information on self-assessment, see Smither, 1998.)

Type of Information Collected: Numerical or Narrative

The type of performance information to collect should also be based on the intended use. If the emphasis is on development, then narrative descriptions are usually the most useful. The descriptions should include specific behavioral examples to guide improvement activities. In addition to using a written description with specific behavioral examples, the manager and employee should discuss the examples to ensure understanding.

Judgment-based ratings, such as a rating on a 1-to-5 effectiveness scale, are also useful when development is the emphasis. Reviews conducted in two major companies have shown that raters vary greatly in the positive or negative focus of their written descriptions. An audit revealed very little relationship between what a manager wrote about performance and how that manager numerically rated the performance. Some managers focused primarily on positive examples of behavior that should continue, others on negative examples of where improvements were needed. A numerical rating helps anchor the narrative description.

A numerical rating also helps anchor verbal feedback. People generally hear information selectively, some focusing on the positive and others on the negative. An employee with a positive focus will hear verbal feedback quite differently than an employee with a negative focus. A numerical rating can help reduce misinterpretation.

To the extent the performance development system uses goal setting and specific action steps, numerical ratings become less important. For example, the process might be for managers and employees to work out goals and define the specific action steps necessary to achieve those goals. The specific action steps jointly developed by the manager and employee can replace the need for anchoring narrative descriptions.

If performance appraisal is the emphasis, then numerical data are essential. The data can consist of ratings based on judgments or metrics (for example, sales completed, costs reduced), or both. If, for example, an organization plans to link performance to rewards such as pay increases or stock options, numerical data are needed. A range of ratings or metrics can be linked to a range of rewards. Because of variability in content, narrative descriptions are obviously not useful in linking performance to rewards. Moreover, using narrative descriptions without numerical data is problematic because such descriptions sometimes reflect the motivation and writing skills of the manager more than the performance of the ratee.

Numerical data consisting of a combination of metrics and judgment-based ratings are particularly useful because they allow assessment of both whether an individual "made the numbers" and how he or she did it. For example, a system based on budget reduction metrics provides valuable information for appraisal, but it does not indicate the customer service and human impact of the reductions. Customer and employee ratings can supplement the metrics, allowing raters to determine if the reduction was done in a way that kept long-term negative impact to a minimum.

Narrative descriptions are also helpful in appraisals that will be linked to rewards. Narrative descriptions that provide specific behavioral examples can aid employees in understanding why they were rated at a particular level. Further, behavioral examples used in narrative descriptions can help managers calibrate their numerical ratings by allowing them to compare what they expect at a particular rating level with the performance other managers expect at that level.

Narrative descriptions can also help address concerns often heard about the use of numerical ratings. Even though numerical ratings are very important when appraisal is the emphasis of a performance management system, the decision about whether to use such ratings is frequently one of the most contentious issues in development of the system.

Those who argue against numerical ratings generally oppose them because of one or two primary concerns. One is that they focus attention on justifying the rating. The concern, for example, is that an employee meeting with his manager will spend the bulk of his time arguing about why he should be rated a 4 rather than a 3. One way to address this concern is to train managers to use narrative descriptions that include behavioral examples. These examples can help provide the specifics they need to explain definitively why their rating is 3 rather than 4.

Other concerns relate to legal defensibility and government audits—that the numbers provide data that can be examined for adverse impact of the appraisal process. This issue can be resolved in large part by training managers about rating errors and the implications of inaccurate ratings, and by reviewing rating distributions for potential adverse impact before the rating process is finalized. The possibility of legal challenges and government agency audits will still exist, but it will be substantially less intimidating when there is relative certainty that appraisal ratings accurately reflect performance for all employees and that rating distributions have been reviewed to catch potential issues before they become bigger problems.

Type of Rating Scale and Form

The use of the performance information—whether for appraisal or for performance development—does not have as much impact on choice of rating scale and form as it does on other decisions about the system. It is important to include a rating scale for both uses (although for different reasons, as noted in the preceding section), but one type of scale is not necessarily better for appraisal than for development and vice versa.

Five-point rating scales usually provide a sufficient range to distinguish levels of performance. Three-point scales require raters to make less fine distinctions in performance, and this is usually both a plus and a minus. For example, some raters will argue that it is a plus because it is quicker to make the rating; they simply determine whether an individual is above, at, or below some midpoint level of performance. Others argue that it is a minus because it does not allow them to differentiate levels of performance sufficiently, which is also a minus from a psychometric standpoint. With only high, medium, and low ratings, variability will be reduced and it will be more difficult to demonstrate a statistical relationship, for example, between performance and pay increase. It will also be more difficult for employees to see a meaningful relationship between performance and rewards. In contrast, a 7-point scale requires finer differentiation of performance levels than raters may be able to make. For example, most managers do not keep performance notes. Without notes about performance throughout the rating period, they may barely have sufficient information to rate employees accurately on a 5-point scale, much less a scale requiring fine performance rating distinctions.

Behaviorally anchored rating scales (BARS) provide a numerical rating and behavioral anchors. The specific behaviors used to anchor each numerical rating help clarify the level of performance each rating point represents, and therefore help increase accuracy and interrater consistency. However, to describe the level of performance at each numerical rating accurately, generally a BARS needs to be developed for each position or group of similar positions. As the similarity between the positions for which a BARS is used decreases, the behavioral statements that anchor the ratings need to be more general. The more general the behavioral statements, the less they describe the specific behavior needed to anchor ratings and therefore the less helpful they are in improving accuracy and interrater consistency.

It takes substantial resources to develop BARS anchors, which require generating behaviors for each rating point on each scale.

For example, a performance appraisal form might include a 5-point scale to assess teamwork, a scale for problem solving, and one for communication. Anchors are needed for each of the points on each of the three scales. Content for the behavioral anchors usually must be derived from input from managers or others who are subject matter experts about the position the BARS will be used for, and this requires a number of meetings. Each of the behavioral anchors must be scaled to verify that it accurately represents the level of performance for which it was developed. This involves subject matter experts allocating each anchor to one of the rating points on the scale. Because so much time is required for its development, BARS is usually used only when there are a relatively large number of incumbents for the position. Unless substantial resources (including time) have been allocated to creating a performance management system, it may not be feasible to develop BARS for a large number of positions or when there are only a few incumbents for one position.

If the performance management system is to be used for a number of distinct positions and there are insufficient resources to develop BARS for each, then behavior standards can be developed to supplement a rating scale. Behavior standards can cut across positions and therefore are much less resource-intensive to develop. For example, behavior standards were developed for use in a fast-paced, high-tech organization in which there were a fairly large number of positions, each of which had a relatively small number of incumbents and changed rapidly along with the rapidly changing industry. The number of distinct positions and the pace of change precluded development of BARS, but the behavior standards were quite effective.

The first step in creating the behavior standards in this organization was to determine the dimensions of performance for which the standards would be developed. Previously, twenty-nine competencies, or behavior dimensions (for example, "dealing with ambiguity"), important to success in the organization had been identified. Functional-technical knowledge and skills was added as a thirtieth competency to represent the specific knowledge and skills needed for each position or family of positions. Four levels of proficiency were developed for each of the twenty-nine competencies, and three to six bulleted behavior statements, or standards, were listed for each level of proficiency for each competency. For the functional-technical competency, four levels of expertise relevant across positions were developed ("general familiarity-skill," "working knowledge-skill," "strong working knowledge-skill," and "expert knowledge-skill"), and each level also had bulleted standards describing the level.

The organization's managers now meet with each employee at the beginning of the rating period to select and discuss the five to seven competencies most important to success in the employee's position and the level of proficiency required for each. This discussion sets expectations for performance and provides the foundation for appraisal at the end of the rating period. The standards are used to anchor the numerical rating and are customized to provide behavioral examples for the appraisal form and the performance discussion. The behavior standards for the proficiency levels below and above the required level of proficiency are used in discussing competencies for which the employee is performing below, above, or at the required level, respectively.

The form and related materials need to be short and user-friendly regardless of whether the system's emphasis is on appraisal or performance development. If managers are given a large amount of material they are likely to put it aside without reading or acting on it. The golden rule is to keep forms and written information to one page front and back and to present information primarily in bullet points. If the form looks too long or complex, managers are less likely to use it correctly (for example, by taking the time to provide the written information important for performance management) or at all. Many companies now use electronic templates for appraisal and development forms. This kind of form can be put on one user-friendly page but managers and employees can still write narrative information in boxes that expand to accommodate the length.

Accompanying materials also need to be short and user-friendly. For example, instructions should be presented as bullet points wherever possible, rather than in paragraphs. This makes them more straightforward and less time consuming to read, and therefore more inviting to those with little time to read lengthy documents. Materials such as behavior standards should be categorized in a way that allows managers to select from higher-level information and drill down to more specific information. Using an electronic medium, as described later, is an excellent way to present behavior standards since it allows a person to drill down easily to the necessary information without having to read a lot of information.

To keep the form short and user-friendly, it is important to evaluate carefully how many aspects of performance need to be rated. It can be tempting to include a rating of overall performance, ratings of various dimensions of performance (such as teamwork, communications, problem solving), and space to provide behavioral examples of each. If the form is completed correctly the employee gets the written behavioral examples needed to improve performance as well as a rating to help anchor the written information.

But problems are likely to arise with this approach. First, if a large number of specific performance dimensions or rating factors are included, the form will probably be quite long and therefore not very user-friendly. A reasonable number—that is, the number tolerated by raters in the organization—should be created to capture the most important aspects of performance. Different forms can be developed for major functions in the organization (for example, finance or information technology) or for groups of positions. Each form would include only the most important performance dimensions for that function or group of positions. In addition, using an overall rating along with ratings of performance dimensions can backfire unless managers are trained to provide the most accurate ratings possible on each dimension and overall. Managers and employees frequently jump to the conclusion that the dimension ratings are, or should be, weighted to form the overall rating. This is not the case, because it is rarely possible to develop an easy-to-use weighting algorithm that would apply to multiple positions. In addition, contrary to what managers usually think, weighted and unweighted dimension ratings tend to result in the same rank order of employees. Weighting dimensions adds administrative burden with no accompanying changes in overall results in the appraisal process.

An alternative to providing a large number of specific performance dimensions is to use one or two overall ratings of performance (such as quality of work and timeliness of work) and provide space for the manager to give examples of behaviors where the employee performed particularly effectively or ineffectively. When this is done, managers usually give examples for the dimensions that have the most influence on the overall ratings. This keeps the appraisal or development form short but also provides the specific information the employee needs to improve performance.

Another way to keep the form short and user-friendly is to use an electronic medium. Electronic performance management systems allow streamlined completion of forms. For example, if the system uses BARS or behavior standards for different positions, an electronic system allows the user simply to select a position or position family from a list to get the correct appraisal or performance development form. This alleviates the need to have multiple paper forms, thereby reducing the likelihood that incorrect forms (hence, incorrect behavioral anchors or behavior standards) will be used for an employee in a given position and eliminating confusion and extra work for managers and employees who will need to find and use the appropriate form.

Electronic forms can be automatically populated with data (such as sales information, time since last performance review, or last performance review rating), reducing the amount of time managers need to spend collecting information. They can also present behavior standards in a way that allows raters to navigate them quickly and use them efficiently. In most systems the rater can either select from a list of behavior dimensions or type in the name of a dimension, and the system provides behavior standards for that dimension. The rater does not have to read through a list of behaviors or even search through a document by category. The rater does not have to type the standard on the form, but instead simply clicks on a behavior standard to place it on the form and then customizes it for the given employee.

Calibration of Performance Ratings

The importance of calibrating ratings to facilitate accuracy and consistency between raters is determined by the primary emphasis of the performance management system. If the emphasis is on performance development, calibration is not as important as if the emphasis is on appraisal. However, as noted previously, ratings are useful in helping to anchor narrative descriptions. The increased accuracy and consistency achieved by calibrating ratings usually helps improve the quality of the ratings, thereby making them more useful in anchoring narratives.

However, if the emphasis is on appraisal, then it is very important to calibrate ratings. For example, if the system is used to make pay increase decisions and pay is to be linked to performance, then a rating made by one manager must mean the same thing as a rating made by another. If not, employees performing at different levels will get the same increase, and this will weaken the link between performance and rewards. The better the calibration process, the more effectively performance can be linked to rewards.

How can performance ratings be calibrated? Other than through the use of BARS, discussed previously, it is unlikely they can be calibrated by using a particular type of rating scale. For example, if a scale is used that measures the extent to which an employee met expectations, some way of calibrating the expectations of different managers is still needed. The expectations of one manager may be high and those of another lower, so employees will be rated in part based on a characteristic of their manager rather than solely on their own performance. The same problem of lack of consistency among managers is encountered if the system is based on setting objectives and rating accomplishment of those objectives. For example, if one employee's objectives are more difficult to meet than another's, and both employees meet them and therefore are rewarded with the same pay increase, performance has not been effectively linked to rewards. Without use of behavioral anchors, rating on a scale ranging from "very good" to "very poor" performance will also have this problem. The same issue comes up if the scale compares the employee to other employees rated by the manager, and this will also add the problem of memory accuracy to the rating process.

Besides BARS, another way to calibrate performance ratings is to have groups of managers (for example, all the managers in a given function or division) discuss their ratings and the level of performance required to attain those ratings. The managers would give examples of performance that resulted in various ratings. The examples would need to be specific descriptions of what employees did and did not do, so that other managers could compare this with the performance of the employees they rated.

Group calibration of ratings takes a lot of time and cooperation between the managers involved, and therefore is likely to work well only in organizations with a strong performance management culture. If the culture is not strong enough to support it, then either training or the behavior standards described earlier can be used to help calibrate performance ratings.

Type and Frequency of Performance Feedback

Ongoing behavioral performance feedback is important whether the emphasis is on appraisal or development. The system should encourage providing specific, constructive feedback in private about behavior that needs to be improved and following up on this feedback at the next performance discussion. The system should also encourage recognition of good performance on an ongoing basis. It takes only a little time to point out effective behavior, thus giving the employee useful performance information and most likely motivating him to continue the behavior. The system should also stress understanding each employee's needs and providing appropriate recognition. For example, some employees value a quick pat on the back and would be embarrassed by more extensive or public recognition. Others thrive on public attention that accompanies positive recognition and might be disappointed with minimal attention.

Managers will vary in their ability and commitment to provide ongoing feedback. Therefore, a performance management system, particularly one that emphasizes appraisal, should encourage one-on-one performance discussions between annual or biannual discussions. Such meetings allow managers to get project updates and to provide feedback before minor problems become major. They can be conducted weekly, or less frequently, depending on employee level and the type of work being performed. The performance management system should stress the importance of the one-on-one meetings and require managers to conduct them as scheduled, giving them the same importance as other high-priority meetings. The system should also stress the importance of discussing performance in these meetings, rather than only focusing on the project update aspect.

Managers will also vary in their commitment to conduct these frequent meetings. Therefore, whether the performance management system emphasis is on appraisal or development, it should include scheduled performance discussions every six to twelve months. If the emphasis is on appraisal, then managers should discuss the rating using examples of effective and ineffective performance and link the rating to reward allocation. If the system is used primarily for development, then managers should also discuss examples of effective and ineffective performance but put the greatest emphasis on improvement suggestions and resources.

If the organization has a strong performance management culture, the performance management system can specify conducting scheduled discussions every six months. This helps increase the likelihood that employees reporting to a manager who does not provide ongoing feedback or conduct the more frequent one-on-one meetings will get feedback in time to resolve problems or assist in development. However, if there is not strong support for performance management, or if business needs preclude frequent performance discussions, it is probably better to set the parameters of the system at less frequent intervals. This should increase the likelihood that performance discussions will be held according to those parameters. Employees will lose faith in a system that specifies parameters that are not met, and the credibility of the system and the performance management culture will be weakened.

The performance management system should also emphasize the importance of keeping notes of good and poor performance examples. The less frequent the performance discussions, the more important it is for managers to keep notes to help them provide behavioral examples useful in improving performance. Notes provide the information they need to give employees specific behavioral feedback. A large distribution company uses an electronic system that allows managers to record examples of good and poor performance directly onto an electronically generated monthly discussion form, and the performance examples are automatically populated into the annual performance evaluation form. The manager can revise the examples if necessary or use them as is on the annual evaluation form. This system makes it far easier for managers to keep notes on behavioral examples in a user-friendly, efficient way, thereby encouraging them to do so and improving the quality of performance appraisal. Other systems allow managers to keep behavioral examples for each employee in a system, then simply click to place the examples in the appropriate place on the electronic appraisal or performance development form.

Both verbal and written specific behavioral feedback should be provided in the annual or biannual performance discussions. However, many managers do not think of performance in behavioral terms. Therefore, providing behavioral examples of performance in written form is a particularly onerous and time-consuming task for them. In addition, most managers are already under tight time constraints. These two factors decrease the likelihood that quality behavioral examples will be used in written performance forms and performance discussions.

Managers are more likely to provide the specifics that will help employees understand and improve performance if they have example behavioral statements to use when completing the appraisal or performance development forms. Electronic tools that provide such examples can be developed or purchased. Some of those available for purchase can be customized (for example, by incorporating an existing form and using organization-specific terminology) and embedded in the organization's electronic performance management system. With these electronic tools, managers fill out the appraisal or performance development form by selecting topics from a list of performance dimensions. They click on the dimension that covers the performance to be noted on the form and are presented with example behavior statements, or standards. They select statements that best articulate the behavior to be noted on the form and then customize them to describe the employee's behavior most accurately. Some tools allow the manager to pick an approximate performance rating (such as high, medium, or low) and then select behavior statements representative of that level of performance.

These tools reduce the amount of time it takes to complete an appraisal or performance development form because they free the manager from having to write behavior statements from scratch. However, a frequent concern about these tools is that managers will produce cookie-cutter reviews. Tests at two large high-tech organizations showed that this is not the case. Managers do in fact customize the statements because they want to provide the specifics to give employees individualized performance information.

In addition to providing specific written behavior performance examples, the tools just described help prepare managers for the performance discussions. If they have behavior examples prepared, they usually feel more comfortable telling employees how their performance can be improved and are therefore more likely to have good discussions.

Electronic tools that facilitate use of specific behavior statements are expensive. If the budget is insufficient to implement one of these tools, example behaviors can be made available in other ways. For example, managers could use the type of behavior standards described previously, in which each of the competencies, or performance dimensions, is provided on a separate card. Managers simply select the competencies to be included on the appraisal or performance development form. Then they select the bullets that most accurately describe current performance and desired performance, customize these to reflect the specific performance of the employee, and include them on the form and in their discussion.

A Web site developed by a distribution company provides another example of how behavioral standards can be made available to managers and employees. This Web site displays the competencies that are important for success. Managers simply click on a high-level area of competency (for example, "leading people") and are linked to a list of specific competencies that make up that area (for example, "manages performance"). By clicking on one of the specific competencies, they can drill down even further to get specific behavior standards (for example, "establishes expectations and performance goals") that describe the competency.

Whether the behavior statements are available in electronic form or on cards that can be sorted to select the most appropriate ones, they provide quality information managers can use quickly and easily to help their employees improve performance. Employees too can use these behavior standards to develop skills and competencies. They can work with their manager to determine the most important competencies for their position and use the standards for that dimension to determine performance expectations and development needs. They can also work with their manager, a mentor, or other knowledgeable person to determine the skills and competencies required in another position they are interested in pursuing. Thus, the behavior standards empower employees to take charge of their own performance and career development.

Mechanisms to Ensure Proper Use of the System

One of the best ways to ensure that a performance management system is used properly is for top management to require it. If top managers champion the system and require its proper use, it most likely will be used properly. If they do not, the system is unlikely to live up to its potential, or worse, will not be used at all. A good example of this type of championing comes from the implementation of a new sales representative performance management system in a large distribution company. The most senior sales executive participated in each of a series of management and employee rollout meetings. He introduced the new system, stressed its importance, explained how he would be using and monitoring the system, and responded to tough questions about the new performance criteria in the system.

Top managers in the organization also need to support the system with their actions. This means they follow all parameters of the system and expect their direct reports to do so, and they include performance management as an important aspect in rating their direct reports. In a strong performance management culture, top management usually does this. The reverse is also true: if top management does this, over time a strong performance management culture is likely to be established.

Another good way to ensure proper use of a new or substantially revised system is to pilot-test it in a small part of the organization. A pilot test will show if it functions smoothly and efficiently or needs adjustments. It will show if managers and employees understand and support the process, or if further communication is needed. When a system is in actual use, it is easy to tell if managers and employees understand it and are using it properly. A pilot test can also provide an opportunity to collect information on reactions to the system, and examples of how managers and employees have used the system to improve performance. This information in turn can be used to market the system before its implementation in the rest of the organization.

Appropriate training of those who will provide performance ratings also helps ensure proper use of the system. For example, raters need to understand and support the philosophy and benefits of the system well enough to be motivated to use it effectively. They also need to be thoroughly trained in the importance of minimizing rating errors and rating inflation, and how to do this. They need to understand why ongoing, constructive, specific behavioral feedback is important and how to give it. (For a discussion on rater training see, for example, Smither, 1998.)

Various types of training can be used for performance management, and it is important to use the type most appropriate for the organization. Classroom training, job aides, or Web-based training can be used; each of these has pros and cons. The best type to use depends on the experience and expertise of the raters using the system, and the resources and level of support for performance management in the organization.

Requiring raters to attend classroom training sends a message about the importance of performance management. In addition, classroom training provides participants hands-on experience as well as an opportunity to interact with others and ask questions in a way they cannot with other forms of training. These benefits are particularly important for raters who do not have much experience with making performance ratings.

However, classroom training is costly. Participants need to take time away from the job, and probably for a longer period of time than if they completed the training at their own pace. It also requires participants to attend at specified times rather than complete training as they can best fit it into their schedule. Strong support from top management down through all levels of the organization is usually needed to get all raters to attend training. Even with strong support, it will be challenging. It is also challenging to cover all the material that needs to be covered in a couple of hours or one half-day, and it is very difficult to get raters to attend for longer than this.

Job aides are relatively inexpensive to develop and can be read at the participants' own pace and schedule. If they are succinct they can be very effective, particularly with raters who have a fair amount of experience in rating performance. Job aides can be used effectively as refresher training and can also be used to facilitate transferring knowledge acquired through other training media to the job. For example, a job aide can list in bullet point format key rating errors to avoid; this can be very effective when used during the actual rating process. However, job aides are less likely to be effective for raters who have little experience in making performance management ratings. It will be difficult to cover all the information a relatively inexperienced rater needs while keeping the job aide succinct. Also, as already noted, novices usually need some hands-on exercises to support learning.

Web-based training is costly to develop, and unless it includes a hot line or chat room it will not provide the same opportunity to ask questions and interact with other raters. However, it does allow participants to complete the training at their own pace and at a convenient time. Further, raters can use the Web site while making ratings, facilitating transfer of knowledge to the job. Sophisticated forms of Web-based training (for example, video streaming) can also incorporate hands-on exercises and rating scenarios.

Web technology also offers some other exciting performance management training possibilities, including communication and real-time feedback on quality of ratings. One organization is using a high-quality intranet Web site to offer widespread training about the benefits of a new electronic performance management system. The Web site employs user-friendly technology to explain what the new system offers managers and employees, how it makes performance management easier, and the importance of performance management to the organization as a whole.

The Web site is part of an overall electronic system that also provides real-time training to help mitigate rating inflation. As raters use the system their ratings are monitored, and they are then given on-line feedback about their rating behavior. For example, if a manager seems to be making rating errors, such as consistently rating at the highest levels, a dialogue box comes up on the screen reminding her to make sure she is rating both strengths and weaknesses. Different reminders appear on the screen depending on the rating patterns identified. This technology trains managers while they work, reducing the need for ongoing refresher training and assisting in transfer of knowledge acquired through other training media to the job.

Monitoring of System Effectiveness

Even if all the suggestions offered in the preceding sections are taken, the performance management system should still be monitored for effectiveness. One way to do this is to track performance management activities. For example, the system can require that completed appraisal or performance development forms be submitted to human resources after the annual or biannual performance discussion. If the organization has an electronic performance management system, the forms can be electronically signed and automatically forwarded to human resources, alleviating the need for paper copies.

Another method of monitoring the system for effectiveness is to have the next level of management review and approve completed appraisal and performance development forms. This can be effective if the manager's manager has sufficient information to evaluate the employees' performance and if the organization has a strong performance management culture. But if the next level does not have sufficient knowledge of employee performance to judge the quality of the information provided or if the organization does not have a strong performance management culture, then this kind of review is likely to be a "rubber stamp" process with little impact. Human resources can review forms for things such as narrative descriptions that match the numerical rating, positive or negatively biased ratings, and use of specific behavioral examples. If an electronic performance management system is used, then the forms can be automatically routed from employee to manager to second-line reviewer or human resources.

If the performance management system links appraisal to rewards, the system can be designed so that, for example, a performance rating must be entered into the system in order for a pay increase to be processed. The relationship between ratings and pay increases or stock option grants can also be monitored. With an electronic performance management system, overall ratings can be calculated and reports can be generated both at group (for example, the division) and at individual rater levels. These reports can help identify rating patterns that have an adverse impact on protected groups. They can be generated in real time to assist raters in the rating process or generated for review by higher levels of management or human resources before finalizing a performance rating cycle. When sufficient data are available, these reports can help identify and assist raters who seem to be rating overly leniently or severely.

Also, information can be gathered to understand manager and employee reactions to the performance management system. A special survey can be used to collect information about rater and ratee perceptions, or questions about the appraisal or performance development process can be included on the regular employee opinion survey. Focus groups can be conducted to discuss the system and gather specific information about what is working well or not working well, or anecdotal information can be collected about the system through interviews. This information can then be used to modify the system so that it becomes more acceptable to users.

Making the Right Trade-Offs

If high-quality performance information is to be obtained, psychometric criteria (for example, reliability, validity, and discriminability of ratings) must be met to the greatest extent possible in the performance management system. But although the system must be as psychometrically sound as possible, it also must meet the organization's culture and business needs. As already noted, it must match the organization's level of support for performance management, the extent of managerial experience and expertise with performance management, and the business need and time frame parameters. Thus, there are likely to be trade-offs to make between comprehensiveness and usability.

If a performance management system emphasizes psychometric soundness at the expense of matching the culture and business needs of the organization, it is likely to fail and its psychometric soundness will become moot. Once managers clearly understand the benefits of effective performance management and the organization develops a performance management culture, the complexity of the system and amount of time it requires can be increased. Managers will make time for a system that helps them improve their team's performance because it will help them do their job more effectively.

But if an organization does not have a strong performance management culture, a system that requires a short amount of time to administer may be necessary. In such a culture, managers are likely to view it as something over and above their "real" jobs and will be unlikely to allocate much time to it. It takes strong leaders and positive experiences with performance management to build a culture in which it is a central part of each manager's job. Until there is such a culture, it is better to take small steps than to implement a comprehensive time-consuming process that will not be used because managers do not take time to do so.

Similarly, if managers have little experience with performance management, it is prudent to start with a very straightforward, user-friendly system, even at the expense of comprehensiveness. If the system is perceived as too complex, or is too complex for the current expertise level, then it is unlikely to achieve the intended purpose. Managers will be unlikely to use it or will not be able to use it correctly.

If key decision makers allocate a specific amount of time to implement a performance management system, it is important to find a way to meet this deadline or negotiate for additional time. If the system developers explain the steps needed to develop a usable, high-quality performance management system, they may be able to negotiate a somewhat longer time frame. But it is important to remember that the decision makers who have authority to increase the time line often do not understand, and may not be concerned about, what must be done to develop a psychometrically sound, valid system. For example, they may support the time required to meet with managers from various areas of the company to determine needs and constraints, to pretest forms and communication materials, and to gain support from managers who will use the system. They may perceive this time as necessary to gain buy-in for the system. But they are not likely to understand or support studies to determine which performance components can be most accurately measured (for example, determining opportunity bias and criterion deficiency) and how these components should be weighted, or the degree of trust in performance management in the organization.

A performance management system that is not implemented in the allotted time frame runs the risk of being abandoned. This will leave individual managers or groups in the organization to create their own processes, or do nothing to manage performance. When individual managers or groups create their own processes it wastes resources through redundant activities and leaves the organization with inconsistent performance data that are difficult (at best) to use effectively throughout the organization. Rather than waste resources, have inconsistent data, or be left without a performance management system, it is better to start with small steps and work toward a more comprehensive and extensive system.

Developers of the performance management system will need to determine which trade-offs can be made. If too many are made or if the wrong ones are made, the system will not facilitate collecting accurate information. But if the developers are too inflexible, the system is also unlikely to succeed. System developers need to have expertise in both the psychometric requirements of a performance management system and the cultural and business constraints within which the system will work. This expertise will allow them to make the right decisions—difficult decisions, but ones that need to be made. If a system is as comprehensive as possible but also fits the organizational culture and business needs, then it can be expected to maintain and strengthen performance and thereby improve productivity and quality orientation.

References

Borman, W. C. (1991). Job behavior, performance, and effectiveness. In M. Dunnette & L. Hough (Eds.), *Handbook of industrial and organizational psychology* (pp. 271–326). Palo Alto, CA: Consulting Psychologists Press.

Bracken, D. W., Timmreck, C. W., & Church, A. H. (Eds.). (2000). *The handbook of multisource feedback*. San Francisco: Jossey-Bass.

Murphy, K. R., & Cleveland, J. N. (1995). *Understanding performance appraisal: Social, organizational, and goal-based perspectives*. Thousand Oaks, CA: Sage.

Smither, J. W. (Ed.). (1998). *Performance appraisal: State of the art in practice*. San Francisco: Jossey-Bass.

CHAPTER 8

Implementing Training
Some Practical Guidelines

Mark S. Teachout
Craig R. Hall

Estimates of the amount of money invested in training and development initiatives are substantial (Van Buren, 2001), with the top fifty training organizations alone investing over $5.3 billion in 2000 (Galvin, 2001). This investment reflects the value for their success that organizations have placed on training and development, a value that is supported by growing empirical evidence that training improves corporate performance (Huselid, 1995), including profitability (Bassi & McMurrer, 1999). Hence, training is a key element in a competitive business and human resource strategy, vital to achieving short-term business results, long-term development, and preservation of intellectual capital. With the large investment in training and the demand to remain competitive, there has never been a greater need for training programs to be implemented effectively.

A Working Definition of Training Implementation

The purpose of this chapter is to describe practical issues that are important to the successful implementation of training programs. Training affects almost all employees in an organization, from entry to exit—new employees learning skills for the first time, employees acquiring advanced skills as part of a learning path or because of a job change or promotion, employees being updated on new policies and procedures. Although significant learning occurs in many ways outside of formal, structured training (for example, challenging work assignments, job rotations), we will not address any of these areas in this chapter. Nor will we address broader educational or career development activities, career tracks, or learning paths.

There are many models of training (for example, Gagne, Briggs, & Wager, 1992; Dick, Carey, & Carey, 2001; Goldstein & Ford, 2002) as well as numerous books and articles on the technical aspects of training from a wide variety of perspectives. But our focus is on specific practical issues that contribute to successful training program implementation. The guidelines we offer are generally relevant, regardless of the reason for the training effort (for example, a new product or a new technology inserted into work processes) or the outcomes expected as a result of it (for example, increased sales or reduced time and cost). We draw on our experiences and the experiences of others to highlight the key factors that affect the value of the training investment.

We define training as a planned event intended to produce relatively permanent changes in knowledge, skills, or attitudes in order to improve work performance and organizational effectiveness. Because training is one of many interdependent subsystems in an organization that produce change, it is more difficult to define the implementation of training. We make a basic assumption that a successful training intervention will change on-the-job behavior in the intended way, will lead to positive changes in work performance and organizational effectiveness, and will be sustained for the intended time period. Because training is a systematic process, we attempt to delineate the key factors that increase or decrease the chances for that success throughout the process.

Training is one of several important change interventions that contribute to improved performance in the workplace. Like other change efforts, a successful training program alters tangible on-the-job behaviors of individuals. Unless individual employees change their behavior and do things in a new way, the training intervention will not have achieved its intended effect. Thus, knowledge is at a premium when it can be transformed into work performance that achieves business results.

The main reasons for implementing training are to respond to new products and services, to make big improvements in efficiency and effectiveness, to redesign jobs, and to infuse new systems and technology into the workplace. We believe that training, like other interventions, should be viewed through a "change lens" in order to achieve the desired change in individual on-the-job behavior and subsequent performance results. Hence, we view the training professional as a change agent as we examine training implementation.

The ADDIE Framework

Exhibit 8.1 depicts the framework we use to organize this discussion of the factors that influence training implementation. Although numerous models or frameworks could be used to discuss the factors that influence its success, ADDIE has been an accepted framework to understand and describe training because of its simplicity and acceptance by the instructional community. The five phases of the ADDIE model are depicted vertically down the left-hand column: *a*ssess, *d*esign, *d*evelop, *i*mplement, and *e*valuate. This is the sequence in which training projects generally unfold. First, a request for training comes from management in an operations area. Analysis—or assessment—determines the nature and scope of the problem. If training is part of an appropriate solution, further analysis may be required, and then the training is designed, developed, implemented, and evaluated. Although implementation is only one of the phases, its success depends on the activities in each phase of a training project. Hence, we use the ADDIE model as an organizing framework for our discussion of training implementation issues.

We use five factors to help focus on key issues of training implementation in each of the ADDIE phases. These factors are shown as column headings at the top of the exhibit. Two of them, *focusing on results* and *managing stakeholder expectations,* are relevant to most interventions, including training. We chose the two other factors, *instructional change* and *technology,* because they can drive significant change and innovation in training, creating the potential for stakeholder resistance but also offering the key to successful training implementation. The fifth factor, *sustainment,* is included to provide tips for longer-term success of the implementation effort. By necessity, some of the factors are given greater emphasis in certain ADDIE phases and less emphasis in others.

Focusing on results refers to the need to understand and define precisely what the training is expected to achieve, and often, what it will not achieve. Essentially, it is necessary to keep everyone's eyes on the ball by using learning and performance objectives.

Managing stakeholder expectations is a multifaceted concept. First, it means understanding all stakeholders' perceptions of the intervention's efficacy. That is, what do they expect will change as a result of training, and importantly, what do they think will not change? Second, stakeholders must understand the amount and type of effort it will take to make the intervention successful—the time and resources that must be dedicated to the project, as well as the physical and psychological change required on their part.

There are many different stakeholders, and they may be equally important inside and outside the training department. Stakeholder groups include management from the client area that requested the training, management and trainees from the client area that will benefit from the training, staff from such areas as marketing, and managers and employees who play a role in the instructional process in the training department, including vendors and consultants.

Instructional change refers to changes in instructional strategies, delivery strategies, and the learning environment. Of specific importance is the extent to which proposed changes differ from current practices. For example, changes in the way training is accessed can vary along several dimensions. There may be a shift from a single location to multiple locations, from an instructor focus to a learner focus, from one delivery medium to another, and from one learning environment to another. Changes in these dimensions signal the need for managing change.

We included a factor specifically on *technology* because of the increased emphasis on e-learning and some of the unique challenges in implementing technology-based training solutions. We define technology as a special subset of media that delivers instruction electronically, including traditional computer-based training (CBT), videoconferencing or teleconferencing, teleclasses, and Web-based instruction. All have a host of support requirements, their development consumes technical resources, and their use usually requires extra training for those stakeholders involved in operating and maintaining the technology.

Exhibit 8.1. The ADDIE Framework.

	Focusing on Results	Managing Stakeholder Expectations	Instructional Change	Technology	Sustainment
Assess	What is the business need? Are appropriate measures of success defined? What are the expected results? What are the potential solutions?	Are expectations realistic? Who has a stake in changing versus maintaining the status quo? How will the client need to change? What training personnel are associated with the change?	What are the current training norms, resources, staffing, and skill levels? How might past practices affect the potential strategies, delivery methods, and learning environment?	Will new technology be used? How? Have life-cycle costs been determined? What are the expected benefits of using the technology?	What is the implementation plan? Will prototypes be used to train the implementation staff?
Design and develop	Does the evaluation strategy match the expected results? Has a formative evaluation been conducted?	Will instructors have to change the way they currently train? Will students be expected to change the way they learn? Will stakeholders be involved in formative evaluation?	What changes will take place? Will stakeholders be engaged in the process?	Will the technology be compatible with the current infrastructure? Are adequate resources available to develop and maintain the technology?	

Phase							
Implement	Have realistic criteria for success been defined? Has a pilot test been conducted?	Were stakeholders involved in pilot testing? Was the scale of the implementation manageable?	Will support be provided for instructors and learners?	Was support provided for instructors and learners? Was feedback obtained from instructors and learners?	Were prototypes used for formative evaluation?	Was technical support provided for correcting bugs? Were instructors prepared to use the technology appropriately?	Were the new processes transitioned from implementation staff to sustainment staff?
Evaluate	Was the training implemented as planned? Were the intended results achieved?	Were data collected from each stakeholder? What worked or did not work for each stakeholder? What stakeholders can be used as champions?		What worked or did not work, and what needs to change?		Were the anticipated benefits realized?	Were the new processes and instruments transitioned to the sustainment staff? Have evaluations been conducted to determine if operational adjustments are needed?

The fifth factor, *sustainment*, is included to highlight the activities necessary for the long-term success of the program. In summary, each cell of Exhibit 8.1 contains a brief depiction of the key issues and questions that must be considered in order to improve the chances for the successful implementation of training.

Assess

Successful implementation begins with the initial response made to a training request. It sets the tone for the relationship with the client, and whether the training professional will be seen as an order taker who delivers training or a problem solver who can develop performance-based solutions. The latter role is desired, because it is a position of greater influence and increases the chances of successful implementation.

The assessment phase is often cited as the source of success or failure in training initiatives. If analysis is insufficient, training efforts are often misdirected and fail to produce intended results. But people are often unavailable to spend time on analysis. The organization's culture and established habits influence perceptions about analysis and how to conduct it.

There are two areas of analysis in the assessment phase. The first is performance analysis, where the nature of the desired performance is described, the sources of performance problems are identified, and potential options are prioritized for further analysis. Assuming there is a need for training, further analysis is conducted to identify the component skills and knowledge associated with desired performance.

Performance analysis is usually challenging because there are substantial barriers to doing it. Rossett (1999) points out that analysis is a difficult activity to justify because it does not have the same appeal as a concrete activity like training. Clients tend to prefer simple solutions rather than commit scarce time and resources to studying a problem. Measurements to quantify performance problems are often missing, precluding a tangible way to measure the positive impact of solutions, even training solutions. The analysis process is often misunderstood even by those who benefit from it.

Focusing on Results

We indicated that it is crucial to focus on performance and business results early in the client engagement, setting the expectations for what the training is supposed to accomplish. Many clients have difficulty specifying results that are clear and measurable, so it is essential to be skillful in eliciting requirements. Exhibit 8.2 provides an example of a "value chain" linking learning to performance to business needs. This format has been advocated by Robinson and Robinson (1995), and it is a convenient way to convey to the client the work environment changes that will be required in addition to training in order to achieve the performance and business results.

During the assessment phase, failure to identify both specific business needs and specific measurable desired results will have a cascading, detrimental impact on the implementation. There will be an inability to focus the intervention, an inability to measure results, and too often an implementation that does not solve the problem or fill the need.

At this early stage it is critical to make sure there is a sharp focus on the expected results—that is, what people will be expected to do as a result of the training. Then, client expectations must be managed in that direction. After a performance analysis has determined that there is a need for a change in knowledge or skills, and that training is an appropriate way to accomplish it, then a deeper analysis should be conducted to identify the knowledge and skills to target. Whether or not a thorough performance analysis has been accomplished, two issues frequently arise that must be managed. First, clients often make requests for knowledge-based training solutions, when in fact they really expect people to be able to perform differently. Training professionals frequently hear: "I think they need to know this." Unchecked, this will result in a laundry list of topics that clients believe each employee needs to know. Worse, the focus is on what people need to *know* rather than on what they need to *do*. Second, many clients make requests to teach their employees knowledge in a classroom setting when the information is already available in other locations, such as on-line help systems. That is, it can be *accessed* elsewhere. To avoid or overcome these two common issues, we developed a simple approach illustrated in Exhibit 8.3. First, we focus clients on what employees need to be able to do to be successful on the job. This avoids premature

Exhibit 8.2. Examples of Needs for an Information Technology Service Center Help Desk.

Business Needs	Performance Needs	Learning Needs	Work Environment Needs
Improve service levels from 78 percent to 85 percent of calls within thirty seconds.	Reduce average call time and increase phone availability.	Learn proper use and time-saving strategies using four service center technology applications.	Communicate results of benchmarking studies to management team.
Increase first contact resolution rate from 79 percent to 85 percent.	• Document calls completely and accurately.	Learn correct call documentation sequencing and problem description.	Management must set expectations for performance and business results.
Maintain high customer satisfaction rating of 4.5 out of 5.0.	• Use service center technology to prefill screens and to identify the problem faster.	Learn how to analyze customer problems using two technology applications.	Management must establish incentives and consequences to encourage and reinforce the use of troubleshooting tools, and to reduce interruptions.
	• Listen for key words to identify problems, context, and solutions.	Learn effective troubleshooting and questioning techniques.	
	• Use effective questioning techniques to narrow the problem.	Learn customer service standards and practices.	Experts must be available to troubleshoot unique and difficult problems.
	• Reduce interruptions of coworkers.	Learn correct transfer procedures to experts.	Management must ensure employees are aware of standards and goals, customer satisfaction, and monthly call and resolution rates, and are provided performance feedback.
	Practice professional courtesy standards at all times.		
	Transfer documented calls to the proper field support expert in a timely manner.		

knowledge-only solutions that are not linked to the specific performance changes desired. Once we gain agreement on what employees must do, we can then determine what they need to know versus what they need to access through job aids or performance support systems in order to do the job. These distinctions help to overcome the expectation that a list of topics will be taught, independent of performance expectations. Again, there is often an expectation on the part of clients that simply imparting knowledge to the individual will change his or her on-the-job behavior and improve performance. Usually there is a need to focus and refocus the attention of others on the desired performance and business results expected from the program. This simple yet powerful approach helps to manage client expectations and provide a sharper focus on the desired performance expected as a result of the training while avoiding a common pitfall of focusing on knowledge only. The distinction between do, know, and access is also important for the choice of instructional strategy and delivery methods in later phases.

It is also vital to identify solutions that would complement the training intervention or would meet the business need without a more costly and time-consuming training intervention. The following example illustrates why other solutions must be identified— because some clients believe that training is a universal solution.

We received a request for a refresher training program to increase sales of a specific product. We asked the client if he knew whether the poor sales had resulted because the workers did not know the products or did not have the sales skills, or for some other reason. The client did not know and accepted our offer to determine the cause so we could tailor the training to the workers' needs. A simple analysis revealed that they knew the products and had the skills, but the organization gave them no clear expectations for selling the product and no information about sales results at the individual level. Yet the client still insisted that we train his staff. After some discussion, he reluctantly allowed us to try something else as long as we agreed to conduct the training as well. We trained two units, while to two other units we gave clear expectations, measures, goals, and feedback but no extra training. Then we compared the two groups' sales results. Over a two-week period both groups increased sales, but the nontraining group improved at a much higher rate than the group that received the extra training. We

Exhibit 8.3. Example of Do-Know-Access Framework for Establishing Employee Development Plans.

Do: What tasks do managers need to do to be successful?	Know: What do managers need to know in order to do the tasks successfully?	Access: What resources can managers access to complete the tasks successfully?
Gather information to create performance objectives for employees.	• Operational goals • Skills employees need to meet the goals • Performance standards that the employee must maintain	• Operational business goals • Input from employees • Performance standards • A list of action verbs for defining objectives • Examples of company objectives
Discuss and document the objectives with each employee.	• Active listening techniques. • Questions to elicit input from employees • How to link objectives to organizational performance measures	• Examples of effective listening techniques and role modeling • Instructions for documenting objectives • Examples of linking individual objectives to performance measures
Establish employee development plans.	• Skills necessary for future performance • Skill development strategies • How to assess current employee skills and identify gaps	• Skill development road map • Tools for standardized skill assessment and gap analysis • Employee current performance evaluation and ratings
Document development plans.	• Where to find development plan templates on the intranet	• Intranet Web site

then implemented these simple procedures in other areas as well, and obtained similar results.

Thus we can often get very powerful results with performance solutions that do not include training, but this requires performance analysis and the ability to influence a client toward performance-based solutions. Ultimately, the client must be willing to participate actively in the solution.

Managing Stakeholder Expectations

Perhaps the greatest challenge to effective training implementation is managing stakeholder expectations. A stakeholder is anyone who has a vested interest in the outcome of the training or the development of the training, or whose resources may be used or affected by the training. We will focus on stakeholders in the client area (clients who request the training and whose personnel are affected by it) and stakeholders in the training department (those who will manage, develop, and implement the training).

Client stakeholders often overestimate the amount of change that can realistically be expected from a training intervention and underestimate the amount of change and effort that they need to make to achieve the desired results. One consulting tactic that has been used successfully to manage unrealistic expectations is the "crystal ball" technique (Tannenbaum, 1997). This involves asking the client to envision a hypothetical scenario in which both parties agree that the training provided is outstanding, yet the expected results are not obtained. The client is then asked to identify reasons why this might occur. An illustration follows.

A senior leader from a large multinational company sponsored an executive development program for managers worldwide. Participants from various business units were taught global marketing approaches. To allow immediate practice and encourage future interactions with fellow trainees, participants would visit a country and gather field data about a product line. They would then make recommendations about how to improve market penetration. Importantly, the product line and market were both outside the responsibilities of their own business units.

The senior sponsor expected the program to help the company gain market share in the country under study. Although this was a worthy goal, it was an unrealistic expectation for the program because program participants could only provide advice to the leaders in charge of the product line under study and had no ability to ensure follow-up or implementation. After using the crystal ball technique and after further discussion, the senior sponsor acknowledged that limitation and revised his expectations accordingly. He said that he expected "program participants would provide useful ideas about the market under study and would apply some of the global marketing approaches to their own markets." At that point, the program objectives and the sponsor's objectives were consistent and realistic. A follow-up evaluation revealed that the sponsor's two expectations were fully met, and as a result the program was extended.

The crystal ball technique permits training professionals to manage expectations in two important ways. First, it helps stakeholders focus on what they can reasonably expect from training alone. This avoids misunderstandings later in the process and possible conclusions that the training was unsuccessful. Second, it can open up a discussion about the other things that must be done (usually a change in work environment factors) in order to obtain the desired business results.

Client stakeholders often underestimate the amount of effort, commitment, and change they will need to make to achieve the results intended by the intervention. Sometimes they have a greater stake in maintaining the status quo. Although there are a host of strategies to use to overcome this kind of resistance, it usually requires involving strong senior management and managing expectations at all levels of the organization. The following is a good example.

A large company's information technology (IT) department was implementing a basic project tracking procedure for its large software projects. The company wanted the employees to record their time against projects accurately so that senior management could determine time allocation and budget information, enabling them to improve resource planning.

An IT team created a training intervention on how employees should report their time that emphasized the need for accuracy. This team then asked the training department to deliver the training to IT employees in the company in a short time frame.

The training department responded immediately. In the first two sessions, student feedback indicated that they believed their managers did not want them reporting their time accurately because it would increase the managers' accountability for project costs, reduce their flexibility in assigning resources, and require them to improve the accuracy of estimating resource requirements. The training was suspended when the training personnel and members of the IT development team who attended these sessions agreed that other action was needed.

After consultation with senior management, the training sessions for the employees were canceled, but training was initiated for mid- and front-line managers to teach them what they would be accountable for and that they would be rewarded for accuracy. The training department trained the managers, and then the managers were required to train their employees on the new procedures, emphasizing the importance of reporting time accurately.

This anecdote illustrates several key issues. First, resistance to change may come in many forms and may be undetectable until implementation is attempted, thus reinforcing the need for a thorough front-end performance analysis. Second, the amount of effort and commitment in this case was greater than senior management (project sponsors) and training personnel realized. Knowing how to report time was only a small piece of what was necessary for the IT department to obtain the performance it needed from employees. The right incentives had to be put in place for the employees, but there also had to be strong expectations and incentives for the managers to provide an accurate accounting of project costs.

It may be equally important to focus on stakeholders in the training department during the assessment phase. Stakeholders who will be associated with the anticipated change may be identified. For example, training designs that incorporate new methods or technology often involve substantial changes from past practices in the training department. It is as important to influence the people in the training department—instructors who must implement new strategies, for example—as the clients. These training personnel will help make the transition from established conventions to new instructional strategies or media. As we will discuss later, stakeholders should be given opportunities to be part of the design and testing of training prototypes during the later phases of design and development. If they are part of the process, it will lay the groundwork for the necessary changes to occur. They can try it out, overcome their perceptions of its complexity, establish its relative advantage over past practices, and develop a sense that it is compatible with their own instructional preferences. At this early stage, it is particularly important to identify the stakeholders who are held in esteem by their peers because they will help to influence others later in the process.

Instructional Change

The assessment phase is also the time to assess the norms, resource requirements, staffing and skill levels required to develop and implement the intervention. This will help to determine how the proposed instructional strategies, delivery methods, and learning environment may differ from existing practices. For example, trainers will be affected if training methods shift from instructor-focused to student-focused strategies. With instructor-focused strategies, the instructor has substantial control over the timing and delivery of content, such as in a lecture-based class. In contrast, a student focus means that learners select the content and control the pace of learning. A student focus tends to put more responsibility for learning on the student, such as with self-study. Between these two extremes are blended tactics, where instruction includes use of self-study methods for acquiring basic conceptual knowledge and work with instructors for more complex skills involving analysis, problem solving, and so on. Blended approaches can save money by using self-study materials for simple learning outcomes. Students are then free to learn only the parts that are new to them while skipping what they already know. Later, the students work with instructors to apply what they have learned to more authentic job scenarios. Instructors do not need to spend time teaching basic skills and can devote more time to helping students develop advanced skills.

Despite the ostensible advantages of such strategies, instructors will not automatically accept them. For example, a company decided to implement computer-based simulations to teach work flow procedures involving the use of computer applications. The simulations were intended to free instructors from lengthy demonstrations and to let students practice the procedures before moving to more complex tasks. Instructors were initially skeptical about using simulations, claiming that they could more effectively answer students' questions as they demonstrated the procedures on the live system. After they had a chance to observe students using the simulations, they acknowledged that students benefited from practice opportunities. But they still expressed discomfort about the loss of control of the lecture situation. In this case, assessment of instructors' preferences would have alerted the instructional designers to include instructors early in their design decisions, and during the development phase when they could try out prototypes of the simulations to become more familiar with their instructional potential.

Technology

During the assessment phase it is premature to select a specific instructional strategy or delivery methodology. But it is typical for clients to request or specify a delivery method, such as instructor-led classroom or Web-based delivery. The training professional may have a good idea that the training is a good candidate for Web-based delivery. This would be the case, for example, if the audience is large and geographically dispersed, the content is relatively stable, the time line is urgent and prohibits the scheduling of facilities and instructors, and the needs are more knowledge-based than skill-based. Because clients are prone to be oriented to solution and delivery, training professionals should be prepared to begin addressing questions about potential technology solutions, focusing on the criteria for making delivery decisions and highlighting the challenges and potential benefits of the technology. Also, they can begin to plant the seeds of life-cycle costs, including support and maintenance requirements for technology. Knowing that these discussions are often unavoidable, the challenge is to keep the "horse ahead of the cart" and remind clients that it is premature to make a final decision on the method of delivery at this time.

Design and Develop

The design phase focuses on the design and development of content in support of specific learning and performance outcomes.

Focusing on Results

Often training professionals develop test materials as a final step, after the content is developed. Occasionally, these materials are developed just-in-time, after a course has been launched but before the scheduled evaluation. We advocate a simple approach: develop the test first. Once the objectives are finalized, the evaluation materials can be developed at the inception of the design phase. This provides a target for success, and there is a greater likelihood that the tests will end up evaluating the right objectives. We have seen many instances where the evaluation fails to match the learning and performance objectives. Although the evaluation measures may need to be adjusted later on, developing them first helps to focus on the intended results and obtain input from stakeholders early in the process.

Managing Stakeholder Expectations

Trainers can prepare for implementation during the design phase by anticipating how the instructional design will affect current training practices. Although the assessment phase sets the stage for design and development by identifying performance goals and potential solutions and stakeholders, the design phase matches instructional and delivery strategies with desired outcomes. The development phase then builds the instruction and tests it for accuracy and usability. Along the way, the stakeholders identified during the assessment phase should be included in design decisions and product testing so that they will adopt the training. If it is not practical to include more than a few key stakeholders during the design phase, then evaluations of the instruction can be used to get stakeholder input. Where feasible, prototypes of the instruction can be used during the development phase to correct design flaws and omissions. This allows stakeholders to try out the instructions, provide input, and gain ownership.

When to include specific stakeholders depends on how the new training design will affect them. Stakeholders may be instructors, students, business managers, and technology staff. Some rules of thumb for identifying which stakeholders to include in design and development are outlined in the next sections.

An important question is whether instructors will have to change the way they currently train. In the training organization, the instructors are the primary stakeholders in instructional delivery, and they will be the ones to accept and effectively implement the new training. Those who are used to having control over the timing and delivery of content often find it challenging to adopt new instructional methods. Implementation success depends on how well they accept the training and the responsibilities associated with sustaining it and making it effective.

Regardless of the strategies employed, if they involve a shift away from established instructional practices, instructors should be allowed some participation in the design process. Early involvement in design decisions will give them a sense of ownership and opportunities to reflect on how they can incorporate the new methods into their daily practice.

It is important to look for wide variance in the way the same course is currently taught across an organization. Instructional methods or strategies may differ in their sequencing of events or the media used to support specific instructional objectives. If the methods appear to be tied to individual styles, then the instructional staff could reject new methods.

In many training organizations instructors develop their own content and strategies for the courses they deliver. A course may feature lectures, electronic media, paper-based materials, in-class activities, and more. Moreover, the delivery sequence usually mirrors the way the instructor believes the content and objectives should be organized for the benefit of the students. Instructors take pride in their strategies and often spend many hours developing and refining them. When someone else comes along with a new way to do it, the personal teaching philosophies that they have developed may be threatened. They may question the rationale for the scope and sequence of the new course and how any new media could be an improvement over their own selections. They may resent having to learn and use procedures for operating new technology. Instructors will need to be involved in new instructional designs so they can develop a feeling of ownership about them. In organizations where the design and development roles are separate from the delivery roles, delivery personnel should be involved in evaluating prototypes of the training during the development phase so they can see the utility of the new instruction and become comfortable using it.

For example, there was variability in the way instructors were training entry-level employees at one company, although the traditional lecture format was used by all. To reduce time and make the instruction more consistent, interactive Web-delivered training was designed to teach basic knowledge and skills. Students used the Web-based instruction in one-hour sessions, which were interspersed with instructor-led classes where they were prompted to apply their knowledge in ways that were relevant to their jobs. Only two of the seven instructors were involved in the design and development of the training. When it came time to implement the new training, the instructors who were not participants in the project expressed doubt about the utility of the strategy during train-the-trainer sessions. During postimplementation evaluations, they were found either to have adopted only parts of the strategy or not implemented any of it, while reporting that they felt their students preferred the lectures over the Web-based training. In contrast, the two instructors who had been on the design and development teams implemented the strategy with substantial success. Both indicated that their success was attributable to the insights they gained from thinking about how to implement the instruction while considering its design. During development they were able to appreciate the instructional utility of the software as they observed target learners using developmental prototypes.

Another important issue is whether students will be expected to change how they learn. If they are expected to take more responsibility for learning than they did in the past, or to put in more effort, such as with self-study, then their expectations will have to be managed too. Traditional classroom instruction is convenient, often seen as a break from work. Managers like it because they do not have to assist with training. Employees disappear into the classroom and then reappear in the workplace. Accountability for training stays in the classroom, with the training department. In contrast, when the same instruction is available electronically, employees can access it at any time, and accountability for learning shifts to the employees. Instead of disappearing from the workplace for hours or days where instruction is managed for them, they must now manage their own time and motivation to complete the program. Organizations are finding that employees tend to drop out of on-line instruction more frequently than classroom-based instruction. A successful transition from classroom to Web-based instruction usually involves more than simply transferring the content on-line. Employees need support while they study on their own. They also need to be able to do it without workplace distractions. Managers who accepted the notion of formal classroom instruction might not understand when an employee takes time to study independently. Top-down management support is required to overcome this cultural change, and specific strategies that permit a self-study approach must be adopted.

Instructional Change

Implementation of new training methods may be compromised if people have not been adequately prepared for changes in the way training gets done. One way to figure out how much effort will be needed to prepare an organization for new training methods is to compare the proposed designs with existing instructional strategies, delivery methods, and learning environments. Then, there are several questions to ask.

Will new training designs change the location and style of the environment? For example, will students attend a video- or teleconference in small groups instead of live lectures in large groups? Will employees do self-study at the workplace rather than travel to a distant office for a weeklong course? Changes in learning environment can affect the quality of learning that takes place there. For example, in one department in a large company management decided to eliminate the expense of having training rooms elsewhere on the company grounds. They chose a conference room in the work area, believing that its comparable size and layout would preserve the original training environment. The room's proximity to the work area, however, and its glass wall, enabled managers to spot and retrieve trainees from class for job tasks. Trainees also got involved in work during breaks, returning to class late or not at all. They reported having difficulty concentrating on learning when they could observe the work area from the classroom.

Another thing to consider is whether the logistics of scheduling, developing, delivering, and maintaining the instruction will change. For example, a company's trainers located at remote offices were accustomed to developing their own materials for companywide courses that were managed from a central office. Management decided to consolidate all design and development of instruction at the company's central office, while restricting remote offices to delivery only. When the central office redesigned portions of company courses and distributed them to the remote locations, the remote instructors responded with sharp criticism to the content and instructional design. Follow-ups with instructors found that they resented what they perceived to be a loss of the central office's trust in their ability to develop and deliver their own content.

It is also important to be alert to instructional strategies that rely on personnel not previously associated with training. Training implementation requires coordination of various support roles. If personnel outside the training department are expected to take on new training tasks, then their expectations about responsibility and effort will have to be managed. For example, will workplace employees or managers provide mentoring to facilitate transfer of new skills for training graduates? Will managers take a more active role in monitoring learner progress in the workplace? Will they have to use new procedures and tools to carry out support roles?

Technology

Will technology that is new to the organization be used to deliver training? Computer-networked technology has become a popular medium for delivering training. Although the benefits can be substantial, this technology usually requires special skills to implement and support. If using technology is a change in the way training is conducted, it can be one of the biggest adoption challenges because it affects several dimensions of the way training is accomplished. In addition, it must usually be integrated into an organization's existing technology infrastructure.

If it contains new training methods, technology-based training will pose challenges for both instructors and students. The human-computer interface adds a level of complexity because learners have to adjust to the navigational conventions of the interface, learn how the content is organized, and become familiar with learning strategies incorporated in the design.

The crucial technology issues, however, are compatibility with the organization's current technology and stakeholders' expectations of its usefulness. New technology-based training comes with a host of support requirements. Its development consumes technical resources. Its use involves extra training to operate and maintain it. Despite the technical issues of supporting it, however, its most daunting aspect can be the extent to which people form unrealistic expectations about its potential to improve instruction and performance. The main reason for using technology is to increase efficiency or output while maintaining or reducing costs. The quality of learning can also improve, but that depends on how easy it is to operate the technology and how well the instructional content is designed to facilitate the expected learning outcomes.

Despite the risks of implementing technology, its operation and effect on training can be validated through formative evaluations using prototypes. Prototypes can address several issues. First, instructors get a chance to try out the technology and become familiar with its instructional potential, which sets the stage for subsequent adoption. Second, it is less expensive to redesign and rebuild simple prototypes than a more complete system. Third, the technology can be tested to see how it can be integrated with the organization's current technology. Finally, unforeseen support requirements often come to light during testing.

Technology development budgets should allow for substantial formative evaluation of prototypes as well as extra technical resources. Development staff that have appropriate experience and training for the computer technology involved should always be used. Prototypes should be used to run tests of the technology on the target support systems to make sure there is sufficient bandwidth, software, and hardware infrastructure. And when technical staff are involved in the prototype testing, they can rapidly make corrections and observe how the learners interact with the technology.

Sustainment

The implementation plan also requires planning and design. The key issue here is how the training will be successfully sustained over time. The plan will depend on the complexity of the instructional design and the technology used for content delivery. The same people who designed and developed the training will probably have a role in implementing it. In most cases, the success of new training methods depends on innovators who develop and begin the training implementation. They usually get things up and running, iron out bugs, and figure out how to overcome difficulties. At some point, this knowledge must be transferred to those whose responsibility it is to run the training after the innovators leave.

For example, a community college was experiencing a high failure rate in its math courses. Students found the classroom environment intimidating and the lecture format boring. An instructor who had experience with a similar student population recommended that the students needed more personal attention and would respond better to interactive instruction that they could follow at their own pace, without fear of embarrassment for asking questions. What was needed was a way to increase interaction with instructors and with the instruction.

A project was initiated with performance expectations of increasing the success rate of math students and increasing transfer of basic math skills to advanced topics. Interactive software for teaching basic math skills was made available in a laboratory setting. Several adjunct faculty were included in the project and later staffed the lab to provide learning support. When a student fell behind, a teacher could intervene and diagnose where he or she was having trouble. However, students needed to have immediate answers, which put high demands on attending staff. Without immediate answers, the students gave up.

Despite its initial success, student performance eventually returned to its low level because the team had to turn the operation over to disinterested faculty who were not willing to relinquish the control they had in more traditional classroom settings. An implementation plan was needed to transfer the skills, knowledge, and commitment of the innovators to a permanent and receptive operations staff.

The moral of this story is that staff must be engaged and trained to carry out and support the instruction after initial implementation. If instructors and support staff get involved early they can see how the new instruction will affect operations. Instruction prototypes can be tested with target learners. At least one test of the full suite of the instruction should be conducted, with delivery and support staff given the opportunity to apply new procedures and skills for supporting learners. Importantly, all participants need to know what the new approach is intended to improve, where the gains will be made, and why.

Implement

Training implementation should not be too ambitious and should proceed in phases: first a pilot test, followed by any necessary revisions, followed by the final implementation. The pilot test is a live implementation, but its main purpose is to test the training for flaws that could jeopardize its success.

Focusing on Results

The first important issue to recognize is that there needs to be a constant focus on the expected results of the intervention—specifically, that there is a common understanding of what successful implementation means. The definition of successful implementation should be clarified at the inception of the project and then reviewed during each phase. The criteria for success should be guided by the performance goals identified during the assessment phase. Realistic criteria should be set to evaluate the implementation. During the pilot test and initial implementation, it is important to avoid ambitious comparisons that set unrealistic expectations, such as, "It is 30 percent better than before." Despite the best plans, anticipated results often do not materialize until the training has sufficiently stabilized.

Planning for implementation should have occurred in the earlier assessment and design and development phases. At a minimum, some stakeholders should have evaluated prototypes of the instruction. The next step is to conduct a pilot test using instructors, target learners, and appropriate support personnel. The pilot test is intended to provide guidance on how to proceed with the implementation.

People who are committed to the project and have the patience to work through problems that will inevitably arise should be included. Pilots tend to have more than the average number of problems, and the participants should be willing to make it work. Key stakeholders who have positive opinions about the training are a good bet; those who have not yet had a chance to try the innovative aspects of the training, or who have been critical of the project during earlier phases, are not. Adoption of the training by instructors, students, and managers is crucial to its implementation. This is a chance to take the training through its paces and get a feel for how it will perform, but supportive participants are needed to make it a success. The implementation budget should allow for additional instructors and other support personnel if more assistance becomes necessary.

Managing Stakeholder Expectations

Participants who have a stake in the training may anticipate implementation but also fear failure. A pilot test allows problems to arise without serious consequences. It lets stakeholders who are accountable for results become more confident about implementing the training with minimal risk of failure. It also provides opportunities to adjust the implementation based on observations made during the pilot test.

The pilot test should be small enough to be manageable but significant enough for stakeholders to gain confidence in the training. The scale of the pilot can be determined based on several factors: the size and complexity of the training project, the geographical dispersion of the audience, the audience size, and the amount of instructional change associated with the training.

The first consideration is the size and complexity of the training project. With a large course involving many topics and learning goals, one part of it should be selected that will be manageable for learners, instructors, and other support personnel—a core part that will be meaningful to stakeholders but does not spread resources beyond the ability to keep it running in case of difficulties. The next consideration is whether the target audience is dispersed at several locations. If they are, it may be implemented in one location first, then phased in at the others. Training that gets developed in one locale often overlooks perspectives that external stakeholders may have. Overcoming initial resistance in one area is easier than overcoming resistance in several locations.

The size of the target audience can also increase the complexity of the implementation. Large numbers of students can multiply the logistics of delivering the training. Using a subset of the student population before deploying the training on a larger scale might be considered.

Instructional Change

The scope of the pilot will also be determined by the amount of change associated with the training. It is important to be particularly careful with the replacement of previous training that sustains established practices among stakeholders. It may be best to replace individual parts of previous courses gradually so that stakeholders can gradually adopt the changes. If new technologies or instructional strategies are features of the new training, gaining adoption of the methods is the first step. They may be used on a limited set of course topics before replacing the entire course. To prepare for the pilot, instructors should be trained on any new instructional strategies. Innovative instructional methods tend to fall short if participants do not know how to use them.

A large enough sample of learners is needed to test the course measures. Gaps should be identified in either the measures or the content that supports the relevant objectives. How well target learners are mastering the learning objectives needs to be determined. Evaluation instruments should be tied to instructional objectives. Where testing detects performance deficiencies, both the test and the instruction should be examined for quality.

Everyone should use feedback forms to note problems quickly. A central collection point for the feedback should be established. Criteria should guide prioritizing of reported problems according to their importance and urgency—for example, a high priority to fixing unclear or inaccurate content and test items.

If new instructional methods are being tested, experienced staff must be on hand to support instructors and learners. Feedback should be collected from instructors and learners periodically to review results of their attempts at implementing the methods. Specifically, the difficulties that instructors and trainees have with the operation of the course, its content, strategies, technology, and measurements should be noted.

After the pilot test, meetings with participants should be held to identify what worked and did not work for them. For each role, from student to instructor to technical support personnel, the critical issues that led to success or failure of course features should be determined. Then problems may be prioritized—those that should be resolved before final implementation and those that may be corrected later. The results from the pilot test may be used to revise the implementation plan before proceeding with the implementation.

Technology

Urgent technological issues may include hardware breakdowns or software improperly installed so that it does not function. Technical staff should be available to correct software bugs and update content and make sure that computers and networks are operating properly.

As we have already discussed, technology can represent significant instructional change. Participants should be trained and given support for using new technology, especially if computer technology is used to deliver content or is a key component of instructional strategies. In one case, a Web-based course was implemented using a collaborative learning approach. Instructors, however, did not engage learners in the planned learning activities or encourage use of the technology. As content experts with years of experience in classroom training, the trainers resisted taking train-the-trainer courses to get oriented to the new methods. Effective use of the strategies and technology required coaching, leadership, communication, and mastery of how to use the strategies, software, and hardware. Consequently, instructors were unable to show learners how to make effective use of the technology. After continuous monitoring was instituted with real-time assistance for trainers in using the tools, the situation improved. Afterward, with the benefit of hindsight, the project director said he would have ensured that trainers were better prepared before implementation.

Sustainment

If innovators are conducting the pilot test, it is important to include anyone who is expected to sustain and support the training after they leave. For example, if instructional designers and software developers were instrumental in testing and implementing the instruction and supporting technology, then personnel who will be charged with operating and maintaining equipment, or who will be facilitating instructors or learners with learning strategies and technology, need to be included. To help plan for resources, areas of difficulty or risk should be identified. Knowing what the potential problems are will enable everyone to manage their expectations about the pilot and be alert to providing crucial support.

Evaluate

Evaluation should determine whether the intended results of the program were achieved and also provide information that will help to improve future offerings.

Focusing on Results

One of the first issues to examine is whether the program was implemented as intended. Often evaluation information is collected, judgments are made about the efficacy of the program, and decisions are made without knowing whether the program was implemented as intended.

For example, an automated instructional system was developed to enhance math problem-solving skills. The system was developed in a centralized location for dispersion to several geographical locations across the country. It was intended to be a self-study program that supplemented instructor lectures, with an instructor available to help learners use the system properly but to answer subject-matter questions only after the automated feedback was exhausted. The expectation was that learning would be improved and that money would be saved because fewer instructors would be needed and more students could be taught at once.

An extensive evaluation was conducted and it was determined that the instruction was no more effective than the traditional classroom instruction. The developers were bewildered, the program sponsors considered the training a failure, and the automated instruction was discontinued.

But in follow-up visits to the regional sites, it was discovered that the automated instruction had been implemented in a wide range of ways. In most cases, the students never learned how to use the feedback component properly. They relied heavily on the instructor for assistance with the subject matter rather than on the system. Unfortunately, the decision to discontinue the automated instruction was made without determining if it was implemented properly. The developers believed that if they had been permitted to do so, the program would have achieved the anticipated benefits.

Managing Stakeholder Expectations

Evaluation is vital to understand whether the intended business results were achieved, to provide stakeholders with information to improve the program, to make decisions about its viability, and to deploy resources wisely. The following is an example of a comprehensive effort to address each stakeholder's expectations.

Senior management in a large geographically dispersed organization wanted to increase the amount of entry-level training for new mechanics so they could be more immediately productive on the job. A large-scale program enhancement was conducted to provide additional practice and feedback on key job tasks during training. Program sponsors expected that the time to upgrade to journeyman would be reduced, enabling greater flexibility in work assignments and reducing the need for supervision of apprentices.

Kirkpatrick's (1994) four-level framework was followed as an evaluation strategy that addressed stakeholder expectations. Results from reaction and learning measures indicated that individuals who received the new training were more satisfied, learned more, and scored better on performance tests than the traditional training group. Changes in behavior were assessed through surveys of trainees and their supervisors at three- and six-month periods after they completed training. Trainee confidence was higher than that of the traditional group. Supervisors believed that the trainees were prepared better and more capable than traditional graduates.

Then, data were extracted from personnel records at a later date to assess the time at which trainees were upgraded from apprentice to journeymen. Results showed that there was no difference between the two groups or with other historical data. In follow-up discussions with supervisors and other management, it was clear that despite the greater capabilities of graduates in the enhanced training, the organizational norms were still quite strong that it took one year to become a journeyman. In addition, program sponsors had failed to communicate to the front-line supervisors their expectations that time to upgrade would be reduced. The stakeholders who had sponsored the program were not satisfied with the results and the program was subsequently discontinued.

This example illustrates an evaluation strategy that addresses the expectations of different stakeholder groups. Unfortunately, the results from follow-up discussions were not used to influence sponsors. In retrospect, some of the front-line supervisors could have been used as champions to convey to program sponsors that the training was successful, but that it would take time for expectations and norms to change about the certification process. Significant benefits to the organization were lost because of this.

Instructional Change

Often there is no thorough analysis prior to program development and implementation because of insufficient resources, an uncooperative client, or an aggressive schedule for a new product rollout. If this is the case, the evaluation phase can be used as a reassessment of training needs. Once trainees have had sufficient time to use the trained skills on the job, the answers to two simple questions can provide a wealth of information: What worked, and why? What did not work, and why? Usually, people need the most help determining how to use the new skills in the context of their job or work flow. The best workers can figure this out, but most will revert to old, established habits if the new procedures do not provide immediate benefit.

Frequently, new procedures are learned but fail to produce results because nothing is changed in the work environment to support and reinforce the expected change. Usually, measuring the expected results and providing feedback on those results is effective in instantiating and maintaining the new behaviors. Once the facts of what worked, what did not, and why have been collected, the system developers can go back to the client and present the case for making the appropriate adjustments.

Technology

During the evaluation of a program that involves some aspect of technology, developers and stakeholders are sometimes eager to declare success and proclaim that the technology worked. Over the years, we have become careful about such claims. As we say, "Design for effectiveness and deliver for efficiency." That is, the effective design of instruction is what matters most, and the delivery choice is in large part a matter of using resources efficiently. Hence, we attempt to make distinctions between the instructional design (for example, using advanced organizers, mental models, sequencing of content, engaging activities), any media used (for example, audio, video), and the delivery approach (instructor, CBT, Web-delivered). Claims such as "the Web-based training worked" are misleading, because clients may believe that the delivery approach is what mattered when it was the design that mattered most for effectiveness and the Web was merely an efficient, consistent way to deliver it. Making this distinction helps to avoid future requests for the same technology without conducting the proper analysis and proceeding systematically through the instructional systems development (ISD) process.

Sustainment

Follow-up evaluation over the course of a program is necessary to ensure that it remains successful and to determine if changes are needed. Once it has been determined whether the objectives and anticipated results were achieved, a longer-term evaluation approach may be warranted, particularly for high-flow entry-level courses. Resources should be devoted to maintaining evaluation instruments, overseeing evaluation processes, summarizing data, and depicting results in a user-friendly format that stakeholders can understand. Others should be shown how to use the data to make changes to the instruction or to make decisions about the investment of resources. We have seen many evaluations carried out with no planned purpose or forethought; data then sit on a shelf, and time and resources are wasted. A good starting point for any effort is to define the purposes for the evaluation first and then determine the specific questions to be answered on a regular basis. Next, the best way to collect information to answer those questions should be determined. Purposes may include validating the content and relevance of the training, establishing the effectiveness of the instructional methods, seeing if the trainees have met the standards, and determining the efficiency of the course (whether time and resources were aligned properly), passing rates, costs, amount of transfer to the job, and return on investment. Although Kirkpatrick's four-level framework has been useful for decades in understanding key elements of training evaluation, it is often misused. Practitioners tend to focus on which level of evaluation they have advanced to (often assuming higher levels are better) rather than on what is needed for the specific training program. For example, if an organization decided to invest in new word processing software, there may be little need to evaluate whether the users are applying all of the functions or whether people can produce better correspondence at a faster rate than before. At most, employees probably need to learn the new functions and get some practice and feedback. Perhaps only a brief assessment of the efficacy and relevance of the practice exercises used is needed. In some cases, if the course is a onetime offering, there may be no need for evaluation or follow-up at all.

Routine, systematic collection of data can help to identify trends and changes in workplace issues in large, geographically dispersed organizations where it is difficult to keep track of new technology and processes. In one company, a periodic assessment six months after new employees completed entry-level training revealed a sharp decline in the frequency with which they performed certain tasks associated with a specific piece of equipment. Field personnel were contacted, and it was discovered that the old equipment was obsolete and had been replaced. If there had not been ongoing evaluation, valuable time and resources may have been spent continuing to train for these obsolete tasks. In another evaluation it was discovered that only a small percentage of graduates reported maintaining a safety-related piece of equipment. Follow-up evaluation determined that work procedures had changed and that only two personnel per unit, a primary and a backup, were responsible for maintaining the safety equipment. These procedures were eliminated from the entry-level training when it was determined that the task could be learned on the job. As a result, time and resources were saved in the entry-level training course.

Conclusion

In this chapter, the ADDIE model was used to illustrate the importance of each instructional phase in the successful implementation of a training program. The assessment phase is vital to the implementation because it sets the stage for the intended results and establishes relationships with stakeholders while managing their expectations. Assessment also identifies the established norms of the organization against which to gauge the change required by stakeholders for the intervention proposed later on.

The design and development phases are important in gaining support from stakeholders, particularly those in the training organization. New training methods are like any other innovation that must pass through phases of adoption by stakeholders. Individuals need to assess the relative advantages of the new training and its compatibility with existing operating norms, become comfortable with its complexity, and try it out or observe it before adopting it. Training implementations must determine who the stakeholders are and how they participate in order to ensure success. Managing expectations about the training is usually a good place to start.

Stakeholders need to be involved in training design decisions. If new designs will change the current methods of training or of supporting learning transfer in the workplace, then the affected staff should be involved in design and development. When considering whether new designs will affect stakeholders, it is important to look for possible changes in supporting roles and any skills that will be needed to support the training. Individuals should be involved from across the organizational hierarchy, including management, instructors, and developers. Well-designed training may fail if these people are not included early and feel some ownership. They must resolve their personal feelings about new training designs and feel that their participation will make a difference to the organization.

Before the implementation phase, an implementation plan should be drawn up. During implementation, a pilot test can reveal hidden problems. Problems should be sorted out—those that need to be resolved before final implementation and those that may be corrected later. Pilot test results could be used to revise the implementation plan before actual implementation.

During the evaluation phase, it is important to be certain that plans address a life-cycle view that mirrors the life cycle of the course and that resources have been devoted to maintaining evaluation instruments, overseeing evaluation processes, summarizing data, and depicting results in a user-friendly format that stakeholders can understand. Others should be shown how to use the data to make changes to the instruction or to make decisions about the investment of resources.

There is an old saying: "You can pay now or you can pay later." In this case, paying now means investing in a systematic process to focus on results; engaging stakeholders in a way that will use their expertise and obtain their acceptance; understanding the nature and magnitude of the instructional change and what it will mean for the stakeholder groups; planning for the use and adoption of technology; and being proactive, planning ahead for the long-term sustainment of the training program. Paying later means ignoring this advice, risking that the program will not be implemented properly and that the investment will not achieve the anticipated results. Those who invest wisely will find the payoffs are well worth it.

References

Bassi, L. J., & McMurrer, D. P. (1999). *Training investment can mean financial performance.* Alexandria, VA: American Society for Training & Development.

Dick, W., Carey, L., & Carey, J. O. (2001). *The systematic design of instruction* (5th ed.). Reading, MA: Addison-Wesley.

Gagne, R. M., Briggs, L. J., & Wager, W. W. (1992). *Principles of instructional design* (4th ed.). Austin, TX: Holt, Rinehart and Winston.

Galvin, T. (2001, March). Training top 50. *Training,* pp. 57–79.

Goldstein, I. L., & Ford, J. K. (2002). *Training in organizations* (4th ed.). Belmont, CA: Wadsworth.

Huselid, M. A. (1995). The impact of human resource management practices on turnover, productivity and corporate financial performance. *Academy of Management Journal, 38*(3), 635–672.

Kirkpatrick, D. L. (1994). *Evaluating training programs: The four levels.* San Francisco: Berrett-Koehler.

Robinson, D. G., & Robinson, J. C. (1995). *Performance consulting: Moving beyond training.* San Francisco: Berrett-Koehler.

Rossett, A. (1999). *First things fast: A handbook for performance analysis.* San Francisco: Jossey-Bass/Pfeiffer.

Tannenbaum, S. I. (1997). *Consulting skills workshop.* Albany, NY: S. I. Tannenbaum.

Van Buren, M. E. (2001). *The 2001 ASTD state-of-the-industry report.* Alexandria, VA: American Society for Training & Development.

CHAPTER 9

Issues in Implementing Large-Scale Selection Programs

Nancy T. Tippins

Implementation of a selection system is as important as the development and validation of the test itself. Many well-researched and highly predictive selection programs are unsuccessful operationally because of problems in the implementation phase of the project. When a careful implementation strategy has been developed, there is more likely to be appropriate and consistent use of the selection tool despite wide variations in test administrator capability, geographic location of users, or supervision and guidance offered to test administrators.

Implementation includes those nonresearch activities necessary to put a selection program into use in the field: decisions about test format, test administration, test scoring, databases, test previews, and test feedback, and development of a test administration guide. For the purposes of this chapter, implementation generally excludes activities related to test development and validation.

In successful large-scale selection programs, decisions about implementation and the research approach are made conjointly. For example, the form of the test (paper and pencil, computer administered, work sample, interview) are chosen before test development even begins. Although it is possible to retool a paper-and-pencil test for computer administration, it is far more efficient to write a test for computer administration from the start. Common problems, such as including items that cannot be administered by the available software, can thus be avoided. Planning for implementation should begin at the same time as planning for the validation research.

Moreover, implementation activities continue once a test is delivered to the field for use. Many aspects of a selection program and its context can and do change. For example, cutscores may be raised or lowered because the applicant population has changed significantly or because the needs of the organization have changed. A change in cutscore will necessitate modifications to the test administration guides, scoring instructions, test interpretation documents, feedback materials, and so on. So implementation must also include subsequent changes to the way in which a selection program is used.

In many respects, implementation is an iterative process. Although the test user can carefully plan research and implementation, both must be adapted to constraints in the environment and the results of the validation study that are revealed after initial planning. For example, a plan to use both a paper-and-pencil cognitive ability measure and a work sample for repair technicians may be modified when the validation research demonstrates the unreliability of the work sample instrument. Many of the decisions about test implementation are interrelated; decisions made early on will affect decisions made later. Decisions about how to use a test score will determine what kind of feedback can be given, as well as the content of test previews and test preparation materials. In some cases, the test developer may have to rethink earlier decisions. For example, discovering during the job analysis phase that resources are not available to train administrators for work sample tasks may cause the test developer to change plans and develop instead a paper-and-pencil, multichoice job knowledge instrument that can be objectively scored.

The purpose of this chapter is to review the steps involved in successful implementation and to alert readers to issues they should consider before moving a selection procedure into operational use. The chapter focuses primarily on paper-and-pencil or computer-based tests of cognitive and noncognitive abilities, but many of the comments are applicable to all forms of testing. Where appropriate, references to the special requirements of other forms of testing, such as interviews or work samples, are made. The chapter is organized by topics associated with the implementation of large-scale selection programs and concludes with a brief discussion of the implementation process and the order in which each step should be considered.

Staffing Process

When choosing an implementation plan, the entire staffing process must be considered. Selection is usually one step in the staffing process, which often begins with targeted recruiting efforts that seek individuals with certain backgrounds and experience and ends with background checks and administrative processing.

Prescreens

In some organizations, all candidates are tested; in others, only those who meet minimum requirements are tested. In setting a policy on whom to test, large organizations often consider the number of applicants for a position, the existence of observable, job-related criteria for prescreening, past experience in teaching fundamental skills that could be learned elsewhere, and reliability and validity of the initial screens. When large numbers of candidates are available for a relatively small number of openings, the organization may not need to test all applicants because the number of test-qualified individuals is likely to exceed the need. In some very large organizations that have infrequent openings for highly desirable positions, a lottery is used to determine those who will be tested. Other organizations test until they have enough qualified candidates to fill their openings.

Organizations often find it difficult to specify the education, experience, or credentials of good job candidates. For many positions, particularly ones requiring little or no job-specific skills, observable prescreen criteria simply do not exist. Other organizations may have had great success in teaching the job to new employees in a cost-effective manner, and they may not wish to eliminate candidates with good work orientation skills in favor of those who may already know something about the work.

An important problem for most organizations that use education or experience as a prescreen is developing a reliable method to assess qualitative information fairly and consistently and to quantify it in some way. The person responsible for selection will have to answer questions like these: Is ten years of experience better than five years of experience? Is ten years of experience twice as good as five years of experience? Are all experiences doing a particular job of equal value? Without probing for information about that experience, there is no way to know how useful or relevant it is in most cases.

A related problem is the validity of the prescreen. Although some experiences appear to be job-related, their relationship to job performance or other important job criteria cannot be demonstrated. In some cases, the lack of observed relationship is due to the measurement problem. A common example is the use of a college degree as a prerequisite to entry-level professional positions. Few organizations have been able to establish a relationship between a college degree and a job performance criterion probably because of the high degree of variability in the demands different college programs place on their students. In other cases, the experience may simply not be related to job performance. Many managers have personal beliefs about what experiences are job-related based on their own experiences. Although there may be some truth in the manager's belief about a particular experience, such beliefs often exclude many other experiences that are equally (or more) applicable. Because the manager lacks firsthand knowledge about these other experiences, they are considered neutral information at best.

Multiple Hurdles Versus Compensatory Models

Sometimes several selection tools are used in a multiple hurdle model, where the candidate must qualify on each element before moving to the next. For example, a candidate might be required to take and pass a paper-and-pencil test battery measuring cognitive skills before being allowed to complete an interview measuring basic managerial skills. Other times, all the selection instruments will be administered at one time with a qualifying score required on each or with a qualifying total score on the battery required. So a candidate for an electrician position might be given a general aptitude battery and an electronics knowledge test. Some organizations will require qualification on each test; others will use a compensatory model and combine the two scores and then compare that total score to the test standard.

Perhaps the most important factor in the decision to use a multiple hurdle approach or a compensatory approach is the degree to which the knowledge, skills, and abilities measured by each instrument are truly compensatory. If job requirements for both problem-solving skills and interpersonal skills have been demonstrated, do good interpersonal skills make up for poor problem-solving skills? A second, closely related question is the wisdom of defining job requirements and then ignoring that information by potentially accepting a candidate who scores very high on one test and very low on the other.

In my experience, the decision to use a multiple hurdle approach or a compensatory model is often heavily based on administrative considerations. The test user may simply find it too difficult to administer one test, score it while candidates wait, provide feedback, and then administer the next component. The administrative problems increase when the period of time required for scoring necessitates allowing the candidate to leave and return at a later time. Staffing organizations may also argue for a compensatory model in order to increase the number of qualified people. Another administrative argument for using a compensatory model involves the adverse impact of an instrument. By combining the scores of a high adverse impact instrument with those of a low adverse impact instrument, the number of people in protected classes remaining in the candidate pool may be increased.

In contrast, some organizations may argue for a multiple hurdles model when one or more of the testing components is expensive to administer. Consider the organization that uses a paper-and-pencil test of general mental ability followed by an electronics work sample and an interview. That organization may find it cost-effective to test a large number of people on the general ability battery and eliminate some of them before moving to measures that require one-on-one testing, like the work sample and the interview. Other organizations argue that a multiple hurdles approach placing the most valid test first results in the most efficient selection practice.

There is no right or wrong answer to this question. The best model to use depends on the nature of the test and the needs of the organization. The industrial/organizational psychologist must use professional judgment to determine the most effective solution for the particular situation.

Continuous Versus Mass Hiring

Some organizations run a continuous staffing program. Openings for jobs are always available or are unpredictable. Consequently, the staffing organization is constantly seeking candidates to fill positions. In other organizations, however, the number of people to be hired is predetermined and jobs are filled during one block of time. The staffing process is turned on to hire a specific number of people and then shut down until needed again.

The test user must think about how the test score will be used in the context of the entire staffing process. Top-down hiring is difficult to administer and sometimes to defend in a continuous hiring program, particularly when the program includes internal candidates. The top candidate for a position on Monday may be the third choice on Tuesday. In contrast, use of cutscores or wide bands may create administrative difficulties when there are large numbers of applicants and few positions. If a large number of applicants meet the test standard, how will the staffing process select from among the qualified individuals? How valid is this secondary selection process?

Internal Versus External Candidates

Another variation in staffing processes across organizations is the population included. In some organizations, internal candidates (that is, employees) and external candidates are treated identically. In other organizations, internal candidates are exempted from some testing processes and may simply move to the job of their choice when there is an opening. In yet others, the skills of internal candidates are evaluated based on their past job performance. For example, employees seeking to move to a customer service job are evaluated on their customer service skills that may or may not have been displayed on their current jobs. (It should be pointed out that there are legal risks in not treating all candidates similarly; however, there are also risks in ignoring past work experience and relying solely on test scores.)

Capability of Personnel

A final factor affecting the organization's decision about the use of a test score is the capability of the personnel in the staffing organization and their other responsibilities. Highly trained staffing personnel who have the time to devote to selection issues may be able to monitor and coach managers using test information to make hiring decisions. Staffing personnel with minimal training and little time may need specific rules that they can follow easily and that reduce the need for decision making.

Use of Test Scores

At implementation, test users must choose one of four options for use of test scores: top-down hiring where the highest scoring individual is chosen first, then the next highest, and so on; cutscores, where everyone at or above the cutscore is considered qualified; banding, where everyone in a band of scores is considered qualified; and individual manager decisions, where managers decide who is qualified based on test information (for example, test score, norms, and expectancy tables) and other information (for example, education and experience). There are also a number of variations on these four basic choices. Some organizations may use multiple cutscores that define a highly qualified group, an intermediate group, and an unqualified group so that they can be more selective in favorable labor markets and less selective in tight labor markets. Only those in the qualified group are hired until labor market conditions change, then the cutscore is effectively lowered and those in the intermediate group may be hired. Organizations that use bands may choose a sliding band so that the width of the band changes each time someone is removed. And organizations that allow manager decisions may establish boundaries for those decisions such as setting a floor below which a score cannot go or requiring compensating education and experiences for individuals with lower scores. Organizations may also mix test score use approaches within one selection program. (For more information on these various approaches, the reader is referred to Guion, 1998.) For example, an organization might use a cutscore with a cognitive battery but use managerial decisions with the structured interview.

Again, there is no one right use of test scores. Cutscores and bands work well in continuous hiring programs where there is a need to label a person qualified or not qualified for some period of time. A top-down hiring process works well when the organization's goal is to identify the best possible candidates for a job and when the hiring process is conducted in well-defined blocks.

Cutscores and bands may be more appropriate when the consequences of an error on the job are high. When a mistake on the job creates the possibility for great harm to the employee, others, or property, the company may need to ensure that everyone in the job has at least minimal skill or knowledge. Compared with top-down hiring, banding may ameliorate adverse impact when the selection process is heavily loaded with measures of cognitive ability. The effects of cutscores relative to banding on adverse impact depends on the philosophy behind the cutscores. Those that are set to select a few of the top scores will usually have more adverse impact than bands, whereas cutscores that establish a floor above which everyone is equally qualified may actually have less.

In tight labor markets and in companies that value filling positions rather than staffing them only with highly qualified individuals, the organization often will prefer top-down hiring that allows it to go as low as necessary to fill positions or very low cutscores or wide bands that define qualified status. In contrast, companies that emphasize high skill levels or are unwilling to go below certain minimum qualifications may resist top-down hiring that would allow them to reach as far down as necessary. Instead, these companies set cutscores appropriate for the skill level required or use top-down hiring with a cutscore that establishes a floor below which no one can be hired.

Some psychologists would argue that statistical prediction is always better than clinical judgments (see Meehl, 1954, 1957, 1965; Wiggins, 1973). Consequently, using rules (for example, cutscores, bands, or top-down hiring) is superior for predicting performance than more subjective models where the manager makes a decision that uses test information in some unknown way. However, in some circumstances the more objective models for test score use are not acceptable. For example, some organizations have only the resources to develop selection programs for the more easily measured skills. Consequently, other important skills and knowledge (for example, interpersonal skills and job knowledge) are not formally assessed. Yet in many situations, a hiring manager may get an indication of the individual's skills in these areas from a résumé or from interactions with the person. In other cases, hiring managers make judgments about candidates based more on short-term business needs than on test scores. For example, a manager may select a candidate who has moderate scores on an aptitude battery over one who has superior scores because the first candidate has extensive education and experience in a relevant field and there is an immediate need for a person with job knowledge.

The culture of the organization may also determine how test scores are used. In some organizations managers are responsible for the people on their team, and this results in a great deal of independence in selections as well as terminations. In other organizations, the idea that an I/O psychologist would determine qualified people (through the cutscore or bands) is offensive. The I/O psychologist must remember too that most managers are not well versed in the I/O literature and remain unconvinced of the benefits of statistical prediction.

Stakeholders

Many different individuals will be concerned about how test scores are used in the organization. Staffing personnel may be more concerned about filling requisitions than identifying highly capable applicants, whereas the members of the training organization and the client organization may have opposite priorities and desire the most competent applicants available. Senior leaders in the staffing organization will also be very concerned about the feasibility of the proposed test score use and the availability of resources to support the selection program. The I/O psychologist responsible for the testing program may opt for an approach to test use that ensures the most consistency across locations and deters charges of unfair treatment. Labor relations, equal employment opportunity (EEO) and affirmative action, and legal departments may also have conflicting needs. Often those responsible for affirmative action are primarily interested in promoting diversity, whereas the overriding concern of the legal organization may be the defensibility of the selection system in case of a legal challenge. To maintain a relationship with union leaders, the labor relations group may need a hybrid form of test use that acknowledges the importance of seniority or extracurricular educational efforts sponsored by the union.

Many individuals have strong personal beliefs about how people should be hired that are independent of the role they assume in the organization. Perceptions about the fairness of testing or the accuracy of judgments about a candidate's background may color the ultimate decision on using test scores. Similarly, the perceptions of candidates may also affect the final use of test scores. Selection programs that include a large number of internal applicants (that is, employees seeking other positions in the organization) are particularly affected by applicant reactions.

One of the most important steps the test developer takes is determining who should help decide how the test scores will be used. Once decided, difficult discussions must occur regarding the balance between the need and desire for highly capable workers and a diverse workforce and the challenges of a difficult labor market. The organization will have to decide whether it is better to let jobs go unfilled than to place less qualified candidates in them. It will have to determine how much adverse impact and associated risk it can accept in its current environment and how much it should tolerate to achieve its goals for diversity. Obtaining consensus on these issues early on will provide the road map for future test use.

Process

The I/O psychologist responsible for test implementation must develop the process to be used to make subsequent decisions about test use. For example, if a cutscore is used, the test user must decide what process will be used to set the cutscore, what data will be needed to facilitate that process, and which people will decide where to set the cutscore.

Bands require similar implementation decisions. (Some would argue that cutscores are simply a two-band system.) The additional question the test user must face with bands is whether a sliding band approach is warranted or feasible. A sliding band in a continuous hiring program may be too complex to administer with the personnel available. If the sliding band is chosen, then the user responsible for implementation must again decide on the process to establish those sliding bands, collect the necessary data, and assemble the right mix of people.

Some organizations try to avoid organizationwide problems associated with adverse impact, affirmative action, diversity, and a capable workforce by giving individual managers the responsibility to achieve these goals and the authority to make decisions based on the needs of their unit. Other organizations believe it is the manager's prerogative to staff the organization in the way he or she sees fit. In these cases, test scores are only one source of information in the hiring process. If discretionary use of a test score is allowed, then the test developer must inform the manager about what a test score means, what constitutes a real difference between test scores, and what risks are associated with decisions that contradict test data. In addition, the test developer must decide what tools should be supplied to assist the manager in making a hiring decision. Discretionary use of test scores also puts a burden on the manager making the decision to specify what other information was weighed in the decision and how that information was used.

When a manager has some degree of discretion in the use of test scores, someone with a lower test score can be selected over someone else with a higher test score—for example, if the former individual has more relevant work experience or education. Legal risks associated with test use can surface if there is no information about the mitigating circumstances that justified overriding the test information. By disregarding test results, the organization is susceptible to the complaint that a valid process was not fairly and consistently applied to all candidates. The I/O psychologist must decide which documentation will be required to support decisions that conflict with the test score information. Ideally, this will include a process to measure accurately and use the information that will override the test score information to avoid the complaint that decisions were made on less valid information.

Interviews

Interviews are often part of large-scale selection programs and do not always yield precise scores, making the use of cutscores or banding questionable in some circumstances. The test developer has a special obligation to explain to interviewers what the test score means, how large a difference between test scores is significant, and how the test scores should be used. Further complicating the decisions on how interview scores are to be used is the fact that many interviews measure constructs that are to varying degrees unrelated yet essential for successful job performance. For example, many interviews for entry-level professional jobs measure problem-solving skills, interpersonal skills, communication skills, and the components of these. Problem-solving skills may be only slightly related to communication skills and interpersonal skills, with much of that relationship dependent on method variance. Some users want complex models that require minimums on each dimension measured as well as a minimum on the aggregated scores. If we assume the validation data support such a model, the test user implementing the interview is left with the difficult task of first developing such a model, gaining buy-in from the relevant stakeholders, and explaining the process to the ultimate users, who are often the interviewers themselves.

Test Delivery

A minor but important component of the implementation plan is the delivery of the test materials to the test administrators for use in selecting candidates. Depending on the nature of the test, these materials might include test booklets, answer sheets, scoring keys, special equipment for work samples, supporting materials for role-plays, computers, and so on. The first questions then are, Who is going to administer the test and where will it be administered? The operational questions become, Who will receive test materials and where are they located?

Test delivery questions are normally worked out between the test developer and the staffing organization that will be responsible for test administration. Often the staffing organization will argue for as much flexibility as possible in who may order test materials and who has access to testing materials. However, experience in large-scale testing programs suggests that materials are most effectively protected when specific responsibility is assigned and access is limited. Thus, an important task in test implementation is to create a process for identifying and authorizing personnel who may order test materials, administer tests, score tests, and access test information databases.

244 IMPLEMENTING ORGANIZATIONAL INTERVENTIONS

Paper Test Materials

The test developer must manage the logistics of test production, which ranges from who is producing the camera-ready copies of tests and answer sheets to who will do the actual printing and ensure the accuracy and security of test materials at every step. Once printed, the test developer then deals with getting the materials to the right person. Maintaining control over paper test documents is a formidable task in large, geographically distributed test programs. The test developer should ensure that someone keep track of the people who are authorized to have access to paper documents and which documents each one possesses. Periodic audits of test materials are recommended. Serialization of the documents is the most effective way of keeping track of each copy of a test or scoring key.

Computerized Test Materials

If a test is delivered by computer, many of the same issues apply. Someone must be responsible for ensuring that the version of the test and scoring program on the computer is completely accurate. Someone must keep track of who has passwords and access to equipment. Although it is somewhat more difficult to steal a computer or a disk containing test materials, it is certainly possible to do so. The test developer must take steps to ensure that the theft of tangible equipment is not likely to occur, and if it should occur that tests and scoring materials are protected. In many test administration programs, this means using passwords that limit access and identify the user as well as encryption that prevents unauthorized users from reading documents.

Computerized tests also have unique implementation issues. Software that will present items and time tests are critical elements of the test development process. However, successful implementation often hinges on making sure users have machines with the right capabilities and facilities to use and store the machines.

Interviews, Work Samples, and Assessment Centers

Interviews and work samples pose slightly different distribution problems because of the number and variety of people involved. Many interviewers and work sample administrators are part of the line operations. Consequently, they may have only cursory training in the need to protect test documents and there may be little or no supervision over their actions with test documents. Apocryphal stories abound about interviewers leaving copies of interviews in their desks for the next incumbent to discover and distribute. Although test developers can do little to monitor the actual behavior of interviewers or administrators, they can ensure that the documents contain warnings about unauthorized distribution and they can emphasize the need to protect these documents in the accompanying training materials.

In contrast, assessment center materials are often less problematic than paper-and-pencil tests, computer-based tests, interviews, or work samples simply because fewer people are involved. Moreover, people working in professionally developed and managed assessment centers tend to be particularly well trained and supervised.

Tests that involve equipment (for example, work samples, physical abilities tests) pose unique challenges related to the calibration of equipment. In addition, after a work sample exercise is completed, the equipment often must be returned to a beginning state. For example, an electronics repair work sample must be "broken" in the same way every time.

Although it may seem trivial, the distribution of test materials is an important element of the implementation process. A test with errors often reduces the predictive power of the instrument and brings into question the entire selection process. A test becomes useless when job candidates have easy access to the test items. In order to ensure a successful implementation and continued use of a selection program, the test developer must make sure that the materials are error-free and securely maintained.

Destruction of Test Materials

During implementation few people think about how test materials should be removed from circulation. Yet answer sheets will be used, test booklets will be damaged, and scoring keys will become worn. It is important to destroy unusable materials in a way that prevents security breaches (for example, supervised shredding or burning). Moreover, managers of a large-scale testing program need to ensure that records of each document's status are kept. Otherwise, there will be no way to tell if the document has been destroyed or is simply missing.

Test Administration

The central question in the test administration sessions is, Who is going to give the test? The background and training of test administrators will determine the complexity of the tests and scoring systems that are feasible and dictate the level of detail that the test developer must provide in the test administrator guide.

Of course, highly trained and certified test administrators are ideal. They follow the rules precisely so that each applicant takes the test under the same conditions, they ensure the accurate retention of all data, they handle unexpected situations appropriately. Yet one of the traditional points of conflict in large HR organizations between the selection research organization and the staffing organization is the capability of individuals assigned to test administration and the willingness of the organization to train and supervise them. The tendency of many is to assign test administration duties to the low-skilled clerical population, provide as little training as possible, and do minimal or no performance monitoring, feedback, or coaching. Although the costs of testing mistakes are high when retesting is required, an unqualified individual is hired, or an aggrieved test taker files a lawsuit, EEO charge, or grievance, the value of professional test administrators is rarely acknowledged. Many HR professionals have no idea of the real costs of testing errors because no such information is collected in most organizations. In my own experience, training is always justified given the costs of correcting testing mistakes, supervising an incapable employee, terminating poor performers, litigating test administration cases, and handling grievances and arbitration related to test administration. Moreover, mistakes tend to be repeated, so it may not be a question of just one person who was hired in error but of some percentage of the hundreds who were tested.

In addition to the very real costs associated with mistakes in test administration are the intangible effects of poor administration practices. Gross mistakes on the part of the test administrator create doubts about the fairness of the entire selection process. Although not every doubt leads to equal employment opportunity litigation, the reputation of the organization suffers. Finally, the test developer responsible for implementation should realize that there does not have to be a mistake for damage to be done to a testing program. Inappropriate comments and attitudes may do an equal amount of damage.

Many test administrators in staffing organizations have an inherent conflict when their goals are to hire people as quickly as possible and to hire qualified individuals. The demand for quick hiring supersedes the need for capable employees. Or to put it another way, failure to hire quickly is more apparent and attributable to the staffing representative than failure to hire capable individuals. Often, the extent of a new hire's inadequacies is not apparent until a considerable investment has been made in hiring and training the individual. Unfortunately, this pressure to fill positions sometimes leads to poor test administration practices such as inaccurate timing and scoring, inappropriate assistance to test takers, and failure to adhere to retest policies.

In the past few years, it has become popular in some large companies to outsource test administration. It is often less expensive to do so because the salaries in large companies are usually higher than in the smaller vendors and because a vendor's test administrators are paid only for the time they work. Theoretically at least, the vendor can afford to provide appropriate training because its employees are entirely focused on test administration and the payback on the training investment is greater. Whether the costs are actually lower and the quality of service higher of course depends on the practices of both the organization and the vendor.

One of the more difficult problems for organizations with offices in far-flung locations is choosing individuals to administer tests in remote sites. Although it is obviously desirable to have trained HR test administrators give every test, it may not be feasible in some locations. An all too familiar scenario is the department secretary administering one test a year with absolutely no training or supervision. Because remote locations have few job openings for higher-paying positions that are filled by employees, and because the secretary is often keenly aware of the boss's preferences for the next placement, he or she sometimes feels tremendous pressure to ensure that a particular employee meet the test standard.

One solution here is to require test takers to go to a central location that has trained test administrators who are free from undue pressure from the client organization. Although some organizations do send test takers to central sites, many are unwilling to cover their travel expenses. Many are willing to accept the risk and consequences of a problem in a test administration session rather than pay for the other solution.

Even if the organization does not encourage test administrator training, the test user must take all steps possible to ensure that every test is administered in a consistent manner. A test administration guide documents how a test is to be administered and scored. If training is feasible, the test developer should develop a comprehensive training course that covers the role of testing in the hiring process and the responsibilities of the test administrator. If training is not possible, a more detailed test administration guide or a self-study guide may provide the same information, although there is no assurance that either one will be read or that questions and confusion will be clarified.

Ideally, the test developer will establish a system to monitor the performance of test administrators and provide feedback and coaching. When the resources for that level of interaction are not available, the test developer must consider other alternatives like group meetings where test administrators bring up recent problems and the group discusses possible solutions. My experience suggests there is no good substitute for face-to-face training.

Another solution to the problems of inadequate resources for test administration is computer administration of tests. Although this poses special challenges in terms of equipment, networks, and security, it does ensure that each applicant gets the same instructions and the precise amount of time allocated. Tests are accurately scored, and data are consistently captured and stored. Test security is generally heightened because the physical materials are difficult to pilfer and hard to read if stolen. Furthermore, a large part of the applicant population simply lacks the skills to hack into a sophisticated computer system.

Interviews, Work Samples, Role-Plays, and Assessment Centers

Administration requirements are very different with interviews than with most paper-and-pencil or computer-administered tests. Far greater skills and training are needed to conduct an effective interview and score it than to administer a written test satisfactorily and score it objectively. The test developer who uses an interview must make sure that all interviewers are properly trained and their performance adequately monitored.

Assessment centers seem to have fewer test administration problems when compared to tests administered in employment offices. Willingness to devote the resources to an assessment center almost always seems to connote a commitment to test administrator-assessor training and supervision.

Work samples and role-plays often have unique training requirements for the administrator-rater and frequently involve line personnel who are experienced in the work on which the sample is based. Many organizations that devote the time and resources to careful work sample development also commit to appropriate administrator training. However, unless the line function that provides the administrators is willing to schedule their most competent and conscientious people to participate, problems in administration are likely to develop. Problems with the administration of work samples often occur some time after the implementation, when the excitement of a special test has worn off and adhering to precise instructions and test conditions seems less important. Some organizations resort to assigning their poorest performing employees to rating and assessment tasks because their presence on regular work assignments will be missed the least. Some organizations have found the problem of using employees as administrators in work samples and role-plays so great that they contract this work out to organizations that hire professional assessors.

Test Administration Location

Another seemingly trivial but important question when it comes to test administration is location. Tests that will be administered in public facilities like job fairs must be transportable. Organizations that conduct off-site testing need to consider carefully whether computerized testing or complex work samples and role-plays are feasible in unknown locations. If the test location is the outsourcing vendor's facilities, that vendor's ability to provide equipment and appropriate facilities at a reasonable cost may be an issue.

Even when tests are given at dedicated testing facilities, problems may arise. The space must be large enough to accommodate the maximum number of candidates to be tested at any one time and comfortable enough to be conducive to good testing performance. In addition, the facility should be conveniently located in the building so that candidates can easily get to the testing room and to rest rooms.

Test Administration Environment

Although knowledge of appropriate testing conditions is basic for I/O psychologists, many test administrators overlook or are unaware of the conditions that allow candidates to perform at their best. The person responsible for implementing a testing program should be very specific about the environment in which the test should be administered. Usually, environmental factors that may affect test performance include noise, temperature, lighting, desk and chair comfort, and spacing between candidates to enhance security and minimize cheating. The I/O psychologist responsible for test implementation should also provide test administrators with detailed instructions on tasks like checking the condition of test materials, reading instructions, answering questions, handling disturbances, accounting for test materials after the testing session is over, monitoring test takers, timing the test, and so on.

Test Administration Process

The I/O psychologist must also establish the procedures to use in actual test administration, including ways to identify candidates and minimize opportunities for candidate misrepresentation. For example, in many companies candidates must show photo identification and sign every test document. There are also procedures for distributing, using, and collecting scratch paper or identifying appropriate timing of breaks. These procedures too may seem trivial, but they can prevent inappropriate testing and ensure the security of test information.

Testing Rules

Every organization has rules about who takes a test, when a person may take a test, and the conditions under which a test can be taken. The test developer in conjunction with staffing representatives, members of the client organization, EEO and affirmative action personnel, labor relations, and attorneys should determine the rules so that they may be consistently applied to all test takers. Some of the common issues that test administration rules address are as follows.

Test Exemptions

An important set of rules deals with test exemptions: Who must take a test to qualify for a position? Who may be exempted? Often companies establish standard test exemptions for anyone who has a valid qualifying test score on file, currently holds the job title, or has formally held the job title for six months or longer in the last five years. Standard exemptions eliminate testing of individuals who have already met the test standard, are already successfully performing a job, or have performed the same job in the recent past, and minimize needless exposure of the test. Although some groups (client organizations in particular) would like to use the selection process on incumbents to identify and eliminate performance problems, most I/O psychologists would argue that such use of a selection test is inappropriate. In addition to test exemptions, many testing programs refuse to test those with no need (for example, curious supervisors) to minimize the exposure of test items.

In companies that use formal selection procedures for upgrade and promotion decisions, exemptions are sometimes granted for subsets of the candidate population. A typical scenario is one in which a job is split in two and the testing requirements for each job are different. The company may "grandfather" those employees in the two jobs and allow them to move to the other job without qualifying on the current testing procedures for some period of time. Often, individuals who have qualified on a selection process that is subsequently changed and who have not yet been assigned the job are exempted from qualifying on the new selection procedure for some period of time for purely administrative reasons. The staffing offices could not handle the influx of large numbers of people who want to be tested on the new process.

Although many companies try to avoid bargaining the terms and conditions of testing programs, some collective bargaining agreements contain statements that contradict the test policies requiring all applicants to meet the test standard. A common example in some companies and some contracts pertains to layoff conditions, where employees who have "bumping" rights are not required to meet test qualification standards when they displace less senior employees in other jobs.

Exemptions for subgroups of employees should be carefully developed with representatives of the staffing, labor relations, and the legal organizations to minimize the problems associated with not applying a selection program to all candidates or trying to equate certain experiences to the skills measured in a selection program. Clients often want a voice in the decision to exempt large numbers of people from a test, particularly when its original purpose was to upgrade the workforce.

In addition to the standard exemptions and grandfathering of subsets of the applicant population, many organizations allow for nonstandard exemptions. Many of these come from the organization's inability to make ADA accommodations in the testing process, so they resort to exemptions from testing altogether and use some other alternative (for example, training performance) for assessing capability. When nonstandard exemptions are made, the test developer must design a process that carefully documents the reasons why. The process for nonstandard exemptions needs to be developed with representatives from a number of organizations, including staffing, labor relations, legal, EEO and affirmative action groups, the client, and the research team.

Waivers

Some companies distinguish between exemptions and waivers. Exemptions refer to groups or classes of people who are not tested because there is some other indicator of their capabilities, such as job performance, scores on the tests used for the job previously, and so on. In contrast, waivers are exceptions to the testing policy and are decided on a case-by-case basis or nonstandard exemptions. Thus ADA exemptions are technically waivers in the organizations that make a distinction. In addition, waivers might be granted as a result of a grievance or arbitration. Although exemptions may be granted to large numbers of people, waivers are usually given sparingly.

Retesting

Most organizations offer two kinds of retesting. The first, corrective retesting, is offered to candidates when something goes wrong with a testing session that is beyond the control of the test taker. For example, a fire alarm goes off in the middle of a session and requires evacuation of the building. Usually, gross errors on the part of the test administrator (for example, the test administrator distributed the wrong test booklet) are grounds for corrective retesting. Although the test administrator should take all possible steps to prevent such problems from happening, the test developer should establish guidelines that explain how to handle these situations once they have occurred. Documentation of such incidents is essential in the event the company is challenged on the exceptions to its testing requirements. In addition, documentation allows the test developer to identify weak test administrators with recurrent problems and coach them appropriately. Documentation of testing incidents may also provide information that can be used to develop better explanatory materials that may prevent future problems.

Many companies allow candidates who fail to meet the test standard to retest after some time has elapsed. Retesting allows for the possibility that the test taker was having a "bad day" the first time he took the test or has subsequently become better prepared to take the test. In order to reduce practice effects and prevent administrative logjams, the test developer should specify time intervals for each retest as well as the form of the test to use. Ideally, alternate forms should be used, and retest intervals should take into account the length of time practice effects last as well as administrative considerations. Unfortunately, alternate forms are difficult to develop for some types of tests, and few organizations research the extent of practice effects on their proprietary tests. Most retest intervals are set with administrative convenience in mind.

Many models for retest intervals exist. Many organizations begin with a reasonably short retest interval to allow for the possibility that the candidate was overly anxious or not sure what to expect and then move to more extended intervals for later retests. A common formula is six months and one year. The candidate must wait six months after the first test before retesting and then one year after the second test and all subsequent test events. Sometimes retests after the third testing event are extended to longer periods of time (for example, three years). The challenge of this variation is the extensive requirement for accurate record keeping and access by all test schedulers regardless of geography.

Another common variation on the retest intervals is to allow substantially shorter time intervals on tests on which the practice effect is relevant to the skill that is being measured. Many companies allow retesting after one week on typing, data entry, and stenography tests and subsequent retesting after one month and three months. An unusual twist is to relate the retest interval to the score achieved. One company allowed immediate retesting if the candidate achieved 95 percent of the test standard. The rationale was that a candidate very close to the test cutscore would likely improve her score on the second attempt when test anxiety was reduced.

When batteries of tests are given, the test developer should determine whether the entire battery must be retaken or whether individual tests may be retaken. Many companies do not allow tests to be taken singly in order to prevent a massive record keeping headache and problems recalculating battery scores. If candidates find it easier to remember a smaller number of items or employ a cheating strategy with fewer items, administration of a single test may also increase security problems. Single-test administrations may also allow a candidate to prepare for one test at a time instead of mastering all the skills required at once.

A related decision for the test developer is the number of times that a test may be retaken. Some companies allow for unlimited retesting to promote the idea that individual development can always occur. Others recognize the limits of developmental activities and require evidence of substantial preparation after some number of retests has been given before allowing another retest. Some allow no retesting at all, particularly when the lack of alternate forms reduces the value of the second test score. Retesting is sometimes eliminated for certain tests (for example, personality tests, biodata tests) on which no significant changes in score should occur if the candidate is answering honestly and accurately.

If retests are allowed, another decision to be made is which scores will be used for selection purposes. Some organizations count only the most recent score, whereas others use the highest score. Using the most recent score can lessen the problem of poor historical records. Using the highest score is often tautologous. The candidate only retests if the original score does not meet the test standard; thus if the more recent score (that is, the retest score) is not sufficient, the original score is unlikely to be. Of course, test standards can be lowered and the highest score may indeed be useful. It is also useful to use the highest score when batteries are administered in their component parts and the highest scores on each component rather than the most recent score on each component yield the highest battery score.

Confidentiality

Many organizations set rules about the confidentiality of test scores and limit who has access to scores. In some organizations, only personnel in the staffing and selection research organizations with a need to know may see test scores. Supervisors and hiring organizations may only be told that an individual is or is not qualified and not given the reason for the person's nonqualification. In some companies confidentiality is so protected that managers are not told that the test is the reason for the nonqualification. In others the manager is told about it in hopes that she will facilitate the individual's development.

In my experience, the best policy is to provide test information only to the candidate, the staffing organization, and the selection research organization. This keeps the I/O psychologist or the staffing manager from having to judge who has a need to know the test score and who will use the information wisely. The candidate is at liberty to share the test information with anyone and make decisions about who will use this information to help.

Whatever the limitations on test score availability, the test developer must design an implementation process that prevents access to test information by unauthorized individuals. That process should also include a procedure for the test taker to release test scores to others.

Other Rules

Most companies have a number of rules for the test administration process itself. Often they will require certain rules to be read to every applicant. A common rule is the "doing your best" rule. Every test taker is asked if there is any reason why he or she cannot do his or her best in the current test session and told that concerns about doing one's best are grounds for rescheduling a test but not for dismissing the results. The purpose of this question is to prevent candidates from later claiming they were unable to perform but did not have a chance to say so, and then demanding a corrective retest.

Another common test administration rule involves test security. Many organizations read statements that tell test takers that cheating in any form is prohibited and candidates are expected to protect the security and confidentiality of the test materials used. Usually the penalty for cheating, theft of test materials, or any other compromise of the testing process is disqualification.

For most of these test rules, three guidelines are applicable. First, the rules must fit the needs of the organization. For example, test exemptions should be given to incumbents who have held the closely related job in recent times if it calms labor unrest or eliminates testing of obviously qualified individuals. Second, rules must be applied to all candidates fairly and consistently. Few companies make unnoticed exceptions to their testing policies, particularly when there are large numbers of internal candidates or a labor union is monitoring the test program. Third, rules should be consistent throughout the company. It is difficult to argue that a practice effect lasts for at least six months on the arithmetic portion of the clerical battery but one year on the arithmetic portion of the craft battery.

Test Scoring

Scoring is an essential step in the testing process. The thorough test developer considers the options for ensuring accurate scoring, selects the one that best fits the test and the context, and provides detailed instructions. The test developer in conjunction with the staffing organization must determine who will score the tests and determine the kind of training, supervision, and monitoring to provide. The availability of qualified personnel and training affect the decision on what kinds of scoring aids to use. If the software is user-friendly enough, computer scoring demands the least amount of training, monitoring, and checking. "Fax-back" scoring technology that allows faxed answer sheets to go directly into a scanner for scoring also requires less training and supervision of the test administrators when the equipment is operated by trained individuals. In contrast, use of scoring keys and templates at each testing site requires training and monitoring to ensure the tests are accurately scored and the keys are adequately protected. Although remote test administrators are often used out of necessity, remote test scorers are generally perceived as an unnecessary temptation. Tests are usually returned to a central location for scoring.

Regardless of the training provided, there should be some method for verifying the accuracy of scoring. Often double scoring for hand-scored tests is used, or regular software and equipment checks are made for computer-based scoring and scanners.

Sometimes several different individuals administer tests, score tests, and process the paperwork. In order to ensure smooth administration of the entire process, the time frame for completion of scoring and dissemination of test information should be established and communicated.

Of all the different test formats, work sample tests, role-plays, and interviews may provide the greatest challenge to accurate scoring. Because the scoring process involves matching an observed behavior or statement to a standard, the test developer must carefully develop rating standards that will be accurately and consistently interpreted by the user regardless of person, time, or location. In addition, the test developer must monitor ratings to ensure that users continue to use the rating scales as written and rater biases do not creep in over time. Normally, complex scoring procedures like those required of interviews, work samples, and role-plays require periodic refresher training or recalibration to the standards.

Test Databases

Under current legal guidelines, accurate record keeping is a clear requirement (see Equal Employment Opportunity Commission, 1978, Section 15). Although it is permissible to store test scores in paper filing systems, most organizations with large-scale selection programs employ some sort of mechanized system for tracking test data to facilitate retrieval and reporting. Decisions about test data storage involve not only the test developer but also the staffing organization that will input the data, the information technology organization (IT) that designs and maintains computerized databases, and the EEO and affirmative action, legal, and labor relations groups that may need to use the data for the company's defense. The most important decisions about data storage are as follows.

Database

Perhaps the most fundamental question is which data will be stored. Obviously, the test score and some candidate identification (for example, name, social security number) should be kept. Less apparent is the form of the test score to keep. In order to prevent errors in interpretation, some test developers provide staffing representatives only the final qualification status (for example, Q/NQ). However, in the event a cutscore or the boundaries of a band change, raw data or the converted scores may be necessary. I/O psychologists usually need access to raw data for research purposes. Moreover, separate databases that require redundant input increase the likelihood that all databases will be incomplete. In order to serve the needs of all the stakeholders, it is advisable to keep all the test score information in raw, converted, and other forms in one database and limit access to the appropriate form of the data.

A related question in some organizations is which data are entered and which are calculated. When tests are manually scored, raw scores are often converted to some other form and test data are entered at a later time. Entering both raw and converted test scores provides an opportunity to check for errors albeit after the fact. Similarly, some organizations choose not to reenter demographic information and pull it from another source (for example, employee database or application). Others reenter such data to create a checkpoint for possible errors.

An interesting problem arises if different demographic coding is used at two different points in time. Periodically, a test taker will designate a race (or sometimes age) that is different from the race recorded in the employment records or the application blank. Because it can be awkward to ask people to clarify their race or age, most managers of large-scale selection programs adopt a consistent rule—for example, using the designated race on testing documents for test records and the other designated race for the other records. Of course, some data will not match up later on.

EEO and affirmative action, legal, and labor relations groups may need data to defend the company against accusations of discrimination, which are usually based on race, sex, or age. Thus demographic variables are usually included. It is important to note that some states prohibit collecting some demographic data. For example, a California state law currently makes collection of data on age inadvisable.

Contact information (address and phone number) is often stored in order to provide candidates with test feedback or contact them for the next step in the staffing process. For the sake of organizational efficiency, test information databases should be designed with the staffing organization so that duplicate data entry and records can be avoided. Again, my own experience suggests that using one central database, minimizing data entry, increases the probability of a complete database.

A final point when it comes to data storage involves tests that are not scored or tests that are administered in some nonstandard way. If a candidate cheats, the test is not scored no matter how much of the test he or she completed. Yet it is very important to record the fact that the individual actually did take the test for the company's own records as well as to prevent inappropriate retesting.

Most tests that are administered in some nonstandard way are the result of an ADA accommodation. The issue of flagging test scores (that is, noting in the test record that the test was given under nonstandardized conditions) is a significant one. Some psychologists argue that once the accommodation is made, test takers should not be penalized by drawing attention to it. Others argue that in employment settings particularly, the nonstandardized conditions make the score difficult to interpret and knowledge of the administration conditions aids the interpretation. The I/O psychologist and relevant stakeholders should carefully consider both sides of the issue and specify what approach to take. My experience suggests that scores that result from accommodated administrations should be flagged, but that information should be available only to the selection research organization.

Data Entry

Entering data into test information databases is often a challenge for staffing organizations. Once a person is disqualified for any reason or already hired, many staffing representatives perceive little need to enter data into a system. Yet maintaining test information is a clear legal requirement. The test developer must work closely with the staffing organization to define who enters the data and set time frames for entering them.

Access

The test developer must also determine who has access to test information. Rules about confidentiality will determine who may view individual test data as well as who is allowed to aggregate test data into reports. In addition, the test developer and the staffing organization should consider the security of test scores in the database and decide who may change test scores already entered. The test developer must work with the IT organization to ensure an effective means of appropriately limiting access.

Retention of Data

Even though electronic storage of data is now relatively inexpensive, most companies have some physical limits to the amount of data they can store on-line. When a company needs to limit the amount of data it keeps on-line, it should consider how long an external applicant is likely to stay on the labor market, how long the test is actually used, and how long it takes for employment discrimination complaints, grievances, and suits to materialize.

The laws and guidelines that affect the retention of selection records vary considerably in their guidance to the test user. For example, the Uniform Guidelines on Employee Selection Procedures (Equal Employment Opportunity Commission, 1978) state that when adverse impact is found in the selection process, records must be maintained for two years after the adverse impact is eliminated. This requirement applies to employers subject to Title VII of the 1964 Civil Rights Act (that is, employers with one hundred or more employees). Data must be retained by sex and for each ethnic group that constitutes at least two percent of the applicable workforce.

Although attorneys' advice varies, seven years is a common time frame for keeping data easily accessible. Companies then add extra time for tests that are used for more than seven years and for applicants who stay in the applicant pool for more than seven years. Some companies keep employee data on-line for the duration of the employee's career because such information may be useful for development or establishing patterns for defense in legal and administrative proceedings or for ADA accommodations. My recommendation based on personal experience is to keep all employee data on-line and applicant data for a minimum of ten years, longer if the tests continue to be used.

Reports

In addition to providing individual candidate information, testing reports provide valuable information about a key part of the staffing process. Certain reports are needed on a regular basis, and it is often helpful to produce these automatically. Other reports are generated in response to specific needs or questions on an ad hoc basis. The I/O psychologist responsible for test implementation must consider who may generate reports and who may receive them and develop a procedure that protects information, yet provides timely reports. The implementation process must also include careful consideration of tools that can be deployed for authorized users to create reports.

Examples of commonly produced reports include individual score reports, office reports, and organization reports. Individual reports usually include identifying information about the candidate, contact information, test score information, and qualification status. Office reports generally provide lists of qualifying individuals and nonqualifying individuals at a staffing location. Organization reports aggregate information across the entire company (for example, the number of people tested, the number qualified). Sometimes adverse impact calculations (for example, the four-fifths rule) will also be reported.

Monitoring

Frequent problems with test information databases are the number of errors and the amount of missing data. Ideally, data entry programs are written to prevent errors in the first place—for example, out-of-range test scores. The I/O psychologist responsible for test implementation needs to consider how the test information database will be maintained and kept as error-free as possible.

Test Previews

Many companies provide basic information about their testing program before the actual test administration. These test previews contain information including the kind of items in the test, the number of items, time limits, guessing strategies, note-taking rules, retest policies, ADA statement, information about the testing session, and general test-taking strategies. The purpose is to provide the test taker with basic information about what to expect at the testing session and inform him or her about basic test-taking strategies. Normally, the intent is not to provide any sort of training for skill improvement or test-taking ability. There is little research to suggest that test previews have any effect on resulting test scores.

Although most agree that providing basic test information is useful, a common problem is distribution to all candidates. In tight labor markets, candidates are often tested as soon as they show an interest in the job, leaving little time to distribute test previews. Many question the fairness of providing test previews to some but not all candidates. Some companies try to remedy this problem by providing everyone a test preview immediately before the actual test administration. However, late distribution reduces the benefit of knowing ahead of time what to expect. The best practice seems to be to distribute test previews in advance whenever possible, but always to provide time for review before the test session for those who did not receive the brochure and to offer to reschedule testing sessions if the candidate wants more time to prepare.

Test Preparation Guides

In tight labor markets especially, many organizations take extra steps to improve the skills of candidates (particularly internal candidates) for their positions. Besides increasing the pool of qualified candidates, companies often generate goodwill among the targeted candidates by trying to increase their skills. Test preparation guides usually provide general information about a test that might also be found in the test preview, more information about the skills and abilities measured, sample items or practice tests, and references to activities that may improve these skills and abilities.

One critical issue the test developer and others in the organization need to face is the value of such materials in improving test scores and presumably the knowledge, skills, or abilities being measured. Although test preparation activities may not always result in enduring skill development, the practice effect generated by sample tests and items should not be discounted. In some cases, a few extra points gained through practice are sufficient for some candidates to qualify.

If the company provides these materials, another important question is their content. Several issues arise here. One is the extent to which test-taking practice should be provided. Some researchers argue that the test should not be taught, whereas others argue that current test practices favor the test-savvy and that the playing field should be leveled. Another issue is the potential compromise of the actual test items. Often the training organization is enlisted to help write the guide and suggest activities that lead to skill improvement. The risk is that items too close to the actual test will be used and compromise the value of the test.

Distribution is also a problem with test preparation materials. Because these materials usually assume that some effort will be made to develop these skills, quick delivery is not the problem it is with test previews. However, the more important question is the physical distribution of the materials. There are sophisticated Web-based training tools that reduce printing and mailing costs, but many candidates do not have access to computers for personal development. For cost reasons, many companies ask whether they are obligated to build the skills of all candidates, just their own employees, or just candidates who have some probability of being hired. The more expensive the test preparation guide, the more salient these questions become.

Whether to provide test preparation materials depends on the organization's resources and its culture. The cost of developing materials that cover the content of a multitest battery is not insignificant. Distribution even to internal candidates alone can be costly. Yet test preparation materials may lessen some of the animosity toward a testing program that excludes large numbers of people and help create a feeling that the company cares about individuals and their career opportunities. Test preparation materials may also be seen to demonstrate the company's commitment to affirmative action. Moreover, in union environments where there is a spokesperson for the internal candidates, the selection research organization is often asked for suggestions on skill development. It is usually easier to develop these tools a priori than to respond repeatedly to questions on score improvement activities. Thus, even when there is little evidence that test preparation materials improve test scores, the cost may be worth the effect on attitudes toward the organization and its selection program.

Test Feedback

Ethically, psychologists should ensure that test takers receive some sort of feedback on their test performance. However, I/O psychologists are divided on the issue of the kind of test feedback that is appropriate and how it should be provided.

The first question the test developer must deal with is the content of the test feedback document. This document usually has several purposes and contains different kinds of information, depending on the organization's goals. It may include information about the candidate's score, information that places the score in context (for example, it is in the sixty-seventh percentile or is average), the candidate's qualification status, next steps in the staffing process, developmental information, and information about retesting. Some companies provide all of this, others only some of it. Some companies also include information on subtest or scale scores and descriptive labels that suggest relative strengths or weaknesses.

Distribution of test feedback is an organizational issue that should be decided by the affected groups. Although written feedback can be an additional expense, some staffing organizations prefer to mail test feedback to avoid unpleasant scenes and difficult questions and to ensure that all candidates receive the same level of feedback. Others prefer to give the feedback face-to-face so that the staffing process can continue promptly for qualified candidates. A few give qualified candidates their test feedback in person and mail the feedback to the nonqualified candidates. My preference is for trained test administrators to give face-to-face feedback to all, unless the situation makes it impractical (for example, large test administration sessions with hundreds of applicants). No matter if the feedback is face-to-face or written, a plan for providing the feedback, handling subsequent questions, and monitoring the feedback process should be developed as part of the implementation plan.

Communications

Communications about the implementation of a new selection process are critical to its success. The people who will be tested need to be informed about the new selection process and rules. The client organization needs to understand the selection process for its future employees and when it will take effect. The staffing organization that administers the testing program needs to know its role. The labor relations organization needs to understand the selection process and may require assistance in communicating it to labor leaders. Perhaps most important, candidates for jobs requiring the selection process will want information about it. The test developer must define all the audiences, the information each needs to know, and the optimum time to receive that information and then come up with a communications plan. A critical component of a communications plan is ensuring the materials are written in a way that each audience understands.

Another important characteristic of a communications plan is its two-way nature. Although the tendency of test developers is to think about what they need to say to others, if they encourage questions and feedback they gain information about potential problems and opportunities to improve the selection process.

Another important communications activity is handling questions about the testing program. The test developer and relevant stakeholders need to decide carefully which information is shared publicly and which is kept confidential. Large employers get frequent inquiries from the press as well as from representatives of advocacy groups. Many want to know what the testing program measures. Some also want sensitive information like pass-fail rates for various subgroups, which creates legal risks. Because many in the general public do not understand the complexities of test scores, a good rule of thumb is to provide the general public with the same information as candidates who take the test.

Test Administration Guide

The test administration guide is designed for those personnel who administer a test, score it, or use the test scores to define qualification status. Consequently, it should include specific instructions on how these tasks are to be accomplished and on the organization's policies and rules for selection processes.

The test developer must decide who has access to the test administration guide and that decision will be influenced by the information included in the guide. If cutscores are considered confidential material, then only those with a need to know cutscores should have access to the guide. Because of the way tasks are distributed in companies, the test administration guide is sometimes divided into smaller documents that provide all the information one person in a particular role needs to have.

Like other facets of the testing process, test administration guides must change as the selection program changes and the test developer must plan for their maintenance. One challenge for test developers is to ensure that everyone who has a test administration guide gets updates and implements new requirements when they should. One advantage of computerized testing is the ease with which all materials and instructions can be updated and old materials immediately removed from circulation.

The test administration guide for a work sample test is similar to that for paper-and-pencil or computerized tests. The main difference is in the amount of detail about test equipment, conditions for testing, and scoring information. Test administration guides for interviews are often mingled with training materials for the interview and include detailed information on conducting interviews, documenting the interview, rating responses, and so on.

Conclusion

Although some decisions must be made before others, there is no set procedure or order of tasks for implementing a test. I have found it helpful to use checklists and review them periodically throughout the test development, validation, and implementation phases, checking off items for which decisions have already been made. Because of the interrelationships among implementation tasks discussed earlier, checked items must be continually reviewed to ensure a later decision has not altered the "right" answer for a decision already made.

Implementing a large-scale selection program challenges the I/O psychologist in many ways and requires an array of skills. The sheer number of decisions to be made and details of processes to be established are daunting. In addition, the number of stakeholders involved, all with different needs and goals, can be overwhelming. The successful implementation of a large-scale testing program will depend as much on the I/O psychologist's project management skills and interpersonal skills as on his or her technical I/O skills.

I offer three final thoughts on implementation of large-scale testing programs that have more to do with managing large projects than with testing per se. First, planning the implementation is the sine qua non of a large-scale test development project. Large-scale testing programs do not manage themselves. If the I/O psychologist neglects implementation, someone else will step in and develop an implementation process that may not be professionally, legally, or ethically acceptable.

Second, problems ensue even with the best-laid plans. Perhaps we misread the environment, make mistakes in judgment, or underestimate the needs of the applicant population or the capabilities of the staffing organization. The I/O psychologists responsible for a large testing program must constantly monitor the selection programs and the people who are affected by it. They must be adaptable and adjust quickly when something is not working.

Finally, consistent treatment is the mantra of test administration. The I/O psychologist must be attuned to how the testing program is perceived. Consistent test policies will foster the idea that all candidates are treated fairly and that decisions are based on test scores rather than some other characteristic that is not job-related.

Additional Resources
Cascio, W. F., Goldstein, I. L., Outtz, J., & Zedeck, S. (1995). Twenty issues and answers about sliding bands. *Human Performance, 8,* 227–242.

Cascio, W. F., Outtz, J., Zedeck, S., & Goldstein, I. L. (1991). Statistical implications of six methods of score use in personnel selection. *Human Performance, 4,* 233–264.

Cascio, W. F., Zedeck, S., Goldstein, I. L., & Outtz, J. (1995). Selective science or selective interpretation? *American Psychologist, 50,* 881–882.

Kehoe, J. F., & Tenopyr, M. L. (1994). Adjustment in assessment scores and their usage: A taxonomy and evaluation of methods. *Psychological Assessment, 6,* 291–303.

McDowell, D. S., Norris, J. A., Kessler, L. L., & Williams, R. E. (1993). *Basic EEO resource manual: Practical guidance for EEO professionals and attorneys.* Washington, D.C.: Employment Policy Foundation.

Murphy, K. R. (1994). Potential effects of banding as a function of test reliability. *Personnel Psychology, 47,* 477–495.

Murphy, K. R., & Myors, B. (1995). Evaluating the logical critique of banding. *Human Performance, 8,* 191–201.

Murphy, K. R., Osten, K., & Myors, B. (1995). Modeling the effects of banding in personnel selection, *Personnel Psychology, 48,* 61–84.

Sackett, P. R., & Roth, L. (1991). A Monte Carlo examination of banding and rank-order methods of test score use in personnel selection. *Human Performance, 4,* 279–295.

Scientific Affairs Committee. (1994). *An evaluation of banding methods in personnel selection.* Arlington Heights, IL: Society for Industrial and Organizational Psychology.

Schmidt, F. L. (1991). Why all banding procedures are logically flawed. *Human Performance, 4,* 265–277.

Schmidt, F. L., & Hunter, J. E. (1995). The fatal internal contradiction in banding: Its statistical rationale is logically inconsistent with its operational procedures. *Human Performance, 8,* 203–214.

Zedeck, S., Cascio, W. F., Goldstein, I. L., & Outtz, J. (1996). Sliding bands: An alternative to top-down selection (pp. 222–234). In R. Barrett (Ed.), *Handbook of fair employment strategies.* Westport, CT: Quorum.

References

Equal Employment Opportunity Commission, Civil Service Commission, Department of Labor, and Department of Justice. (1978). Uniform guidelines on employee selection procedures. *Federal Register, 43*(166), 38295–38309.

Guion, R. M. (1998). *Assessment, measurement, and prediction for personnel decisions.* Hillsdale, NJ: Erlbaum.

Meehl, P. E. (1954). *Clinical versus statistical prediction.* Minneapolis: University of Minnesota Press.

Meehl, P. E. (1957). When will we use our heads instead of a formula? *Journal of Counseling Psychology, 4,* 268–273.

Meehl, P. E. (1965). Seer over sign: The first good example. *Journal of Experimental Research in Personality, 1,* 27–32.

Wiggins, J. S. (1973). *Personality and prediction: Principles of personality assessment.* Reading, MA: Addison-Wesley.

CHAPTER 10

Going Global
Additional Considerations Inherent in Cross-Cultural Implementation
Scott L. Eggebeen

The preceding chapters have discussed the technical and practical details of specific human resource interventions. This chapter will consider the added challenges that come with global implementation. Its structure will be somewhat different than that of previous chapters because of its unique overarching nature. This chapter will address general human resource practices across borders and provide more detail on the cross-cultural implications of specific interventions. It will look at the issues underlying many different types of global interventions. Local cultural and geographic differences play a role in the success or failure of all the interventions discussed in this volume. These differences are subtle threads in the fabric that make up an international organization.

It is difficult to summarize all that is relevant in such a short piece. Indeed, one might imagine an entire volume of the Professional Practice Series to address the multitude of cross-cultural implementation issues alone. Nevertheless, we would be remiss not to include at least a general overview of such an important topic. As the reader is likely aware, whole volumes have been published on international business issues (Bartlett & Ghoshal, 1991; Brake, Walker, & Walker, 1995; Phatak, 1992; Prahalad & Doz, 1987). In addition, several authors have considered global human resource

270

management specifically (Brandt, 1991; Dowling & Schuler, 1990; Fulkerson & Schuler, 1992; Schuler, Fulkerson, & Dowling, 1991). And finally, recent publications have begun to focus on industrial/ organizational psychology in a global context (Aycan, 2000; Earley & Erez, 1997; Ronen, 1997).

Several sources offer good overviews of cross-cultural organizational issues that provide a basic framework to guide the practitioner (Cascio & Bailey, 1995; Erez, 1994; Harris & Moran, 1996; Triandis, 1994). For example, a chapter by Erez in the *Handbook of Industrial and Organizational Psychology* (Erez, 1994) points to the need for a new, broad four-factor model: cultural values and norms that serve as a criteria for evaluating management practices; types of managerial practices and motivational techniques in the work setting; the self as a function of self-regulating processing, and as the interpreter and evaluator of management practices; and employees' work behavior. In the same volume Triandis (1994) examines some of the theoretical and methodological problems in defining and measuring culture and studying its effects on industrial and organizational processes.

But the scientist-practitioner is often flung into real-life situations well before a complete, tested framework for activities has been established. In the rush to corporate globalization, this is certainly the case. Many companies seek to export current operations and practices before they understand the complexities of working in different cultures. Although past behavior may often be a good predictor of the future, when translating expected behaviors into an entirely different cultural context, the outcomes may be unexpected.

Most successful multinational organizations seek a tense balance between corporate "centrism" and local or regional authority. At worst, this can be a sham—a plaque displaying corporate values that is ignored or mocked locally. At best, however, it can provide a helpful web in which to hold together all the pieces and unify them into a larger entity.

Global consistency may mean a unified and efficient organization, but geographical tailoring adapts practices to the local cultural needs and business requirements. In a specific geography, significant legal as well as social obligations are often linked to the ability to achieve business objectives in that region.

To put it simply, one must understand and be attuned to the social, cultural, and moral choices explicitly or implicitly underlying human behavior. Therefore, although it might seem preferable simply to focus on the technical components, it is important to address also these social and interpersonal issues in order for interventions to flourish globally. Many readers will already be aware of some of these challenges based on their own painful past experiences. By collecting such lessons learned, one can create a kind of map to guide practitioners. If not a complete treasure map to an ideal implementation, it can at least be a general reference on some suggested approaches and potential minefields.

Changing Forces Affecting Practitioners

In his groundbreaking book *Global Paradox,* John Naisbitt (1994), a noted futurist, suggested that allegiances are shifting from nationalism to arrayed small economic alliances. Technology and travel are viewed as forces that are leading to the inevitable globalization of communication, information, and commerce. In essence, one could interpret this to mean that a form of feudalism is returning in corporate form. Large corporations are breaking down into globally aligned entrepreneurial units, whereas smaller companies are bonding together to create competitive global alliances. At the same time, events such as protests against the World Trade Organization point to a growing backlash against the trend toward globalization. Individual-country nationalism is reemerging in response to pressures and influences—the Internet, for example—to create one large global village.

Naisbitt describes these two competing trends as a global paradox. The push toward one large global economy has in turn led to a stronger need for differentiation, which he refers to as tribalism. Both forces are present and growing. The only logical way to deal with these divergent forces seems to be to incorporate both into all solutions. This is also the case in cross-cultural human resource interventions.

One must try to unite an organization through similarities and facilitated by technology. At the same time, it is essential that individual countries and regions feel that their unique differences are acknowledged and accommodated.

Much of the research simply acknowledges that each country has unique differences that must be taken into consideration. Several frameworks have emerged to identify constructs or dimensions on which the different cultures may vary. All of these provide helpful ideas. Similarly, simple personality inventories such as the Myers-Briggs Type Indicator (MBTI) can provide helpful frameworks. But they can be overinterpreted and perhaps provide too simplistic a solution to a very complex topic.

A holistic plan or process flow for implementing global human resource initiatives is something different. Practitioners need a hands-on guide to help them make projects run more smoothly and quickly and feel more certain of reaching the intended outcome. This chapter will attempt to begin such a guide for implementing human resource solutions globally.

Critical Variables That Determine Tailoring Needs

It is hard to generalize about which cross-cultural variables are most essential to address. Much depends on the makeup of the institution and the specific project. Nevertheless, there are a few variables that one might initially consider in project development, such as the following:

- Makeup of the workforce *(level, type, and number of workers; percentage of locals and expatriates)*
- Languages *(common international business practice or native tongue)*
- Locations *(how many, how substantial an employee base in each, how geographically distant from other units)*
- Intervention type *(for example, training program or profit-sharing plan)*
- Legal implications *(for example, the degree to which the intervention has legislative oversight)*
- Compliance *(the degree to which a solution is mandatory)*

Here is an example of how the makeup of the workforce is relevant. Consulting firms and investment banks have the luxury of employing top-tier MBAs. Many of these individuals were trained at a select set of primarily U.S. business schools. As a result, they have shared experiences, meet consistent screening criteria for entry, and offer an expected level of skills and abilities. Even though these educational programs accept people from diverse classes in many different cultures and geographies, their graduates turn out to be strikingly similar in many ways. This situation allows for a high degree of global consistency in HR solutions.

In contrast, large manufacturing corporations may employ primarily local nationals who have little or no experience outside their location of birth and traditional culture. These employees may also have little educational background and not speak the language of the headquarters country. Industries with little high-level specialization will likely find that much more local tailoring will be necessary to accommodate those at the lower levels with minimal multinational experience. The challenges associated with interventions in these environments are consequently quite different from those in the first situation.

If the workforce does include a large percentage of local nationals, it is essential that all materials, handouts, and communications be translated into the local language. This is not just a matter of literal word-for-word translation but a highly specialized activity that requires the expertise of someone with substantial experience in the culture. Concepts, ideas, and normative references are directly tied to the culture from which they emerge. It is essential to involve someone who is familiar with the local cultural concepts in coming up with the ideas as well as the communications.

This is certainly true in testing and employee surveys. The grassroots group Fair Test suggests that making a simple analogy to a cup and saucer may be seen to be highly correlated with socioeconomic status. Consequently, it could be viewed as a biased test item. Similarly, associated references can also be connected to cross-cultural norms. It is essential not to translate selection instrument items or survey questions word for word; there must be awareness of potential differences in contextual meaning.

In addition, people in different cultures are more or less open to communicating in person or on paper. The results achieved through a carefully facilitated focus group may be very different from an anonymous mailed survey. In Thailand and Malaysia, for example, there are likely to be very low response rates to employee surveys simply because many local workers are not familiar or comfortable with the format. Simple responses to questions posed directly in a focus group, such as yes or no, can also result in confusing interpretations. For example, Singaporean employees might prefer to say yes simply to avoid disagreeing in public.

Common 360-degree feedback mechanisms also presuppose a degree of willingness on the part of respondents to comment openly and directly. In some cultures, open criticism is neither valued nor accepted, even if it is constructive. Thus, techniques used in one location are not necessarily applicable in all locations in a global organization. It is important to look at the needs of the whole organization as well as the needs of the local culture to find an appropriate balance.

Types of Issues to Consider

Cross-cultural implementation brings one face-to-face with a broad set of complicated challenges. Practitioners have to make difficult decisions about ethics, diversity, open communication, fairness, equity, and appropriateness of behavior. There is no one appropriate method to deal with these challenges. Each project must address a unique set of cross-cultural issues.

A few examples may provide insights into the unexpected complexities. For instance, the Thom McAnn brand has traditionally sold shoes with a nearly illegible trademark signature printed inside the shoe. But when the company tried to sell this footwear in Bangladesh, a riot ensued in which more than fifty people were injured. The signature was mistaken as Arabic script for *Allah*. Outraged locals concluded it was designed to desecrate the name of God by walking on it—an insult in any culture, but especially in Bangladesh, where the foot is considered unclean (Morrison, Conaway, & Borden, 1994).

How easy it is to make critical mistakes if there is no awareness! In Saudia Arabia, simply crossing your legs and accidentally showing the sole of your shoe to your host may be considered a very serious insult. Unfortunately, these avoidable kinds of mistakes are all too common.

Another often-cited example involves General Motors' attempt to market a car in Latin America under the brand name Nova. In Spanish, *no va* means something like, "It doesn't go." Thus, translation does not resolve the issue; the idea itself needed to be rethought to bring forward another image more in line with the intent. Field testing the ideas in local markets and contexts may also help companies to discover confusion and areas that need clarification or reconsideration.

Translating Meaning, Not Just Words

Many organizations make the mistake of assuming that simply translating memos and documents into the local language will ensure that the messages received will be consistent. Many concepts, however, are not universal. Consequently, simply translating into a different language does not necessarily result in the intended action. It is important not to wait until the end of a project to translate. Instead, a much more fundamental question should be raised early in the process: How is it best to build ideas and communicate the prescribed set of issues in the context of those to be influenced? This approach may suggest that a memo or package from headquarters may not, in fact, be an option at all.

Besides basic translation services, it is important to seek input into how the tone, style, and structure of communications may be perceived. A thorough audience analysis from other points of view can raise a wealth of issues to avoid, assign relative weight and intensity of messages and meanings, and uncover fundamental flaws in the way a project has been conceptualized.

Ethics and Values

There are also many ethical and values issues to deal with. Different societies have significantly different views on gifts, honesty, and social engagement. Simple practices such as entertaining clients at social and cultural events can be a minefield. For example, compensation and rewards programs suggest what is of value to the company and who deserves to have what percentage of it. In developing countries, the population may take for granted stark contrasts in socioeconomic status. In contrast, in highly modernized societies expansive social welfare programs may attempt to establish at least a minimum standard of living for all. To give equal or different bonuses to two employees of different social class structures in a country may be either perceived as laudatory or reprehensible, no matter the technical merits of the solution.

Diversity and Discrimination

Ethnic, cultural, and racial differences also often come into play. Most cultures have unwritten social rules that determine who may participate and who may not. An uninformed employer in Brazil might put Paulistas and Cariocas on the same work team. This scratches only the surface distinction between these two Brazilian groups, not noticing perhaps significant local social and cultural distinctions between them. At an even a broader level, an employer might include both groups with Chileans representing Latin America, even though these groups do not share a language or culture, let alone a similar view of themselves and their appropriate social class positioning.

The more important the initiative, the more concern there will be over which people to include in it. In some countries, women are still not normally selected for specific types of work assignments. Similarly, in Latin American cultures, family structure and "connectedness" to certain social echelons are seen as very important for an individual to be considered worthy of certain types of assignments.

The first mistake of many well-meaning business managers is to trivialize these issues or try to ignore them. The worst thing to do is try to teach others "better" ways. Demonstrating an interest, awareness, and acceptance of deeply held personal beliefs may in fact be the price of admission to gaining influence.

Standards of Discipline and Punishment

In some cultures, general compliance is mandatory. Authoritarian regimes have zero tolerance for alternative approaches. Those who do not comply are openly criticized and possibly publicly humiliated. Other, more laissez-faire societies follow a live-and-let-live philosophy. Here, a mandatory appraisal system with consistent performance criteria can conflict with local cultural values and be almost impossible to implement globally.

Whatever consistency is expected must be followed up. Putting in a solution that will not be monitored and reinforced can begin a very slippery slope to denial or lack of deference to organizational hierarchy—perhaps having the opposite effect of what was initially intended.

Communication Parameters

All societies have communication parameters. Willingness to discuss certain topics, to criticize others, to acknowledge wrongdoing, or even to agree or disagree varies. Saving face may be one of the most important social obligations. In such cultures it may be more natural to withdraw than to confront that which is perceived to be misguided or foolish behavior. Expecting others to conform to one's own cultural norms and standards presupposes that there is a right and wrong as related to the initiating culture. Because all organizations are headquartered in a particular country and have an overwhelming number of staff in that country but smaller numbers elsewhere, it is common to try and export the social value structure. However, it is important to distinguish the very real need for consistent corporate norms (for example, no bribes) from local cultural choices, and then apply the minimum requirements.

Fairness, Equity, and Appropriateness

When employees are hired, they should understand the corporate choices and values for which they are signing up. This helps alleviate potential individual conflicts with corporate standards in the future. At the same time, the institution must accept and acknowledge the existence of alternative points of view and try to impose a minimum of absolutes. Thinking through the cultural values associated with an implementation at its inception can be a valuable way to prepare for the conflicts that may emerge as the project progresses.

Some cultures value equity whereas others emphasize equality, and these values correlate with individualism and collectivism. Consequently, the very notion of what is fair needs to be researched and understood.

Identifying and Using Expertise

Because the territory is so vast and diverse, the savvy practitioner must assemble resources—books, videos, and professional society documents, as well as legal assistance and the assistance of colleagues with global human resource experience and experts in cross-cultural communication. By all means, practitioners should not proceed alone in trying to adapt an intervention across geographies.

One particularly useful source to start with is *Kiss, Bow, or Shake Hands* (Morrison, Conaway, & Borden, 1994). This volume profiles the cultures of sixty countries. Each profile includes a brief overview, as well as detailed sections on behavior style, negotiating techniques, protocol (greetings, gestures, forms of address, gift giving, and so on), and business practices. It can provide HR professionals with a basic safeguard against common social gaffes, as well as give them notice of expectations and help them anticipate potential points of conflict.

Legal Counsel

Also necessary for a thorough understanding is detailed regulatory knowledge as well as research capabilities in specific geographic markets. Although the United States may once have had more detailed and complex work rules and workplace legislation, this is not necessarily the case today. For example, Germany allows a small group of employees to form together in a work council to address an issue, and the company generally must respond.

Consultants

Consulting firms can provide comparative data. For example, compensation standards may be quite different from country to country. In some places, a car is part of a standard executive package. If an organization did not offer such a perquisite, it would lose many talented recruits for a position simply because of the issue of implied social status. Several large multinational consulting firms benchmark international differences, particularly in the largest economic centers. They also catalogue legislation and government requirements. For example, a small capacity reduction or downsizing in several countries in Asia faces differences in government reporting requirements, allowed and expected termination benefits, and mandated notice periods. Although costly, one strategy may be to provide a standard package for all affected personnel that is higher than the expectations in any individual country. Or the company could provide the minimum expected in each country. This means finding a delicate balance, much as with a compensation structure, trading off internal equity with market competitiveness. Employees will be impressed by standards that are above requirements, but practically speaking an organization that needs to downsize is usually not looking for opportunities to be more generous than necessary. However, its behavior also sends a signal to all other employees about how they can expect to be treated. This affects commitment and satisfaction, and often productivity.

Experienced Colleagues

Other large multinational corporations may have experience in dealing with particular issues in a specific geographical area. It is often valuable to try to find out what has worked and what has not worked for other companies, or at least how they have tried to address a particular problem. Generally, other international human resource managers are at least aware of difficulties that they or others have encountered. Another set of eyes on a project plan can be most valuable and allow HR professionals to profit from the intellectual capital already gained by their colleagues.

Internal Best Practices

Finally, one can also review the course of other initiatives in the organization before moving forward. What worked well and what did not? Why was a particular global implementation successful, or why did it fail? Many organizations do not even collect internal lessons learned and best practices and so face the same problems over and over again.

Tailoring human resource interventions globally may mean making unique trade-offs and compromises. Nevertheless, many resources are available to provide benchmarks and best practices. It is a good idea to seek out these resources proactively. Although many organizations may revile a "not invented here" scenario, the benefits of doing so can outweigh the disadvantages, even if the resources simply point out challenges to solve or options to cross off the list.

Of course, all of these suggestions involve additional costs—potentially substantial sums. However, this must be considered as part of the cost of doing business globally. The cost may be much higher if a solution is ignored or rejected. Experienced global human resource professionals can be differentiated by their acknowledgment of the many attempts that have been scrapped or circumvented, and their relative skittishness at the idea of a quick and easy adaptation for a different culture. Taking such a stance prevents them from making promises to deliver outcomes that are not easily attained.

Specific Interventions in a Global Context

Although the other chapters deal with these specific interventions, this section provides brief synopses of issues that may need to be considered when trying to implement them globally.

Performance Appraisal

- Performance review may be one of the areas where global consistency is most desirable but also most difficult to achieve. For instance, semantics have much to do with the success or failure of competency models. Subtle differences in meanings and interpretations can affect implementation success.
- The culture of raters and interviewees will affect their willingness to talk openly and give difficult messages.
- Managers have a vested stake in the perceived success of their staff. In some cultures, it may be important for them to be seen as positive and supportive, so it can be very difficult to get them to deliver straightforward messages. In Japan, for example, a manager may choose to step down as having failed the team rather than openly criticize and terminate a long-term employee.
- Many organizations have tried to implement appraisals that include input from multiple rating sources. This can be extremely difficult to do, however, because subordinates are often unwilling to criticize their elders and those receiving the

feedback may be easily insulted if it comes from subordinates. In such cases, the performance improvement objectives are thus null and void.

Recognition and Rewards Systems

- Different countries have unique provisions about pay and rewards. In some, almost any arrangement is legally acceptable; in others, very specific payments must be made to the country in addition to the employee. Staff may be hired and fired only with specified government permission through official agencies.
- Local authorities may regulate severance and termination payments and benefits. It is advisable to contact local authorities or have external partners (for example, consulting firms) do so to get up-to-date information on requirements.
- Pay practices must be aligned with local market norms to be competitive and attract and retain top performers. This may mean setting up unique local perquisite programs in addition to or in place of a consistent global framework.
- Some organizations have attempted to set up one international payroll company in one location to pay all staff in different countries. Increasingly, however, this has come under scrutiny because of the potential for lost tax revenues in specific countries if an individual employee spends a large portion of time working in a host country, whether officially stationed there or not.
- Much like currency traders, international compensation managers must be attuned to currency fluctuations and the relative values of money as international rates go up and down. Accruing specific amounts may not be accurate or sufficient if not pegged to local currency markets.

Assessment and Development, Career, and Succession Planning

- Although corporations generally want to develop individuals through international assignments, doing so can cause difficulties with local nationals and result in limited bench strength when expatriates return to their country of origin.
- Local aspirations for personal growth and development vary. Organizations often assume that drive and career advance-

ment will be seen to be equally desirable and expected. This may not be the case. Merely identifying high-potential employees can make individuals uncomfortable.

- In various countries, leaders may be chosen for an organization based on their age, social class, political orientation, or even family membership. Simply appointing senior executives in some countries can be difficult because of local expectations about the religion and marital status of leaders. Respect is an essential element of leadership, so organizations have to be aware of those things that are necessary to put leaders in place who followers will respect.

Global Assignments

- Work authorization rules and citizenship provisions in each country will determine who is allowed to perform which types of activities. Organizations must be extremely careful in creating and communicating what could be perceived as an expectation that expatriates are more skilled or have higher potential than locals.
- Standards of living may be dissimilar based on local taxation levels and government benefits provided. In many cases, equalization packages must be created for expatriates to allow them to maintain a standard of living that is equivalent to their previous one. This often involves complicated accounting and tax calculations provided by companies through independent experts (for example, individual financial advisers are provided as a part of the total compensation package).
- Many organizations provide little cultural training for managers assigned to new international locations. This can initially be cost effective, but in the long run it may be very expensive in terms of opportunity costs because the failure rate is quite high. In fact, many trailing family members may be more crucial to the success or failure of a global assignment than the managers themselves. Often family members have a difficult time adapting to the cultural norms in schools, social clubs, or volunteer activities. If the trailing spouse is not allowed to work, it may be particularly daunting for him or her to find meaningful engagement, dialogue, and social interaction, especially if the individual does not speak the language.

Employee Surveys

- In some countries it may be considered rude to ask many questions or pointed questions. Different cultures are comfortable with various levels of disclosure. Topics that may be openly discussed in one country may be completely off-limits in another (for example, comparative levels of pay).
- It may or may not help to make responses to instruments anonymous. In some cultures, it may be considered dishonorable if comments are not attributed. In others, employees may only feel safe providing input if they are assured their feedback will not be directly attributable to them.
- It is essential to understand levels of criticism. An American may get many comments and complaints in France that would appear to be highly critical or even condescending in the United States. It could be a serious mistake, however, to conclude that French employees are generally more dissatisfied. Instead, their behavior may reflect a cultural comfort level with certain kinds of criticism.

Recruiting and Selection Systems

- There are significant differences in educational systems. Even those receiving the same degree (for example, Ph.D.) may have very different training and experience levels. Building extensive relationships with local recruiting channels (for example, universities or their equivalent) is essential to understanding and acquiring top talent locally.
- In many countries, positions in organizations are tightly tied to social rank, status, personal affluence, and "connectedness." Recruiting for top talent in these countries may require much more social interaction at key nonbusiness functions; this may be necessary merely to talk with potential candidates of a particular social status.
- Interviewing content and styles may not come across in similar ways in other cultural contexts. Structured, formal, hard-hitting competency questions may be expected in one culture but discourage applicants in another.

- In some countries, it is common for individuals to send pictures with résumés as well as samples of their writing. Details of family, age, and religious and political affiliations may be included. In the United States, these items would not be considered valid in employee selection.

Cross-cultural research is emerging to help companies understand these specific issues. For example, a simple personality instrument such as the MBTI has shown both similarities and differences in different countries. It is illuminating to contrast U.S. managers with Japanese. Although the percentage of individuals representing different personality types may be similar in the two countries, the percentage of those with a specific personality reaching management positions may be somewhat different because of accepted social norms and standards of appropriate behaviors for the role prescribed by the local culture.

McCrae and Costa (1997) suggest that underlying constructs such as personality trait structure may transcend country and language boundaries to some extent. For example, the five-factor model (FFM) was tested in German, Portuguese, Israeli, Chinese, Korean, and Japanese samples and compared with an American factor structure. The authors concluded that the structures were closely reproduced. This led them to hypothesize that personality trait structure may, in fact, be universal.

Training

- Many organizations make the mistake of mandating worldwide training programs that are not adapted to the cultural sensitivities of some of the countries involved. Forcing employees to sit through sessions that clearly miss the mark may cause more difficulty than not training them at all.
- Deference to teachers and learned elders varies greatly. Thus, programs designed to use the Socratic method of discussion and debate may be greeted with silence from participants, even if the instructor attempts to elicit strong reactions from the audience.
- Learning styles too can vary by culture. Some educational systems embrace harsh graders and tough instructors, pushing

individuals as far as possible. In others, learning is an enlightened pursuit not meant to be rushed but instead to be an introspective and reflective process. If a program does not adapt to the particular norms, it risks losing the majority of learners early on.

- It may be difficult to evaluate training in cultures where knowledge is considered a gift to be treasured, not criticized.

Employee Relations

- In different locations, work rules and standards may apply in unexpected ways. In issues such as sexual harassment, while conducting investigations, one must untangle different perspectives and beliefs from the facts of the situation.
- When it comes to disciplinary action, saving face and honor is of utmost importance in some cultures. In others, termination of workers may occur at almost any time for any reason without regard for the impact or impression it may create.
- Responding to challenges by employees can be dictated as a part of government legislation. Those involved in employee discipline must be certain they understand the level of severity and acceptable punishment. Some cultures approve of rigorous responses to mistakes or misdeeds that might be considered barbaric by others.
- Gifts given for special anniversaries or outstanding performance are not always received as they are intended. Being singled out of a group can be viewed as highly embarrassing and reflect poorly on an individual, demotivating rather than motivating both the individual and the group.

General Process Dynamics

To carry out global interventions successfully one has to gain agreement on three fronts before implementation: the problem is truly a significant one that is consistently understood across the various cultures; solving the problem in a particular way would be mutually valuable for the institution and the individuals in the cultural context; and there is agreement on the extent to which the solution must be adhered to in order to achieve the expected payoff.

Building Support Through Input

There are many tips and techniques for cross-cultural negotiations at the highest level, but it is essential to have a method and process that convinces key stakeholders that their views have been heard and acknowledged. Disagreements between team members can be resolved more quickly if they understand from the start that they are responsible for bringing each other together to resolve significant issues. This avoids criticism by those who do not feel vested in a successful outcome.

It is also very important to set the stage for conflict. Everyone on the project team needs to understand that diverse ideas and suggestions will be welcome. The tone and style of interactions must demonstrate intellectual respect. It is essential to elicit the various points of view and then explore their relative merits in discussion. Investing more time up front can be worthwhile because common, uniting goals and objectives will be established. If there is awareness of and attention to the cultural norms and values of participants, it suggests that their views were at least considered and an attempt was made to work some if not all suggestions from each participant into the solution.

The challenge, of course, is to keep this from becoming a bureaucratic exercise that does not move toward an effective solution. Careful planning and coordination can help. All participants need to be aware of key decision points, forced choices, and expected progress deadlines. When and where input will be allowed, how decisions will be made, expectations to support conclusions once decisions are made, and shift of emphasis to the next phase of the assignment can be documented and communicated.

Providing several opportunities for input in different styles and formats can also be quite helpful. Individuals in certain cultures, particularly in Asia, often find it uncomfortable to confront directly and openly. One must try to find forums for input (both public and private) that match local norms.

Focus groups can be used to test reactions and get opinions on issues in a relatively safe space. It can be invaluable to ask participants how they see the issue, what solutions they might consider, and what they see as potential barriers to implementation. However, focus groups may not work if individuals will not speak openly in such a forum, which is the case in certain cultures.

The best solutions come from diverse teams with widely differing perspectives. Cross-cultural implementations that follow the same principles similarly get the best results. The reality, though, is that they often take longer, are more difficult to achieve, and involve careful management of conflict.

Valuing Diversity of Opinion

There are many cultural differences to contend with, but underlying them all is the fundamental human desire to be respected, considered, heard, and acknowledged. In this regard, many very difficult challenges can give way to one universal culture of mutual respect and consideration.

The right individuals should be involved from very early in the process, even perhaps before the problem is fully detailed. It can be valuable to have a team of people provide input and counsel on a project. This can be accomplished in a number of ways. An advisory board, a review body, a working group, and a steering committee can all help to make sure the effort meets with the least resistance on implementation. The idea is to pull together input from multiple key stakeholders. However, these options differ markedly in expected decision-making authority, override power, responsibility for work, and championing of results.

Identifying and Including Local Champions

At a minimum it is advisable to have local team members from all relevant geographies and cultures understand the full nature of the problem, the alternatives to be considered, the challenges presented, and the hypothesized solution before final development and implementation. An advisory board can serve this purpose well. Its main function is to respond to ideas presented, identify potential difficulties, and provide feedback on alternative solutions. In the basic sense, the advisory board has no official decision-making power but it provides a way for the project leader to anticipate reactions and justify decisions. The advisory board can meet or hold conference calls when key milestones are met to comment on progress and raise other concerns.

Appointing a regional implementation leader for each location ensures that someone is responsible for thinking through the challenges inherent in tailoring to the local culture. This not only builds local support but also shows that headquarters believes that local input is relevant.

Historically, many large multinationals have relied heavily on a central corporate push to get policies and procedures out to field locations. Although this approach had the advantage of using hierarchical power to drive acknowledgment and acceptance, many of these solutions were tightly held before implementation rather than discussed with relevant constituencies. Thus, when they were implemented, many important issues came up or the goals were ignored regionally. One may avoid such difficulties with a project management model that includes multiple concentric circles of influence to provide input and agree on decisions before moving forward. The downside is that more time and significant resources are required. The chosen solution, however, has a much higher possibility of being accepted and used appropriately. In many companies, it is interesting that groups learn quickly that everyone cannot have their way on everything. This forces give-and-take and consensus, as well as an awareness of issues and motivations and other points of view.

Expecting Disagreement and Resolving It

Conflicts must be anticipated and proactively managed. Before problems arise, resolution approaches can clarify how disagreements will be negotiated. Specific cross-cultural research can help in this regard. For example, Kimmel (2000) notes that international meetings and negotiations depend on human perception and behavior. Relatively low levels of cultural awareness can contribute to or cause destructive conflict. Intercultural exploration uses differences in mind-set to develop new opinions and approaches, build relationships, and create unique solutions.

Tinsley (1998) developed three models for resolving conflict drawn from the literature: deferring to status power, applying regulations, and integrating interests. Tinsley suggests that one can begin to predict the conflict models of Japanese, German, and American businesses from their group rankings on three dimensions of cultural variation: hierarchical differentiation, explicit contracting, and polychronicity. Preference for a model was reported to be influenced by culture, which filters information and guides members toward using a particular approach more consistently.

For example, in negotiations German managers may take a long time to come to agreement, but once they believe a decision has been made it is generally considered final and intractable. In contrast, although Japanese managers may push for consensus, even after the contract is drawn up they may not consider the decision to be final. It can be reopened to interpretation and renegotiated as appropriate. American managers move very swiftly to a conclusion with a focus on short-term impact, and once a contract is signed it is often seen as a legally binding irrevocable document. Such differences clearly can cause conflicts—over the speed of the process, the finality of the solution, and the general level of agreement and compliance required.

Elsayed-Ekhouly and Buda (1996) demonstrated differences in the ways U.S. and Middle Eastern (from Egypt, Saudia Arabia, Kuwait, and the United Arab Emirates) executives handled interpersonal conflicts on five key conflict-handling styles: integrating, obliging, dominating, avoiding, and compromising. Results showed that cultural orientation affects executives' responses to conflicts. Middle Eastern executives used more of an integrating and avoiding style, whereas U.S. executives were more likely to use an obliging, dominating, and compromising style.

According to Porter (1997), trust is increasingly important for flexible and efficient team performance. Thus, an understanding of how trust is developed and interpreted by others can be essential for all team members. Although diversity adds to a team's resources, it also may lead to different interpretations of behaviors and thus inhibit trust among project participants.

A General Model for Global Implementation

Overall, a schematic model (Figure 10.1) may prove helpful by outlining the stages in which the global HR professional will want to raise questions and adapt solutions. The model is not meant to be all-inclusive or applied in the same way to all global initiatives. But it may serve as a guide for some of the critical issues to be considered. Specific choices may be forced later or earlier, depending on the project. The model is designed to be iterative, however, to suggest that one may cycle back through the choices several times to achieve the best solution.

Figure 10.1. A General Model for Global Implementation.

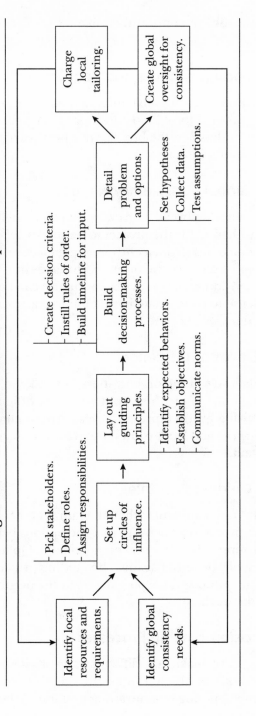

The specific elements and choice points in the model are as follows.

Identify Local Resources and Requirements

At the beginning of any global intervention it is essential to choose credible sources of local help and support. Articulate participants who clearly understand the broader perspectives of the groups they represent should be selected.

Identify Global Consistency Needs

Before considering broad alternatives it can be helpful to create a set of "must-haves" for the project to be successful. The minimum expected outcomes (from a corporate perspective) that will signify the accomplishment of the intended intervention is a good place to start. Then additional areas of congruence can be defined where it makes sense to consolidate in relation to scale, scope, or volume of transactions.

Set Up Circles of Influence

At multiple levels in the organization, key stakeholders should be aligned together to provide input and relay official communications. Involving group representatives early on eliminates the element of surprise and lends extra support for the challenge of change management.

Lay Out Guiding Principles

It is helpful to create tenets that all team members will look to as the project progresses to ensure that the options being chosen and the actual approach follow the intended path. Options and choices can continually be tested against the guiding principles as a way of unifying the group and keeping it true to the original mission and intent of the work.

Build Decision-Making Processes

Before the group makes any difficult trade-offs it is essential to clarify the methods by which it will settle on solutions and move forward despite opposing or contrasting positions. Whether it is group consensus, majority rule, or committee chairperson dictum, the method of resolution must be clear and consistent.

Detail Problems and Options

As the previous chapters in this volume have suggested, the elements of the problem, symptoms, alternative approaches to solving it, and criteria for success should be established and possibly pilot-tested.

Charge Local Tailoring

Where it has been agreed that some local differentiation is required or valuable, a subteam that includes local representation should be assigned to prepare a plan and return to the larger team with suggested changes. With approval, this group becomes the local implementation team.

Create Global Oversight for Consistency

As the old adage put it, "If it doesn't get measured it doesn't get done." Unless a reinforcing mechanism is put in place to test for global consistency, local tailoring can drift along into completely different approaches. A follow-up process and minimum standards for how global compliance will be evaluated must be specified. There may be occasional follow-up visits, surveys, or training evaluation. A mechanism for communication on exceptions can also be helpful to provide a protocol to keep all engaged in making only those changes that remain in line with the original intent.

Issues will undoubtedly come up during a pilot implementation. These can be collected and reentered in the beginning stage of the model to adapt and refit the solution accordingly. Provided the organizational structure is stable, periodic ongoing meetings of the design team can be held to make additional decisions on changes to the implementation parameters.

Conclusion

When it chooses to implement human resource initiatives globally, an organization must make complex trade-offs. Although there is no single way to address these challenges, this chapter has offered a road map that shows obstacles and barriers to success that can be minimized or eliminated.

Common Elements in Effective Global HR Implementations

Successful global implementation projects seem to have a number of factors in common, including the following:

- Clear and open communications about intent, process to be followed, time for input, and intended consequences
- A structured project management framework that provides detailed work activities, inputs for decision making, milestone dates when review and approvals will take place, and expectations of all critical team players
- Multinational teams that both gather input and review hypothetical change options and trade-offs
- Clear goals and directives that support the value proposition for both the employees and the organization, and a value proposition that is appealing to all

Steps to Take to Increase Chances of Success

Globalization requires human resource professionals to be very flexible, informed, and skilled cross-culturally. It increases the complexities involved in implementing a human resource solution tenfold. But if one takes a series of steps and actions, it will likely lead to a better end product and a smoother implementation process:

- Include and implement through local or regional champions.
- Pretest communications and concepts with experts on and natives of the local culture.
- Gather extensive reference sources on specific cultural working situations and conditions.
- Study the contextual factors for the program.
- Do not translate language; instead, create similar, culturally relevant concepts.
- Seek input from those most affected by the intervention to be sure the desired response actually occurs.
- Balance the need for organizational consistency with local tailoring, being flexible where possible.

- Ensure that the approach is culturally relevant to the intent of the initiative, not just feasible to achieve.

Lessons Learned

Practitioners can draw some basic lessons from the suggestions and descriptions of mistakes presented here. In general:

- Seek broad understanding and communication early on.
- Use inclusive project team approaches to build buy-in.
- Anticipate tailoring problems through early field testing.

If the working approach makes the necessary accommodations and balances local needs with global consistency, human resource interventions can become successful organizational unifiers.

References

Aycan, Z. (2000). Cross-cultural industrial and organizational psychology: Contributions, past developments, and future directions. *Journal of Cross Cultural Psychology, 31*(1), 110–128.

Bartlett, C. A., & Ghoshal, S. (1991). *Managing across borders: The transnational solution.* London: London Business School.

Brandt, E. (1991, Spring). Global human resources. *Personnel Journal,* 38–44.

Brake, T., Walker, D. M., & Walker, T. (1995). *Doing business internationally: The guide to cross-cultural success.* New York: McGraw-Hill.

Cascio, W., & Bailey, E. (1995). International human resource management: the state of research and practice (pp. 15–36). In O. Shenkar (Ed.), *Global perspectives of human resource management.* Englewood Cliffs, NJ: Prentice Hall.

Dowling, P. J., & Schuler, R. S. (1990). *International dimensions of human resource management.* Boston: PWS-Kent.

Earley, P. C., & Erez, M. (1997). *New perspectives on international industrial/organizational psychology.* San Francisco: New Lexington Press.

Elsayed-Ekhouly, S. M., & Buda, R. (1996). Organizational conflict: A comparative analysis of conflict styles across cultures. *International Journal of Conflict Management, 7*(1), 71–80.

Erez, M. (1994). Toward a model of cross-cultural industrial and organizational psychology (pp. 559–607). In H. C. Triandis & M. D. Dunnette (Eds.), *Handbook of industrial and organizational psychology* (Vol. 4, 2nd ed.). Palo Alto, CA: Consulting Psychologists Press.

Fulkerson, J. R., & Schuler, R. S. (1992). Managing worldwide diversity at Pepsi-Cola International. In S. Jackson (Ed.), *Diversity in the workplace*. New York: Guilford Press.

Harris, P. R., & Moran, R. T. (1996). *Managing cultural differences* (4th ed.). Houston, TX: Gulf Publishing.

Kimmel, P. R. (2000). Culture and conflict (pp. 453–474). In M. Deutsch & P. T. Coleman (Eds.), *Handbook of conflict resolution: Theory and practice*. San Francisco: Jossey-Bass.

McCrae, R. R., & Costa, P. T. (1997). Personality trait structure as a human universal. *Annual Review of Psychology, 52*(5), 509–516.

Morrison, T., Conaway, W., & Borden, G. (1994). *Kiss, bow, or shake hands*. Holbrook, MA: Bob Adams.

Naisbitt, J. (1994). *Global paradox*. New York: William Morrow.

Phatak, A. V. (1992). *International dimensions of management* (3rd ed.). Boston: PWS-Kent.

Porter, G. (1997). Trust in teams: Member perceptions and the added concern of cross-cultural interpretations (pp. 45–77). In M. M. Beyerlein, D. A. Johnson, & S. T. Beyerlein (Eds.), *Advances in interdisciplinary studies of work teams* (Vol. 4). Greenwich, CT: JAI Press.

Prahalad, C. K., & Doz, Y. (1987). *The multinational mission: Balancing local demands and global vision*. New York: Free Press.

Ronen, S. (1997). Personal reflections and projections: International industrial/organizational psychology at a crossroads (pp. 715–731). In P. Earley & M. Erez (Eds.), *New perspectives on international industrial/organizational psychology*. San Francisco: New Lexington Press.

Schuler, R. S., Fulkerson, J. R., & Dowling, P. J. (1991). Strategic performance measurement and management in multinational corporations. *Human Resource Management, 30*, 365–392.

Tinsley, C. (1998). Models of conflict resolution in Japanese, German, and American cultures. *Journal of applied psychology, 83*(2), 316–323.

Triandis, H. C. (1994). Cross-cultural industrial and organizational psychology (pp. 103–172). In H. C. Triandis & M. D. Dunnette (Eds.), *Handbook of industrial and organizational psychology* (Vol. 4, 2nd ed.). Palo Alto, CA: Consulting Psychologists Press.

CHAPTER 11

Concluding Comments
The Role of Organizational Culture in Implementing Organizational Interventions

Elaine D. Pulakos
Jerry W. Hedge

Organizations are continually changing to meet the competitive challenges they face. One way they respond to these challenges is by implementing interventions and making innovations for long-term viability and growth. But successfully implementing change is difficult because of the inherent complexities of organizational systems and the human tendency to resist change. The chapters in this volume offer specific, practical steps and strategies to facilitate implementing a wide variety of organizational interventions.

Some common themes emerged in the implementation discussions in this volume. For example, the authors discussed the need to have sponsors and champions and to obtain buy-in for interventions. This is critical because, ultimately, any intervention will need to be adopted by organizational members to be effective; they must be motivated and willing to embrace the new system or process. The authors also discussed the importance of communicating with organizational members, giving them opportunities to provide input, and acknowledging their views. They mentioned strategies such as delivering consistent messages, making a compelling case for change, managing stakeholder expectations, delivering the right messages to the intended audiences, and so forth.

In addition, the chapters contained many substantive, specific, and practical suggestions for dealing with the idiosyncratic issues and problems that plague implementation of the various interventions they discussed. This is the unique contribution of this volume, because earlier discussions of implementation offered general prescriptions on implementing change and being innovative rather than focusing on issues, problems, and steps that are specific to particular interventions. The fact that each type of intervention has its own idiosyncratic steps and decisions makes the topic of implementation much more complex, something that cannot be easily captured by one-size-fits-all generic models.

One complexity that the authors discussed in this volume is organizational culture. Certainly, when new systems and processes are implemented in different countries, there are significant challenges from different business models, regulations, values, language, and so forth. But even organizations in the same country have unique cultures that significantly affect implementation efforts. The authors thus stressed the importance of designing systems, processes, and interventions to be compatible with the organizational culture. However, the implications of cultural variables for the implementation of specific organizational systems and processes have yet to be fully explored. Although this was beyond the scope of the present chapters, key cultural variables can (and should) have a significant impact on the decisions that are made in both designing and implementing interventions. Accordingly, in this concluding chapter we look at cultural elements and their implications for the design and implementation of effective organizational interventions.

Importance of Cultural Elements in Organizational Interventions

Many managers, consultants, and implementers have learned about the importance of organizational culture the hard way—by experiencing a failed intervention that was then traced back to a mismatch with some aspect of the organization's culture. Hammer and Champy (1993) discussed several examples of such potential mismatches for a reengineering intervention. If one is dealing with a company that operates by consensus, the top-down nature of reengineering is likely to be an affront to that mode of thinking. Likewise, in a company with a short-term orientation, organizational members may find it difficult to shift their focus from quarterly results to the longer-term horizons that reengineering demands. Or an organization with a bias against conflict may find reengineering's challenge to long-standing rules and procedures unacceptable. Attempts to implement a reengineering intervention in such organizational contexts will likely fail before the intervention even has a chance to take hold. Thus, either matching an intervention to the organization's culture or changing the organization's culture to ready it for the intervention should be the critical first step in any implementation process.

Certainly, matching an intervention to an organization's current culture is easier than trying to change aspects of an established, ingrained culture. Thus, to the extent possible, key aspects of an intervention should be designed to match relevant dimensions of the organization's culture. In some circumstances, however, interventions are designed to support cultural changes that are deemed necessary to achieve broader strategic goals or changes in the organization's direction. In these cases, it is critical to ensure that the intervention is compatible with the desired end state. The process of changing an organization's culture is a complex and elaborate one that has been discussed by previous authors (see, for example, Connell & Ryan, 1998; Katz & Miller, 1996; Martin, Beaumont, & Staines, 1998), and thus will not be our focus here. What has received much less attention are the key cultural elements that are most likely to affect organizational interventions and consequential changes in human and business outcomes. Accordingly, we next turn to a discussion of the cultural factors that are most likely to affect organizational interventions.

Key Cultural Elements in Organizations

An organization's culture consists of some combination of practices, assumptions, and values that organizational members share about appropriate behavior (Cooke & Rousseau, 1988; Gordon & DiTomaso, 1992; Schein, 1992). These beliefs, assumptions, and values work in a normative fashion to guide behavior. O'Reilly and Chatman (1996) have defined culture as a system of shared values defining what is important and norms that guide members' attitudes and behavior.

Although others have discussed different aspects of organizational culture (for example, Dyer, 1985; Hofstede, 1991; Schein, 1992; Tucker & McCoy, 1988), a recent content analysis of the literature by Detert, Schroeder, and Mauriel (2000) revealed a relatively small number of dimensions that seem to underlie most existing discussions of organizational culture. These dimensions are truth and rationality; time; motivation; stability versus change; orientation to work, task, and coworkers; isolation versus collaboration or cooperation; control, coordination, and responsibility; and internal versus external orientation and focus. We review these eight dimensions in the next sections and discuss examples of how differences on these dimensions are likely to affect the design and implementation of organizational interventions.

Truth and Rationality

This cultural element concerns the beliefs that people hold about what is real and not real, and how this reality is discovered. In some organizations, truth is derived from systematic, scientific study that relies on hard data, research, and rigorous problem solving. In other organizations, truth tends to be discovered more through experience and intuition.

This cultural feature has implications for the types of interventions that are likely to be adopted. For example, organizations that rely on data and analysis are likely to be more amenable to systems and processes that produce and use data rigorously, such as selection systems that use systematic scoring and test-use procedures, performance management systems that yield ratings and other numerical data on employees, and compensation systems that closely tie performance measures with pay outcomes. Organizations that discover truth more through intuition and experience may not be as inclined to collect data systematically or to use rigorous data. Instead, they may prefer systems and processes that allow more subjective judgments to enter into decision-making processes. For example, they may be more interested in making selection decisions based on interviews than rigorous test data, or they may prefer performance narratives to ratings. An organization's orientation on this cultural element can thus affect the design of several of the interventions that were discussed in this volume.

This cultural element also has implications for how one should communicate about and pitch—or sell—an intervention to the organizational members. If data, research, and rigorous analyses are highly valued, then communications should focus on such things as bottom-line measures and expected outcomes, evidence from other organizations or the research literature that the intervention will be effective, and the decision-making processes that were used in choosing the intervention. Members of data-driven organizations may also be less tolerant of the softer exercises that are sometimes used to support implementation (for example, team building exercises and exercises designed to increase interpersonal skills). Instead, they often react more positively to substantive intervention activities that deal with the mechanics of the intervention, how it will work, and the outcomes they can expect. In organizations where truth comes through intuition and experience, communications and activities to bolster implementation should be more experiential in nature, focusing on building consensus and support through human interaction, discussion, and discovery.

Time

This dimension refers to how time is determined and measured, what kinds of time exist, how important time is, time horizon, and so on. Time horizon is important because it helps to determine whether organizational members adopt long-term planning and goal setting or focus primarily on the here and now.

Time is a focal point in the implementation of many interventions, and a key variable is how much time organizational members are willing to devote to the activities required by a new system or process. For example, if one were implementing a skills assessment, selection, succession planning, or performance management system, an important consideration would be how many hours people are willing to spend routinely on such things as completing evaluation instruments, providing feedback, and other tasks related to these systems. The answer will depend on the culture for these types of systems in the organization. Furthermore, it takes strong leadership and positive experience with the benefits of such systems to build a positive culture for them.

One must begin by evaluating the perceived utility of the intervention under consideration and the tolerance of organizational members to devote time to it. The systems developed should be designed with these organizational realities in mind, because this will increase the probability that the intervention will actually be adopted. What is ultimately implemented may be smaller or different in scope than originally envisioned, but the intervention can always be expanded as organizational members gain experience with it and grow to appreciate its value.

Another aspect of time that is clearly important for an organizational intervention is how long organizational members and decision makers are willing to wait for it to be implemented. Many of the interventions discussed in this volume can take several months and up to a year (or more) to develop and implement. Organizations that operate in a strategic and methodical mode are more likely to understand the time involved in implementing complex interventions, and they may be more likely to spend the time needed to ensure success. Such organizations are also more likely to implement processes and systems that have a longer-term focus—for example, succession planning.

Organizations that operate in a more reactive mode often shy away from interventions that are designed to have a longer-term impact. They are also likely to expect faster turnaround for interventions they want to put into practice, but this may limit the rigor and comprehensiveness of the intervention developed. There are obviously significant trade-offs that must be made if the decision is to develop and implement an intervention quickly. A key role of implementers is to provide guidance to their organizations on what trade-offs are possible without risking failure. In reactive cultures, they will more regularly have to weigh the pros and cons of quickly implementing something that may provide only a partial or less than optimal solution. Such cultures are also more likely to embrace the latest industry fad and push for its rapid adoption without carefully considering the fit between the intervention and the organization.

Motivation

This dimension of culture encompasses ideas about whether people are motivated from within or by external factors, whether people should be rewarded or punished, and whether output and effort can be changed by manipulating another's motivation.

Beliefs about what motivates the organization's employees can have a significant impact on both the design and implementation of many types of interventions. These beliefs certainly affect the development and implementation of effective reward contingencies, for example. If workers are intrinsically motivated, establishing a system to increase productivity that uses external reward contingencies will likely not be effective. However, rewards can help encourage a desired cultural change. For example, if organizational leaders have decided that they need to move away from a risk-averse culture, then new forms of rewards such as bonuses or stock options might encourage more risk-taking behavior.

Another example, this one concerning TQM, was discussed by Detert et al. (2000). If one were interested in implementing TQM in an organization, one should first ascertain whether the organizational beliefs about motivation are compatible with the TQM philosophy—namely, that people are motivated to do a good job but are often thwarted by the system (Dean & Bowen, 1994; Hackman & Wageman, 1995). The TQM value, therefore, is that performance problems are attributable to faulty business processes and not to people. If an organization's culture around motivation is not consistent with these ideas, then a TQM intervention will not be well matched to that culture and will likely fail. Many other examples could be offered for how organizational beliefs about motivation might affect the design and long-term viability of various interventions, but the primary point is simply to ensure compatibility between the intervention and relevant aspects of these organizational beliefs.

Stability Versus Change

Closely tied to ideas about what motivates human beings are ideas about individual desires for stability versus change. Some people are open to taking risks whereas others need stability and security. Similarly, at the organizational level some companies push for constant and continuous improvement and have an institutionalized belief that they can always improve. Others are more risk-adverse, not inclined to rock the boat, and satisfied with being "good enough."

An organization's standing on this dimension will have a significant effect on its overall readiness for any type of intervention. If an organization has a climate for continuous improvement, implementers should focus their communications on demonstrating how a new process, program, or procedure will facilitate this. Assuming such a case is successfully made, little more may be necessary to sell the intervention and motivate organizational members to adopt it. But if an organization prefers the status quo and is resistant to change, much greater effort will be needed to convince organizational members about the merits of a proposed intervention and to motivate its adoption. It is thus important to evaluate the readiness of an organization for change early in the implementation process and to plan steps and strategies that are compatible.

Orientation to Work, Task, and Coworkers

This involves ideas about the centrality of work in human life and the balance between work as a productive activity and a social activity. Individuals who view work as an end in itself focus on the task or results, with a primary concern on work accomplishment and productivity. Others view work as a means to an end, with productivity a less important goal than the social relationships they develop at work. This organizational culture dimension could have ramifications for a number of different interventions. For example, in the training arena, a culture oriented toward social relationships may not readily support implementation of a technology-based training medium that encourages isolated, individualized learning. Conversely, a training solution that embraces relationship building as a key component may not fare well in a task-based company.

This dimension also has relevance for how interventions are positioned and sold to organizational members to facilitate adoption. To obtain buy-in for an intervention in an organization with a results orientation, developers should focus on showing how the new system, process, or procedure will enhance productivity and competitive advantage. In contrast, if they are selling an intervention to an organization where the social value of work is high they should demonstrate how it will enhance work processes and other desired outcomes.

Isolation Versus Collaboration or Cooperation

This cultural element involves the underlying beliefs about the nature of human relationships in a work context and how work is most effectively and efficiently accomplished. In some organizations almost all work is accomplished by individuals and collaboration is viewed as inefficient. In other organizations, collaboration is viewed as key to achieving higher productivity and better decisions and outcomes. In these circumstances, work is likely to be organized around teams.

This cultural feature is particularly relevant in the design stage of organizational interventions. For example, if an organization values individual contributions, reward systems that focus on team performance and outcomes will not only fail to be embraced but will likely serve to diminish individual motivation and productivity. But if an organization wishes to promote teamwork and collaboration, then a reward system that reinforces individual contributions will thwart that goal. In another example, it would be difficult to use successfully a performance appraisal system that incorporates coworker evaluations in an organization that measures and rewards individual contributions. Because employees are inherently competing with each other in this type of environment, there would be a lack of trust and possibly even a lack of credibility in coworker ratings. The point is that many interventions make implicit or explicit assumptions about the amount of individuality or collaboration in an environment. It is important to evaluate the features of planned interventions from this perspective to ensure they are properly matched to the organization's culture before implementation.

Control, Coordination, and Responsibility

This cultural element has to do with the extent to which control is concentrated rather than shared. In organizations where it is concentrated, decision making is centralized and formal rules and procedures are established at the highest levels to guide the behavior of others. Other organizations have looser controls and fewer rules and procedures, organizational members have more flexibility and autonomy, and power and decision making are shared.

This cultural feature has significant implications for both the design and implementation of organizational interventions. In designing performance management, selection-promotion, reward, training, and most other systems, type of control must be taken into account. If individual organizational units have a great deal of autonomy, then attempts to design and implement common, centralized systems are likely to meet with great resistance, largely because of perceptions of loss of local independence and control. In these situations, there is often a prevailing mentality that "if it's not developed here, it's no good." Thus, even if a common system will work equally well across organizational units, implementation success may necessitate offering local customization or options and working extensively with individual units to gain their support.

However, organizations characterized by centralized control are more likely to be willing to accept common systems developed at a corporate level. All else being equal, implementation in a structured, hierarchical organization where control is centralized and organizational members are accustomed to following orders tends to be less complex than in those where control is more dispersed. The key stakeholders will also differ in organizations with different control structures, as will their expectations and attitudes about decision making and communications relevant to the implementation process.

This dimension also has implications for the design of specific components of interventions. For example, in a hierarchical organization, employees may be very uncomfortable with performance management systems that formally incorporate peer, and especially, subordinate ratings. Similarly, a flexible and nontraditional reward system may not be well aligned with a highly structured, bureaucratic organization. Thus, the organization's orientation toward control, coordination, and responsibility must be considered, and in fact should be an important factor in an intervention's design parameters.

Internal Versus External Orientation and Focus

This dimension reflects the extent to which the organization believes it controls—or is controlled by—its external environment and also whether its orientation is fundamentally internal or external. For instance, in some organizations it is assumed that the key to success is to focus on internal people and processes. Innovation tends to come from within, based on what managers, engineers, and other employees believe will improve their existing products, processes, and systems. Other organizations are focused on external constituents, customers, competitors, and the environment. In these organizations, innovation is based on what external stakeholders want, and improvements to products and services are judged by external benchmarks. These organizations also tend to search actively for ideas outside their traditional bounds.

Again, this cultural feature has implications for both the design of the intervention and the strategies that will be most effective in implementing it. If an organization is externally focused, then selling the need for an intervention that is based on customer feedback or competitor analyses will likely have a greater impact than it would on an internally focused organization. Externally focused organizations are also more likely to be influenced by the latest business fad in the industry.

Conclusion

Although previous authors have consistently discussed the importance of culture in the implementation of organizational interventions, relatively little effort has been made to identify key cultural dimensions and their practical implications for implementation success. Using a framework offered by Detert et al. (2000), this chapter has provided some initial thoughts on how cultural elements can affect various interventions. Clearly, however, more work is needed to understand the cultural factors that are most relevant to each type of intervention as well as how an organization's standing on these factors should drive design and implementation decisions.

Although the eight dimensions discussed here provide a useful framework for thinking about organizational interventions, not all will be equally relevant to a particular intervention, and other cultural aspects may be relevant to specific interventions and should be considered in designing them. For example, global interventions also require consideration of the key cultural elements of all of the different countries in which implementation will occur.

Similarly, even in a single organization some cultural elements may vary from unit to unit—an R&D unit in a technology company may be highly flexible and characterized by low formalization, centralization, and standardization, whereas a production unit may be much more centralized, formalized, and standardized. So even in the same organization, implementation may need to be customized to fit different cultural characteristics.

It is important to keep in mind that the elements of culture can affect interventions in two significant but different ways. First, they need to be taken into account in designing specific components of interventions to ensure compatibility between system features and the environment in which implementation will occur. One caveat, of course, is if the intervention is specifically intended to support changing some aspect of the organization's culture. Second, the cultural characteristics of an organization should play a prominent role in deciding how an intervention will be introduced and sold. Management is more likely to be convinced of its merits and utility if the selling approach fits the organization's cultural context and shows how the implementation supports the organization's strategic goals and orientation.

From a purely practical perspective, there is considerable merit in conducting a cultural analysis before designing any organizational intervention or planning its implementation. This involves collecting information, through focus groups or questionnaires, on the key elements of culture that are relevant to the intervention and assessing where the organization stands on these dimensions. Collecting this information and using it to make both design and implementation decisions will help ensure the intervention's compatibility with the environment and hence the potential that it will be adopted by organizational members and effectively used.

References

Connell, J., & Ryan, S. (1998). Culture change within a regional business network (pp. 129–145). In C. Mabey, D. Skinner, & T. Clark (Eds.), *Experiencing human resource management.* Thousand Oaks, CA: Sage.

Cooke, R., & Rousseau, D. (1988). Behavioral norms and expectations: A quantitative approach to the assessment of organizational culture. *Group and Organizational Studies, 13,* 245–273.

Dean, J. W. Jr., & Bowen, D. E. (1994). Management theory and total quality: Improving research and practice through theory development. *Academy of Management Review, 19,* 392–418.

Detert, J. R., Schroeder, R. G., & Mauriel, J. J. (2000). A framework for linking culture and improvement initiatives in organizations. *Academy of Management Review, 25,* 850–863.

Dyer, W. G., Jr. (1985). The cycle of cultural evolution in organizations (pp. 200–229). In R. H. Killmann, M. J. Saxton, & R. Serpa (Eds.), *Gaining control of the corporate culture.* San Francisco: Jossey-Bass.

Gordon, G. G., & DiTomaso, N. (1992). Predicting corporate performance from organizational culture. *Journal of Management Studies, 29,* 783–798.

Hackman, J. R., & Wageman, R. (1995). Total quality management: Empirical, conceptual, and practical issues. *Administrative Science Quarterly, 40,* 309–342.

Hammer, M., & Champy, J. (1993). *Reengineering the corporation: A manifesto for business revolution.* New York. HarperCollins.

Hofstede, G. (1991). *Culture and organizations: Software of the mind.* New York: McGraw-Hill.

Katz, J. H., & Miller, F. A. (1996). Coaching leaders through culture change. *Consulting Psychology Journal: Practice & Research, 48*(2), 104–114.

Martin, G., Beaumont, P., & Staines, H. (1998). Changing corporate culture: Paradoxes and tensions in a local authority (pp. 73–94). In C. Mabey, D. Skinner, & T. Clark (Eds.), *Experiencing human resource management.* Thousand Oaks, CA: Sage.

O'Reilly, C. A. III, & Chatman, J. A. (1996). Culture as a social control: Corporations, cults, and commitments (pp. 157–200). In B. M. Staw & L. L. Cummings (Eds.), *Research in organizational behavior* (Vol. 18). Greenwich, CT: JAI Press.

Schein, E. H. (1992). *Organizational culture and leadership* (2nd ed.). San Francisco: Jossey-Bass.

Tucker, R. W., & McCoy, W. J. (1988). *Can questionnaires measure culture? Eight extended field studies.* Paper presented at the annual convention of the American Psychological Association, Atlanta.

Index

gies' impact on, 136–138; and link between pay and performance, 143–144; linked with HR systems and organizational strategies, 134; and money's motivational power, 135–136; open vs. closed, 148–149; and pay philosophy, 147–149; resistance to changing, 134–135; steps in designing and implementing, 144–164; succession planning's link to, 100, 102; training about, 161–162. *See also* Reward systems

Conaway, W., 275, 279

Confidentiality, of test scores, 255, 260

Connell, J., 299

Consultants: change, 15, 16, 17–18, 36; as resource for global implementation, 279–280

Control, as element of organizational culture, 305–306

Cooke, R., 299

Corporate incentives, 141

Cost: of information technology (IT), 118–119; of testing errors in selection programs, 246–247; of training and development initiatives, 198

Costa, P. T., 285

Cost-of-living increases (COLA), 141

Craiger, P., 125

Crisis management, as approach to mergers and acquisitions, 58–59

Critical success factors (CSFs), in mergers and acquisitions, 61, 62

Cross-cultural implementation. *See* Global implementation

Cultural due diligence, 55

Culture. *See* Organizational culture

Customers, information about, for IT project implementation, 114, 116–117

Cutscores: defined, 238; necessary decisions when using, 241; when to use, 239

D

Daimler-Chrysler merger, 45

Dannemiller Tyson Associates, 38

Dean, J. W., Jr., 303

Detert, J. R., 300, 303, 307

Dick, W., 199

DiTomaso, N., 299

Diversity: and global implementation, 277, 288; and pool-based succession planning, 85; as value involved in organizational change, 14

Dorsey, D. W., 110

Doty, H. D., 150

Dowell, B. E., 78

Dowling, P. J., 271

Doz, Y., 270

Due diligence: cultural, 55; hurried, in mergers and acquisitions, 53–54

Duncan, R., 6

Dyer, W. G., Jr., 300

E

Earley, P. C., 271

Eggebeen, S. L., 270

Eisenstat, R. A., 2, 3, 5, 10

Elsass, P. M., 43

Elsayed-Ekhouly, S. M., 290

Emery, M., 34

Employee input: to build support for global implementation, 287–288; as source of information for performance management system, 177–178; for succession planning, 93–94

Employee relations, in global implementations, 286

Employee satisfaction, with compensation system, 143, 159

Employee stock ownership plans (ESOPs), 157

Employee surveys, global implementation of, 274–275, 284

Employee value proposition (EVP), 138–140

Organizational change, 12–41; assumptions contributing to, 21; business case for, and compensation system change, 145; conditions for successful implementation of, 3, 5–6; don'ts for implementing, 33; failure of implementation of, 2–3; history of focus on, 13–14; leadership for, 21, 26–28, 33; measuring implementation of, 39–41; methodologies for, 34–39; model of process of, 15–21; participation in, 29–30; personal adaptation to, 28–29; planning for, 30–33; resistance to, 3, 4, 25–26, 32, 134–135; stability vs., as element of organizational culture, 303–304; systems perspective on, 23–25; types of, 14–15; values involved in, 14; vision-driven vs. gap-driven, 22–23

Organizational culture, 297–308; activity for clarifying, 67–70; defined, 299; dimensions of, 300–307; due diligence team's perspective on, 55–56; and implementation of information technology (IT), 129–130; importance and effect of, in organizational interventions, 298–299, 308; innovation implementation success as affected by, 7; integrating, in mergers and acquisitions, 43, 63–70; and performance management, 195–196

Organizational innovation: defined, 6; factors affecting implementation success of, 6–8; models of process of, 6

Orientation: internal vs. external, as element of organizational culture, 306–307; to work, 304

O'Toole, J., 104

Overtime pay, 141

Ownership, as necessary for organizational change, 14

P

Paese, M. J., 106

Park, M. V., 12

Participation: to deal with resistance, 26; as essential for change implementation, 29–30

Pay for performance, 140–141, 152–157; individual incentives, 141, 153; merit pay, 140–141, 152–153; variable pay plans, 153–157

Pay grade systems, 151

Pay mix, 148

Pay philosophy, 147–149

Performance, link between pay and, 143–144

Performance analysis, in assessment stage of implementing training, 204

Performance appraisal: calibration of performance ratings in, 186; collecting numerical and narrative information for, 179–180; defined, 167; emphasized in performance management system, 172–173, 174; frequency and timing of, 175–176; global implementation of, 281–282; sources of performance information for, 177–178. *See also* Performance ratings

Performance development: collecting numerical information for, 178–179, 180; defined, 167; emphasized in performance management system, 173–175; frequency and timing of, 176; sources of performance information for, 176–177

Performance management, 167–197; calibration of performance ratings in, 185–187; champions of, 170–171, 191; collecting numerical vs. narrative information for, 178–180; comprehensiveness of system for, 195–197; defined, 167–168; electronic, 185, 189–190;